SOUTH SIDE GIRLS

D0862932

SOUTH SIDE
GIRLS

GROWING UP IN THE
GREAT MIGRATION

MARCIA CHATELAIN

DUKE UNIVERSITY PRESS *Durham & London* 2015

© 2015 Duke University Press

All rights reserved

Printed in the United States

of America on acid-free paper ∞

Text designed by Amy Ruth Buchanan

Cover designed by Natalie F. Smith

Typeset in Garamond Premier Pro by

Graphic Composition, Inc., Athens, GA

Library of Congress Cataloging-in-Publication Data

Chatelain, Marcia, 1979–

South side girls : growing up in the great

migration / Marcia Chatelain.

pages cm

Includes bibliographical references and index.

ISBN 978-0-8223-5848-0 (hardcover : alk. paper)

ISBN 978-0-8223-5854-1 (pbk. : alk. paper)

1. African American girls—Illinois—Chicago—
History—20th century. 2. African American girls—
Illinois—Chicago—Social conditions—20th century.
3. African American girls—Migrations—History—
20th century. 4. Chicago (Ill.)—History—1875–
5. Chicago (Ill.)—Social conditions—20th century.
6. Chicago (Ill.)—Race relations—History—
20th century. I. Title.

F548.9.N4C438 2015

305.23089'96073077311—dc23

2014040374

ISBN 978-0-8223-7570-8 (e-book)

Cover image: Girl with newspaper fashion supplement,
Chicago's Southside, 1947. Photograph by
Wayne Miller. Magnum Photos.

Duke University Press gratefully acknowledges the
support of Georgetown University, which provided
funds toward the publication of this book.

For my mother, Mecthilde Boyer,
her sisters, and their mother.

For Valerie Yapelli
and her incredible legacy.

CONTENTS

PREFACE

For one glorious year, while an assistant professor at the University of Oklahoma (OU), each Friday afternoon I ceased being a scholar and became a Girl Scout. As a Girl Scouts Pathways volunteer, I brought the Girl Scouts curriculum to third and fourth graders at a predominately black elementary school on Oklahoma City's northwest side. Each week, equipped with worksheets on self-esteem and the words of the "Girl Scout Promise" carefully memorized, I listened to the girls articulate their varied interests and whisper secrets about each other, and I accepted their invitations into learning about their dreams for the future. "Dr. Marcia, I went to the OU girls' basketball game." "I'm going to be a veterinarian and take care of puppies." "I'm going to be a teacher, like you."

Of all the moments I shared with the girls, among the songs celebrating friendships, the games designed to instill confidence in them, and the skits directed by me and the co-leader that filled the hour-long meetings, I was most struck by one gathering in the winter of 2009. I often led the Scouts through a quick current events lesson, and on the tail of a presidential inauguration I had a few questions for them. First question: "Who are the new president and first lady?" "Barack Obama and Michelle," they answered with such enthusiasm I feared the librarian would ban us from the library indefinitely. I had no idea what was in store when I asked the second question. "And who are their daughters?" In a burst of energy that can only be described as ecstatic and never appeared again even on Girl Scout Cookie Day, the girls jumped up and down and cheered: "Sasha and Malia!" The mere mention of the first daughters led to a flurry of facts and anecdotes they had undoubtedly gleaned from months of watching campaign coverage and the historic inauguration with their parents. "I liked their coats!" "Their hair looked so pretty!" "Their dad got them a dog because he won!" While the adults around them celebrated the election of a black president ("My mommy cried when she saw the president on TV"), the girls reveled in the presence of two black girls—just like them—living in the White House. Although Sasha and Malia Obama's race and gender may be the only things they had in common with this boisterous cohort in a state where their father did not win the majority of the popular vote, the girls perceived no distance between themselves and the little girls who clung to their parents on Inauguration Day. The privileges the Obama girls had enjoyed up to the day their family moved to the White House and the life that awaited them in Washington, DC, may not have been conceivable to these Girl Scouts in Oklahoma City, but these facts were not important. They felt like they were also members of this family, and that the Obama sisters could be their friends or fellow troop members.

This book is an exploration of black girls who came of age in a time and place that could scarcely imagine a black president. Yet they did live in a world that provided them with possibilities for improving their lives when they or their families made the decision to leave the South and pursue the promises of the Great Migration, the mass exodus of African Americans from the South to the urban north. I focus on Chicago, a major hub of black political, economic, and cultural success. I consider the moments, rhetoric, and activism that centered on black girls' lives and futures in a rapidly changing, and sometimes dizzying, city.

As a native Chicagoan, I grew up surrounded by the legacies of the Great Migration—the electrifying gospel music integrated into traditional Catholic mass, the essays of Richard Wright assigned in high school English classes, and the racial segregation that hampered far too many of my school friendships. As a teenager coming of age in the 1990s, I constantly heard of a war on black boys in news media and read about it in newsletters produced by black community and civic organizations responding to a rise in gang violence and juvenile crimes. I longed to hear substantive and thoughtful conversations about black girls and their battle scars. Now, as a historian, I have uncovered the many ways that black families and communities struggled to define black girlhood and make girls feel safe and hopeful in a moment when Chicago was both a place of refuge from Jim Crow and a site of struggle against northern racism. These girls, like my Girl Scouts in Oklahoma City, also dreamed of what they could be, grappled with disappointments, and sought security. They searched for spaces where their ideas and promise could be reflected in the world around them. This book presents their stories.

ACKNOWLEDGMENTS

One day in 1950, nine-year-old Janie White's mother appeared before an employee of the Chicago Commons Association and inquired about opportunities for her daughter. A social worker at the settlement house noted her visit and described the mother as "anxious to have Janie well cared for and to have experiences." After working on this book for several years, and poring through the life stories and testimonies of dozens of girl migrants to Chicago, this passage has remained with me. Mrs. White's anxiety about her daughter's access to meaningful experiences, in this instance the Chicago Commons camping program, and clear intention to have her daughter "well cared for," reminds me so much of my own mother, Mecthilde Boyer. An immigrant from Haiti, my mother shared Mrs. White's tenacity.

Throughout various moments in writing and revising this book, I imagined my mother when I was nine years old, heading off to a second, maybe a third, job before dropping me off at a racially and ethnically integrated day camp or dozing off in the parking lot of my Catholic school as she waited for me at the end of my school day and prepared to return to her work day. The archive does not indicate how Janie felt about her mother's persistence and insistence that she have access to the type of opportunities readily available to many classes of white girls, nor do we know if Janie's mother believed she was ever truly successful at securing all of her hopes for her daughter. Yet if I use my own experiences to propose an ending to the story, I imagine Janie enrolling in college, perhaps joining the civil rights movement in the 1960s, and one day sharing with her own daughter recollections of how much her mother's furious advocacy meant to her.

My mother always soothes life's anxieties with a humbling faith in God, and she greets life's challenges with an incredible sense of humor and timing. I am forever grateful to my mother's commitment to the spectacular, unbelievable, and thoroughly amazing for her children.

When my mother couldn't collect me from school or deliver me to a speech tournament in a far-flung Chicago suburb, my big brother Ronald or my sister Regine stepped in and saved the day. Growing up, my mother reminded, scolded, and sometimes threatened us to be friends with each other, noting that "when I'm gone, all you will have is each other." My brother's wife, Lupita, and his children, Emmanuel and Anastasia, have made our hearts fuller and our family happier. Hailing from a family of eight children, my mother counts siblings, and our endless networks of aunts, uncles, and cousins, as God's greatest blessing. From my father, Pierre Chatelain, I inherited the ability to focus on the future in the middle of turmoil and chaos, and this has served me well in many instances. I am grateful for the generosity of my other parents, my in-laws Fred and Elaine Yapelli for their endless support and encouragement. During the revision process for this book, our family mourned the loss of my uncle, Paul Boyer, an educator with an incredible sense of humor. Uncle Paul appreciated what he perceived as my seriousness; I appreciated his ability to bring a lack of seriousness in moments of joy and pain. I am deeply saddened that I cannot share this accomplishment with him.

When I think about the many friends who have supported me through this process, I am reminded of Emily Dickinson's declaration "My friends are my estate." My vast wealth includes so many confidantes and inspirations. They encouraged me through every step of my various professional and personal journeys, they answered the phone when they knew I was on the other end of the call filled with anxiety, and they encouraged me to see the big picture of my life when I wanted to measure it in moments of self-doubt. I am especially grateful to Wendi Adelson, Monica Bell, Anitra Cottledge, Sean Greene, Cynthia Greenlee, and Mark Powell for their warmth, love, and good humor when this book, and so many other endeavors, felt impossible. Kimberly Juanita Brown dutifully read every reader report for me before I had the courage to look at the feedback myself. My sister in the academic struggle Sheyda Jahanbani constantly reminded me that things were going much better than I imagined when every setback felt like a catastrophe. Izetta Mobley has supported me through every academic and personal turning point. Beth Pickens's loving support over the course of two decades of friendship makes me wish everyone could have a friend like her. Hentyle Yapp's persistence and downright perfection has lovingly nurtured my creativity. My portfolio has also been enriched by the love of Andrew Allan, Angela Howell, Beata Leja, Mike Watters, and Jamila K. Wilson. My dear friend, Matthew Baugh, S.J., one of the many Jesuits in my life, exemplifies what it means to walk in the "greater glory of God" every day.

This book began as a doctoral dissertation in Brown University's Department of American Civilization, under the direction of and imbued by the support of the finest scholars of U.S. history and American studies. I started with a seemingly simple question: "What about girls?" And I was fortunate to have a dissertation committee as intrigued and excited by the answers as I was. My dissertation chair and committed mentor Mari Jo Buhle modeled professionalism and rigor. Mari Jo's painstaking attention to my writing, and her role in shaping my desire to craft relevant and impactful scholarship, is at the heart of why I remained committed to completing graduate school and this book during the roughest times in my life. James Campbell's seminars were invaluable in teaching me how to teach and to think on my toes. I have yet to see anyone as masterful and engaging as Jim in a classroom. Matthew Garcia's mentorship has evolved into a true friendship. Matt's commitment to young scholars of color is seen throughout the academy, as I and many of his students have followed his example to use our voices as academics to effect change in our fields and communities.

Throughout my time at Brown, the kindness and support of my family at the Center for the Study of Race and Ethnicity in America (CSREA), especially Drs. Garcia and Evelyn Hu-Dehart. The CSREA became my siblings, and Matthew Delmont, Stephanie Larrieux, Mireya Loza, and Mario Sifuentez, and other dissertation fellows, support staff, and work-study students kept me well fed, entertained, and hopeful that graduate school would indeed end some day.

Financial support is key to this kind of undertaking, and I was able to accelerate my graduate school experience with a Harry S. Truman Scholarship, monies from the CSREA, and a Black Studies Pre-Doctoral Fellowship at the University of California-Santa Barbara (UCSB). Each summer of my graduate school education I packed up my belongings and drove from Providence to Columbia, Missouri, where I taught some of the state's brightest high school students in the Missouri Scholars Academy (MSA). Reconnecting with my Missouri friends, especially Sue Crowley, Laura Hacquard, and Jill Rait, prepared me for the next hurdle. The UCSB's Department of Black Studies faculty and staff, especially Ingrid Banks, Gaye Theresa Johnson, and Claudine Michel, provided me with a beautiful setting in which to work on my dissertation and excellent feedback while I prepared for the job market. I was also privileged to teach a group of wonderful women at Santa Barbara in the course "Africana Girls in the U.S. and Abroad." Receiving the Truman Scholarship in college changed my life, and Executive Secretary Andrew Rich has provided the right advice at the right time in my academic journey. I love being able to be part of an ever expanding community, and Foundation staffers Louis Blair, Tonji Wade, and Tara Yglesias have been part of so many fond Truman experiences.

When I initially shared with other scholars and history enthusiasts that I was going to write about black girls during Chicago's Great Migration, I was immediately asked "How do you find sources?" Half of the challenge of uncovering the voices of the marginalized is to work with people who believe that it is possible. I was fortunate to have the assistance and feedback of the librarians and research staff of an array of institutions, especially the University of Illinois-Chicago Special Collections; the University of Chicago's Regenstein Special Collections Library; the Geneva History Center; the Harold Washington Library Neighborhood Research Collection; the Chicago History Museum (where Michael Glass is perhaps the friendliest person to ever work at a front desk); the Schomburg Center for Research in Black Culture at the New York Public Library; the Carter G. Woodson Regional Library's Vivian C. Harsh Collection; the Library of Congress; the Roosevelt University Library; Howard University's Moorland-Spingarn Center; the University of California Library System; and the University of Oklahoma Libraries provided excellent advice on sources, hours of photocopying, and endless energy for what was sometimes an overbroad topic. The CampFire USA organization's Chicago office, now closed, gave me carte blanche to conduct research in their offices; I am grateful for their trust and interest in my search for records of black girls' participation in the camping group.

After collecting treasures from libraries, archives, and reading rooms across the country, I often retreated to coffee shops, fast-casual restaurants, and late-night diners to read through stacks of copies, synthesize archival findings, and write my analysis of Chicago's black past. As I plugged away on first drafts, and then first, second, third, and fourth revisions of sentences and passages in search of the perfect paragraph, I was greeted and fed by incredible men and women. I am deeply grateful to the patient wait staffs, short-order cooks, and night-shift managers who brewed pots of coffee, flipped pancakes, and directed me to booths located next to electrical outlets so I could work for hours on this project. Food service, not unlike the home health aide work my mother did for nearly forty years, can be backbreaking and exhausting, and I was always touched by the smiles and the questions I received as I crafted this book in banquettes and booths in Chicago, Oklahoma City, Williamsburg, Virginia, and Washington, DC.

My first faculty position at the Joe C. and Carole Kerr McClendon Honors College at the University of Oklahoma provided tremendous support in helping me return to archives to strengthen the research for the book. I was fortunate to receive research funds, a semester leave, the Honors Research Assistance Program (HRAP), and a Research Council Junior Faculty Research Grant during my four years there. My three HRAP students—Rachel Edgren, Elizabeth Rucker, Keyonna Wynn—provided research assistance of the highest quality. My colleagues welcomed me with open arms, offered wonderful career advice, and lovingly bid me farewell after I accepted a position at Georgetown University. Julia Erhardt, who is both mentor and friend, provided invaluable suggestions on my book proposal and helped me navigate the intensity of the first years on the tenure track. Sarah Tracy shared great insights on research and publishing and shared her friendship during my years in Oklahoma City. Ben Alpers, R. C. Davis, Barbara and Chris Howard, Randy Lewis, Carolyn Morgan, and Melanie Wright made my Oklahoma years incredibly fruitful, and their support through my early career can never be fully repaid. David Chapell, Rob Griswold, and Fay Yarbrough reached out and extended their hands to me across the OU campus and academic disciplines to help me craft this book, balance teaching and research, and made a second home for me in the History Department.

My service to the Girl Scouts of Western Oklahoma, and the tremendous women dedicated to the Girl Scout mission of "building girls of courage, confidence and character" reminded me why exploring girls' history, as well as girls' futures, was vital to my academic and personal commitments. Ann-Clore Duncan, Kay Goebel, Diana Rogers Jaeger, Karen Luke, Cathy Stackpole, and Linda Whittington are among the most dedicated advocates for girls, and they continue to inspire me, and my academic pursuits.

When I accepted a faculty position at Georgetown University, I was immediately welcomed and embraced as part of a team of outstanding scholars and colleagues. My fellow members of the History Department, especially Tommasso Astarita, Carol Benedict, David Collins, S.J., Jim Collins, David Goldfrank, Michael Kazin, Chandra Manning, Bryan McCann, Joe McCartin, Aviel Roshwald, Adam Rothman, Howard Spendelow, and John Tutino extended advice on navigating processes big and small, invitations to lunch to simply talk about family and apartment searches, and the continued tradition of some of the best junior faculty mentoring at the university. Angelyn Mitchell's vision made possible a position in African-American women's history at Georgetown, and I am grateful for her leadership of African-American studies. Kathleen Gallagher, Jan Liverance, and Djuana Shields also embraced my complicated questions and concerns very quickly, easing the transition from Oklahoma to Washington, DC.

Funding from Georgetown's Academic Summer Grant Program, Junior Faculty Research Grant, Gervase Undergraduate Research program, and Grant-in-Aid funds made it possible to complete this project with the help of an outstanding undergraduate assistant, Yongle Xu, and graduate students James Benton and Paula Hopkins. African American Studies at Georgetown provided funding for the last-minute details for the book, and program assistants Khadijah Davis and Esther Owolabi provided endless support to me in this and so many other projects. I owe my deepest gratitude to my colleague Katherine Benton-Cohen, who helped me complete the final laps of what at times felt like an endless marathon, and her comments and insights helped me to organize my thoughts and maintain my focus by ensuring that each paragraph of this book has a "girl in it." Maurice Jackson and his family have embraced me and welcomed me in ways that have exceeded my greatest expectations of a colleague and friend. Carole Sargent from Georgetown's Office of Scholarly Publications has been a consistent source of advice, support, and cheerleading. Carole's finesse with the publishing process, her ability to calm the most frayed nerves, and her generosity of spirit in helping others become as successful as she is makes her a rare presence in the academy. Comments on the manuscript from Grey Osterud made this book an actual book; Grey finds the center and, more important, helps you rediscover your initial curiosity for your subject. Comments from Susan Cahn, James Grossman, Tim Mennel, Kevin Mumford, Clara Platter, Megan Taylor Shockley, and the thorough and direct readers from Duke University Press, helped shaped a series of anecdotes, hunches, and ideas into a solid narrative about the importance of listening to girls and pondering the many dimensions of girlhood. The annual Conference of Ford Fellows facilitated my first contact with Duke University Press. I am most grateful to the National Academies' support of the Ford Foundation Diversity Fellowship, and to Ken Wissoker for deciding to come to the conference. I contend, and many agree, that Ken is the most "with it" editor in book publishing today, and I'm thankful for his introducing me to Gisela Fosado. Gisela is a model book editor—she is clear in her feedback, prompt in her responses, and generous with her encouragement. The Duke Press editing, production, and marketing team—Sara Leone, Lorien Olive, Martha Ramsey, Willa Armstrong, and Natalie Smith—treated my book as if it were their own, and I always looked forward to an e-mail message from the Press.

This book, and all the ambitions I hold as a scholar and person, are dedicated to my dearest friends, who are now departed, but not forgotten. Vanessa Lynn Kolpak, a Georgetown University graduate who knew me from my teenage years in Chicago, left the world on September 11, 2001. Vanessa remains with me in spirit. Every time I enter a Georgetown classroom, I am reminded of her deep intellect, compassion for others, and obsession with making her friends feel smarter, more talented, and much better than they could ever fathom. Without fail, when I shared news of an achievement, small or large, with her, she replied: "Tell me the details, so I can brag about it." Equally supportive of my endeavors was scholar Christopher Michael Bell, who died on December 25, 2009. Before he was a nationally renowned AIDS activist and author of groundbreaking essays on race and disability studies, he was my college friend, Chris. When he was a Chicagoan briefly, we dined at some of the city's finest French restaurants during my visits home. I often read Chris's journal articles and our e-mail exchanges in order to remind me that his fight for justice and equality lives on in the vast community of scholars and friends who miss him deeply.

And finally, thank you to my spouse Mark Yapelli, who has supported me through the ups and downs of this project since the early days of our journey together. I'm most grateful for his sense of humor and his overwhelming pride in all that I do.

"I WILL THANK YOU ALL WITH ALL MY HEART"

Black Girls and the Great Migration

Four days after the *Chicago Defender* declared May 15, 1917, the Great Northern Migration Day, a teenage girl in Selma, Alabama, asked its founder and editor, Robert Abbott, for help. The girl's letter to the nation's most influential black newspaper of the time captured the desperate conditions of life in the South and expressed her hopes to escape to Abbott's beloved Chicago. In the pages of the newspaper, Abbott promised that African Americans could secure well-paying jobs, send their children to modern schools, and revel in social freedoms unknown to most Southern girls. She wrote:

> Sirs I am writing to see if You all will please get me a job. And Sir I can wash dishes, wash, iron, nursing, work in groceries and dry good stores. Just any of these I can do. Sir, who so ever you get the job from, please tell them to send me a ticket and I will pay them When I get their, as I have not got enough money to pay my way. I am a girl of 17 years old and in the 8 grade at Knox Academy School, But on account of not having money enough I had to stop school. Sir I will thank you all with all my heart. May God Bless you all.[1]

Later that summer, another seventeen-year-old girl asked Abbott and the *Defender* staff to assist her exodus from Alexandria, Louisiana, and she exposed the family tensions sparked by her desire to migrate. "There isnt a thing for me to do, the wages here is from a dollar and a half a week. What could I earn Nothing. . . . I am tired of down hear in this, I am afraid to say. Father seem to care," she observed, "and then again don't seem to but Mother and I am tired tired of all of this.[2] Henrietta Ray Evans realized the other letter-writers' dreams of moving to Chicago. Her mother decided it was time for Henrietta's family to see if all the stories about "up North" were true; Henrietta later remembered vividly the preparations to leave the South. Her mother purchased new clothes for her, and she bid farewell to her friends Eddie and Georgiann, who told her dear friend that she "hate[d] to see me go away." They boarded "the IC train to Chicago" on a Saturday night, and during the journey she befriended a fellow teenage girl traveler. After the family disembarked at Chicago's Union Station, Henrietta's godfather collected the newcomers and led them to a home on "a very beautiful street." The family celebrated with dinner and a party. "I had a very good time."[3]

These pleas and recollections illustrate the many factors that motivated and shaped African American girls' and teenage women's experiences of the Great Migration, the transformative period between 1917 and 1970 in which more than seven million blacks fled the South and settled in northern and western cities in search of better jobs, schools, and social protections.[4] This book examines what happened to some of the girls and teenage women migrants who arrived in Chicago hoping that Abbott's, and the *Defender*'s, stories of the "promised land" were indeed true. As African American parents and community leaders experienced major changes in their economic, social, and cultural lives during the Migration, their outreach to girls led them to define black girlhood in relationship to their anxieties about urbanization, as well as their greatest hopes for the era.[5] In addition, Chicago's community leaders scrutinized black girls' behaviors, evaluated their choices, and assessed their possibilities as part of a larger conversation about what urbanization ultimately meant for black citizens. This book also looks at how adults constructed notions of girlhood in times of crisis—from institutional challenges to scandals to national crises, as well as how girls shared in collective dramas and personal regrets about migration. The strategies and language of social outreach were also claims to and hopes for black girlhood in a time of progress and peril.

Girls who migrated to Chicago with their families were able to do so because of a series of political and economic events that drew southerners to northern cities. Chicago's booming industries and their need for workers to supplement labor losses during a wave of anti-immigration legislation in the post–World War I era brought unprecedented opportunity for black men and women to seek out industrial work. As these northern industries flourished, the agricultural world of the South unraveled for black workers. The advent of the cotton picker and the boll weevil's agricultural reign of terror reduced the need for unskilled black labor in the South. With the expansion of the Illinois Central Railroad's routes into the Deep South, migration became an increasingly possible and desirous option for teenage girls from Selma to Alexandria, as well as others who followed suit, seeking a new life in the North.

The Great Migration roughly encompasses two periods: the First Migration, between 1910 and 1940, and the Second Migration, from 1940 to 1970. I mostly examine the first half of the Migration, when Chicago's African American population grew from 44,000 in 1910 to 234,000 in 1940.[6] In these years, Chicago's social scientists, urban reformers, and journalists engaged in rich conversations about the nature and importance of black girls to the larger culture of the Great Migration. They also debated black girls' influence on the emerging consumer, popular culture that grew in response to the rise in black population and urban employment, the expansion of (mostly segregated) educational opportunities for black children, and academic analyses of changes in black family dynamics in the city.

The Migration transformed neighborhoods in cities like Harlem, Detroit, and Chicago nearly overnight as black populations formed enclaves, opened stores, christened new churches, and most important, developed new identities as black urbanites. The majority of girls included in this study lived in the center of black Chicago life in the neighborhoods of Chicago's South Side, known as the Black Belt. The Black Belt was initially a small enclave south of Chicago's downtown that grew southward from nine blocks between Twenty-Second and Thirty-Fifth Streets to an area encompassing seventy-three blocks to Ninety-Fifth Street along Lake Michigan to the east.[7] I focus mostly on girls living and working in the city's South Side communities of the Second and Third Wards, particularly Bronzeville. Bronzeville was the commercial heart of black Chicago where girls and their families could patronize the black-owned Douglass National Bank, dine in Jim Crow–free restaurants like the Elite, enjoy movies at the Regal Theatre, and attend events at the "colored" Wabash Avenue branch of the Young Men's Christian Association.[8] I also include some stories of African Americans in suburban Chicago towns, for example Harvey and Evanston, where girls lived in institutions isolated from the mass of black Chicagoans but were still connected to them through the city's women's clubs and philanthropic circles.[9]

I chart the varied approaches to understanding black girls and defining black girlhood during the Great Migration. Black clubwomen's advocacy for girls revealed their belief that black girlhood was indeed multifaceted and critically important to black survival and progress. Clubwomen, in conjunction with the pioneers of urban ecology and urban sociology, religious leaders, and girls themselves, guided Chicago's Migration community in a struggle to validate and protect black girlhood. I not only look at institutional and adult responses to African American girls and discourses on black girlhood but also excavate Chicago's rich archives to reveal how girls themselves encountered these dynamic changes. Although black girls' narratives have not appeared in the bulk of scholarship on the Migration, they left behind powerful stories of hope, anticipation, and disappointment. These girls shared the concerns of the masses of southerners who heeded Abbott's call to head North—including a lack of educational opportunities, a sense of stagnation in the South, and low wages earned at the jobs that were necessary to support their families. Girls' reflections of the Migration encompassed a keen awareness of the racial terror of Jim Crow, visions of attending school and working outside the system of domestic labor, a prevailing sensibility that the North could provide respite from racial and sexual violence, and a deep desire to ensure economic security for their families.[10]

The city itself was also an ever-present influence on the way leaders crafted narratives about black girlhood. Many of the programs, ideas, and rhetoric surrounding African American girls in Chicago argued that the city was both an impediment and solution to improving their lives. In light of the dismal lot of many black girls in the South and the slight relief migrating to cities offered, these contradictions sometimes befuddled the most dedicated public servants. The city's role was not the only source of ambivalence about urban black girlhood. Reformers asserted that black girls were children in need of protection from the deleterious elements of urbanization. Yet they believed that girls, through their self-presentation and successes, could also carry the weighty responsibilities of race progress in the hopeful period after Emancipation. Scholars have explored the varied and related conditions in the South that pushed migrants toward cities like Chicago and assessed the northern opportunities that pulled them away from the familiarity of southern life, but girls do not appear in significant ways in Migration scholarship. Historians have pondered how the Migration reconfigured African American families and gender roles, but no study has contemplated the impact of the Migration on African American girlhood.[11] Through an examination of different ways Chicago's black cultural and community organizations reached out to and characterized black girls and girlhood, I reveal the racial, gender, and class tensions that arose from these attempts to understand black girls in an urban context.

The near absence of girls' lives in Migration history scholarship may be a matter of a belief that they are not present in the archive, or that by virtue of their race, gender, and age they could not contribute much to the period. Yet the fields of African American women's history and the history of childhood and youth provide us with the analytical tools and models to remedy girls' erasure in Migration studies. Historians of African American life and culture constantly confront the challenges of archives in chronicling the life of people who were not among the elite and most powerful classes, who have left few papers and publications to us because of their lack of education, low literacy rates, and working-class status. Historians of childhood and youth insist that children's dependency on adults does not necessarily preclude them from being historically significant actors.[12] Still, the questions of how to access their movements, their ideas, and even their formation into a recognizable constituency are especially challenging. Girlhood as a subject of inquiry can be researched by examining theories on childhood, evaluating school practices and curricula, and analyzing discourses on child psychology and psychosexual development. Yet research on actual girls' lives presents a number of vexing obstacles for the historian. Girls experience their own girlhood as a stage of life; it is not a fixed category. Girls do not bequeath material to research institutions, and material on juveniles is often classified or redacted to protect identities.

African American girls present an even greater set of obstacles to learning about their lives. Darlene Clark Hine's concepts of African American women's interiority and culture of dissemblance theorizes the strategies employed by black women to conceal their innermost thoughts and trauma while presenting a composed and open public persona.[13] These protective defense mechanisms were very likely passed down from migrant grandmothers and mothers to their daughters, nieces, and protégées in social outreach programs. Black women warned girls about the consequences of disclosing deep personal information to outsiders, as one migrant woman from the Mississippi Delta did when her children attended an integrated school in Indianapolis. "When our children went into those white schools, them white people wanted to know everything about them, their mamas and daddies and what was goin' on in they home, even if nothing appeared to be wrong."[14] Disparities in school attendance between white and black children also limit the archive of black girlhood. Black girls have fewer editorials in school newspapers, photographs in the glossy pages of yearbooks, and carefully locked diaries to allow a historian to excavate their passions and private thoughts. Many girls' footprints are subsumed within the giant steps of adults; yet, their interactions with institutions, social science research, media, and educational bodies have created an alternative archive that provides a steady backbone for research on black girls and girlhood.

The archive's challenges cannot excuse historians from engaging girls, or children, entirely. As Wilma King has demonstrated in her research on black children, the historian must work creatively and exhaustively to find black children's voices. Nor can historians believe that race's predictive and all too often devastating function in the period invalidates age as a useful and mutually constitutive category of analysis. At the heart of this study is a question that structured activism and discourses during the Migration: whether black girls were really ever girls in the era of Jim Crow, rampant urban poverty, and gendered inequality.

Black girls' ideas and perspectives are presented as much as possible throughout this book. Their voices have been extracted from a wide array of sources in order to present a picture of girls' participation in schools, churches, families, and communities. My sources range from the traditional—the *Chicago Defender* and other black periodicals, the records of National Association of Colored Women's Clubs affiliates—to locations where African American girls' voices are "buried" in larger studies, including the national survey of the White House Conference on Child Health and Protection and the diaries of social work students reflecting on practicum with interracial clubs at settlement houses and camps.

GIRL PROBLEMS

Black southerners' many reasons for choosing migration are clear to us today, but girls' specific role in animating the decision to migrate is an important consideration in deepening our appreciation for black girls' history. A May 1910 news brief communicated the dangers surrounding poor, black girls in the South. A newspaper reported that a ten-year-old "child nurse" in Demopolis, Alabama, was jailed after a "wealthy planter" accused her of poisoning her two charges, a three-month-old baby and a two-year-old child. The story claimed that the poisoning was the girl's retaliation because her employer denied her time off to go to Birmingham for a day trip. The jail was "heavily guarded" to protect her from a "possible attempt to lynch her."[15] The severity of this incident by no means reflected the behavior of most black girls who worked as domestics in white households in the South. The details of this anecdote do capture the complicated position of black girls within the Southern labor market and judicial system. The girl's massive responsibility for the care of two children and, if she indeed poisoned the two children, her highly reactive, and perhaps impulsive, response to being deprived of a day trip are weighted by a social context in which she is also in danger of lynching at the hands of a mob. Her status as a wage earner was not necessarily unusual for her time and place, but the severity of the alleged crime and the community's response undoubtedly frightened other black families about their own daughters' vulnerability in their workplaces and heightened their reception of the reports of how differently black girls lived in the North. Well-paying jobs allowed for daughters to enjoy the schools open to black children. And, most important, Chicago was a place where lynching was not a threat for child or adult alike—although, as the 1919 riots demonstrate, racial violence was not entirely out of the realm of possibility in the city.

The child nurse's story points to three important and related issues black girls in the South faced: a lack of educational opportunities and consistent schooling; the entry of girls into the labor market at a young age; and sexual vulnerability and constant threats to their personal safety due to racist practices of bosses, and little protection from the police or courts. Girls in the South entered menial labor jobs early in their lives, accompanying their mothers to jobs in "white folks' kitchens" or working sharecropped land. If migration could not keep girls out of domestic

BLACK GIRLS AND THE GREAT MIGRATION 7

service entirely, at the very least they would be better compensated for their efforts in the North. According to a 1916 *Defender* editorial, African American girls and women earned between "$5 and $7 a week with room and board, as maids, nurses, and cooks" in the North.[16] Those wages were twice as much as those offered in the South, and tales of friends and relatives who had already left the South suggested that working conditions were far better in cities. Families saw migrating as an opportunity to ameliorate their present status, and for the first time they could dream about controlling their own futures and changing their children's lives.

Higher wages were not the only reason why parents yearned to move their children to the North. The future of their children was another powerful factor in the decision to migrate. Migration promised the possibility of better schools and longer school attendance. Pro-Migration newspapers publicized multi-grade schools for black children. Poor black children in the South attended one-room schoolhouses until the harvest season or the need to send a child to work cut short the school year or the educational process altogether. One migrant girl told investigators that her school, "which was in session only three months a year," had "100 to 125 children under one teacher." The report concluded that the girl was academically and developmentally delayed due to a lack of formal schooling.[17] Future Chicagoans were undoubtedly moved by the *Defender*'s reports of African American youth attending schools such as the Wendell Phillips High School, established by black Chicago in successful protest against school segregation decades before the start of the Migration, as well as stories of adult courses. A 1913 article described a night school class as "but one of many . . . enacted in the big city," with "students from six to sixty earnestly seeking knowledge, the one thing that makes us what we are."[18] Readers learned that girls could take courses as diverse as foreign languages, stenography, art, and "everything essential in the world today . . . merely for the asking."[19] James Grossman's Migration study of Chicago notes: "For the first time since the heyday of the Freedmen's Bureau Schools, black Southerners could entertain expectations that their children might receive an education that would enable them to compete with whites."[20]

Black mothers in the South, traumatized by their own experiences of sexual victimization as girls, thought the North could provide more protections for their daughters. Many believed that Southern working and living arrangements made girls extremely vulnerable to sexual advances and abuses from both white and black men. As one oral historian recorded in her work on Mississippi women migrants, for some, "the need to migrate had less to do with their desire to be in the industrial work place than with the pains they suffered as young girls."[21] Another woman from Mississippi knew that she could not leave the town of Moss Point unless she and her daughters all had good, safe jobs. She requested that Abbott find "a first class cooking job or washing job" for herself and work for "three young girls ages thirteen to sixteen years."[22] One migrant remembered: "The country was a place where people lived so close together in their physical and housing space, and it was the perfect place where little girls, because they were always working around grown men, were at a risk of being sexually abused in the fields . . . So, I left because I wanted my children to be safe."[23] The potential for their daughters to live free from sexual violence eased the pangs of homesickness and the sacrifices that accompanied leaving the South.

As for fathers, the constant fear of economic reprisal from employers and the chilling effect of lynching impeded African American men from "standing up" to white men's abuse of the girls and women in their lives. Therefore, implicit in the rhetoric of freedom in the various articles and stories about migration was a guarantee that African American men could realize the role of patriarch. In a letter to the *Defender* in the fall of 1917, a migrant to Philadelphia put it this way: "Don't have to mister every little white boy comes along. I haven't heard a white man call a colored a nigger . . . since I been in the state of Pa." With the opportunity to be the man in his household, and in the community, a black father could simultaneously give his daughter a chance to be a girl for the first time. Black girls who worked as child servants and teen nurses lived in a world where white men could provide for the protection of female family members and the larger culture buttressed white men's oversight over their wives and daughters. Like their fathers, black girls may have also believed that moving to Chicago would allow them to assume a new role, to live like the beloved white daughters of the households they worked in, the same daughters they befriended as children and later deferred to when they became their household workers.[24]

BLACK GIRLS AND WOMEN'S REFORM CULTURE

Parents alone could not create a new meaning of African American girl-hood, or make a case for its importance to the larger community of migrants. Institutions such as black women's clubs, orphanages, and recreational programs made the public case for African American girls through their interventions with newly arrived girls. Some needed homes, others schools and jobs, yet all compelled race women, or black social reformers, to refute the disparaging characterizations of black girls that stemmed from the racialized, sexual stereotyping of black women. The stereotypes of African American female sexuality as unbridled and deviant shaped what girls could expect from their allies and adversaries of all colors. White community leaders and philanthropists, including the heads of community agencies and public charities that reached out to migrant girls, believed their interventions could reform individual black girls' propensity for sexual immorality. Black organizations steeped in racial uplift ideologies—a communal investment in overcoming stereotype through a commitment to piety, industriousness, and chaste living—believed that black girls needed to represent their race by limiting their expressions of sexuality and desire and displaying the values of the black middle class.[25] In order to engage the public in reconsidering black girlhood, community leaders had to refute what scholar Susan Cahn describes as a lack of recognition of child status for black girls. Cahn's comparison of black and white girls in the New South concludes that "upon puberty the African American girl moved instantly from child status to an image of a sexually promiscuous, enticing woman or the older, rotund, asexual Mammy."[26] Even regarding black girls' "child status," leaders in law enforcement, state legislators, and white social reformers who supported age-of-consent laws for white girls did not equally value African American girls. A black girl's age often failed to inspire widespread concern or compassion in matters of sexual assault, education, and labor protection.[27]

Chicago's thriving reform culture organized itself around black girls and young women's educational, employment, and social needs. Chicago's women reformers were among the nation's most organized and sophisticated, with leaders establishing settlement houses, orphanages, and the nation's first juvenile court. Initially serving millions of southern and eastern European immigrants who arrived in Chicago in the late nineteenth century, white women reformers responded to the black migration with similar approaches. White women working alongside black women recruited volunteers to welcome "friendless" young women, advocated for more schools and sought to eliminate truancy, and crusaded against vice in Chicago's beer gardens and late-night cafeterias, where they believed girls and young women were most susceptible to sexual exploitation.[28]

White women reformers, like Hull House founder Jane Addams, often used their experiences with immigrants to shape work with black Chicagoans. Addams concluded that although black and immigrant families needed similar services to quell poverty and inculcate their children with sound, American (meaning middle-class) values, she recognized that racial discrimination, even in the North, limited girls' ability to fully realize Chicago's many promises.[29] In a 1911 article in the National Association for the Advancement of Colored People (NAACP) publication *The Crisis*, she wrote: "A decent colored family, if it is also poor, often finds it difficult to rent a house, save one that is undesirable, because it is situated near a red-light district, and the family in the community least equipped with its social tradition is forced to expose its daughters to the most flagrantly immoral conditions the community permits."[30] Addams's belief that the city held the power to guide girls' behaviors was common among urban reformers, who sought to physically and morally cleanse the city and its inhabitants. Yet black reformers, even those most steeped in racial uplift thinking, were not eager to endorse the notion that black families inherently lacked "social tradition" and were entirely unable to properly protect their daughters. Black women reformers instead believed that the poor simply needed the right influences to redeem themselves and perfect their families.

Addams partnered with a cohort of Chicago's black women reformers; many of them were among the city's "old settler" community. Old-settler women formed social clubs, mutual aid societies, and churches based on their shared heritage and status as the black elite of the Midwest. Concerned that they might be associated with Southern migrants, old settlers reified their identities to consolidate their class privilege over poor blacks. In 1905, Hope Ives Dunmore established a formal Old Settlers Club and required members to prove that they had been in Chicago for at least thirty years.[31] Historian Ann Meis Knupfer's research on African American women's clubs emphasizes the rich diversity of clubs that sprang from the old-settler activism in Chicago. Knupfer identified 150 active women's clubs in Chicago by 1915, with interests ranging from literacy to child care to antilynching campaigns.[32] These clubs set the tone, goals, and methods with which black institutions conducted outreach to girls.

Old–Settlers Club member Irene McCoy Gaines, a Republican Party activist and onetime political candidate, settled in Chicago in 1892 and attended high school in the city. Gaines was among the strongest advocates for black girls in the Black Belt, establishing a black chapter of the World War I girls group, the Minute Girls, and girls' recreational programs at the YWCA. In a 1920 editorial, Gaines depicted black girls' needs as "one of the most absorbing questions that confront the negro to-day" and pled with readers to raise funds for the estimated ten thousand Black Belt girls who did not have access to "a single swimming pool or gymnasium."[33] Old settlers were perhaps inspired to conduct outreach to migrant girls because their own daughters lived lives drastically different from those of girls from the South. Old-settler girls, although constricted by some of the city's racial policies, sometimes attended schools with whites, attended girls' club teas, and debuted at balls and cotillions. Old-settler women's outreach did not advocate for equality among their girls and the masses of needy migrant girls, but they did arouse these women's sense of civic and Christian duty to protect these girls from some of the most dangerous elements of city life, particularly in the workplace and Black Belt neighborhoods.[34]

The influential network of black and white women reformers shaped the conversations and methods used to evaluate and determine the risks to and moral fitness of black girls. Reformers identified nefarious employment agents, the city's saloons and streetcars, poor families, and even girls' own moral failings as exacerbating girls' problems. They often shared many concerns and believed to be in common cause, but the realities of race and racism in Chicago made their alliances tense, and at times combative. Battles across racial lines among women—as well as gendered and class lines among African American leaders—shaped the discourse and action around black girls. I examine these fragile relationships and ties throughout this book so as to present a fuller picture of how racial uplift operated among a specific constituency—black girls and teenage women.

Historians of gender and urbanization have provided valuable insights into middle-class, civic, and community leaders' interventions in the lives of girls and young women through studies of maternity homes for unwed mothers, girls' courts and juvenile justice facilities, and rescue campaigns to eradicate prostitution.[35] These types of women's social outreach work created a space for educated women to professionalize their maternalist missions, which established that women had a special role to play in urban reform because of their innate sense of compassion and moral authority on family issues. Their crusades and the mechanisms of social policing these women established in the process was a response to the late nineteenth and early twentieth century's construction of "the girl problem," an umbrella term for young women's behaviors and practices ranging from girls and single women enjoying public amusements to having premarital sex to committing crimes. This wide expanse of legal and illegal acts raised concerns in industrializing cities because these behaviors challenged gender roles in the family and workplace, destabilized racialized expectations of white female virtue, and exacerbated notions of black female deviancy.[36]

My central concern extends beyond moral panics about girls, in that I explore the ways reformers and leaders made a case for the state of black girlhood. Driven by impulses that characterized girls as in need of protection in some contexts and deeply deviant and troubled in others, Chicago reformers regarded black girls in a variety of ways, but at the root of all these representations were contestations about power in a changing city. This book incorporates these conversations about morality and family decline in the period of black urbanization and focuses on how black communities constructed the notion that black girls, like their white counterparts, existed as vulnerable and in need of investment. Black girlhood also represented promise and problems for black community leaders. This book captures how Great Migration era leaders, institutions and girls conceptualized black girlhood, and the accompanying tensions that outreach work to girls engendered between whites and blacks, men and women, the rich and the poor, and their sometimes contradictory efforts and perspectives. I look beyond the surface of "girl problems," and the attendant practices and policies of the state and its apparatuses of control, to consider how black institutions, leaders, and families understood girls and teenage women as cultural and social symbols, and how the political and rhetorical uses of girlhood often failed to adequately serve or protect girls.

Scholarship on the history of children and childhood in the United States alerts us to the constructed nature of this stage of life and the way race and class have served to undermine children of color's access to this category. Any project about girls and girlhood leads to the inevitable question as to who is a girl. Can a particular age delineate girlhood and womanhood? Girls' studies scholars and historians of girlhood in the United States have argued that girlhood is a culturally created and constantly shifting category, shaped by culture, religion, and family structure.[37] For the purposes of this project, I define girls in accordance with the ways girlhood was defined by child protection laws, age-of-consent legislation, and mandatory school attendance policies in the first half of the twentieth century. Louise de Koven Bowen, a settlement house leader and head of Chicago's Juvenile Protective Association, broadly characterized African American girls as unmarried and in the teenage years or younger. By 1913, the *Reference Book on Juvenile Welfare: A Review of the Chicago Social Service System* referred to "dependent and neglected children . . . as any boy under seventeen or girl under eighteen years of age." Girls younger than eighteen were subject to laws and policies that dictated their employment protocols, ability to legally consent to sex, and access to social services.[38] The *Reference Book* lamented a lack of concern for older teenage girls, which it blamed on "lax parenthood, sometimes indifferent and sometimes ignorant of dangers." This inattention to children caused "young girls to troop the streets unescorted in the evening. The girl question is largely one outside of school hours. Social workers save children up to the age of 16 or 17, and often sorrow begins where the law maximum ends." The guide concluded that the liminal period of early womanhood, or late adolescence, was particularly vexing: "The question of the girl between 16 and 20 is growing more and more perplexing to the parent."[39] I found some teenaged women in the archive who were fourteen and married during the Migration era, but the majority of the girls in this book are eighteen or younger, unmarried, and dependent on parents or institutions for either some or all of their livelihood.

I do not adhere to a rigid definition of girlhood, but I use the context of the time period to ascertain who was considered a girl, and therefore eligible to access girls' programs and guidance on growing into womanhood. This method does not necessarily yield a uniform definition either. During the Migration, the Illinois age-of-consent law determined sixteen as an appropriate age in which young women could engage in sexual activity, which was representative of most states. State legislatures, influenced by women activists from the temperance and social purity movements, set the age of consent as young as fourteen and as old as eighteen in their campaigns to reform rape laws.[40] Girls younger than fifteen who became mothers or married are often described in black sociologist E. Franklin Frazier's *The Negro Family in Chicago* as engaging in early marriage and eliciting concern from truant officers and social workers. Fifteen years of age demarcated girlhood in the majority of Frazier's work on family life, and he included labor statistics for African American girls as young as ten, pointing to the role girls had to play in the economic survival of their families, even if community and family still deemed them children.[41] Middle-class status and high school attendance prolonged girlhood among the daughters of the most affluent African American communities, and outreach programs for girls enrolled in high school often assumed a level of economic dependence among these girls.

Chapter 1 opens with the early Migration years and discusses the brief but insightful history of the Amanda Smith Industrial School for Colored Girls as an entry point to discuss girls at the margins of Bronzeville, also known as the Black Metropolis. Founded by evangelist Amanda Smith in 1899 as the state's first orphanage for African American children, her school triggered heated debates about what black girls needed, due to their status as orphans, dependents, or delinquents; their institutional care; and the purpose of urban industrial education. Community leaders determined that if the school's girls received loving care at the boarding school, a solid domestic education, and avenues for employment after graduation, they would be poised to become race mothers, who would transform black families and futures. The school's strong sense of mission and benevolent leaders could not shield it from a range of problems, from financial insolvency to conflicts among its benefactors — African American clubwomen and white philanthropists. The two factions held different perspectives on racial integration of girls' institutions, the fitness of African Americans to lead outreach initiatives, and the potential threat black girls posed to their white peers. These racial and ideological divides fueled tensions surrounding the question of who knew what was best for African American girls. The battles were as much about the meaning of black girlhood as about the fates of dependent, delinquent, and destitute girls themselves.

In chapter 2, I focus on the way the image of black girls figured in the growing marketplaces of Chicago, as it related to the commercial spaces where girls exercised their rights and privileges as consumers and the religious market, where storefront churches, new spiritual movements, and old-settler congregations coexisted uneasily and all had their own means of evaluating and reaching girls. The chapter unfolds with the years leading up to the sexual exploitation scandal that disrupted one of Chicago's black religious communities, the early Moorish Science Temple of America (MSTA), a New Negro movement religion often characterized as an amalgamation of Islam, Eastern religions, and black nationalist politics. Churches and religious organizations provided much-needed social and spiritual relief to migrant girls and families. In a departure from scholarship on racial uplift, which focuses almost exclusively on Christian churches and their outreach, I examine why migrants were drawn to the Moorish Science Temple and similar groups. Although not explicitly a girls' group or an organization traditionally associated with racial uplift, the Moorish Science Temple demonstrates the important role gender, women, and girls played in sustaining and unmaking a powerful, African American religious, economic, and political formation in Chicago. I examine the complex dynamics of the Temple's idyllic framing of black girlhood and the scandal that exposed the Temple to scrutiny from black elites. The Moorish girls' programs reveal the way religion and commercial markets contributed to the public perceptions of black girlhood, female sexuality, and a burgeoning commercial beauty culture in Chicago.

The economic vitality that fueled 1920s commerce and Chicago's many job-creating industries came to a screeching halt after the nation plunged into the Great Depression after the stock market crashed in the fall of 1929. The Depression and the New Deal era are the backdrops to chapter 3's engagement with how black girls figured in the responses to the economic calamity in Chicago. I discuss the way black sorority women organized vocational guidance programs for girls in the interwar years, the campaigns sparked by black leftists to use economic boycotts to create clerical jobs for black teenage women, and the opportunities available to black girls in Chicago's National Youth Administration Resident School for Girls. In focusing on three movements, I discuss the emergence of black girls' school culture and the distance between movement rhetoric about education's equalizing effect and the realities of girls' educational and occupational opportunities. Although these three approaches varied, they all obscured the social realities of black girls across a wide economic spectrum and reveal that the promises of a northern education were often unrealized by even the most motivated and talented girl.

In chapter 4, I examine black girls as citizens in Chicago's New Deal era, as the Second Great Migration strained the city's limits of acceptance and resources. I look at two ways adults and authorities viewed black girls as citizens, as a way to examine their participation in, and resistance to notions of, being good citizens. First, I uncover African American girls' participation in the Camp Fire Girls, a national camping organization established in 1910 by Progressive Movement activists Charlotte and Luther Gulick. The couple promised that Camp Fire prepared girls for the women's work of a modern era while emphasizing the frontier values and skills of the past—the tending of the pioneer campfire and the care of the home. Although the national organization did not explicitly bar African American girls from membership, Camp Fire regularly ignored the contributions of African American groups and racism within the organization's local councils. Black Camp Fire groups reinterpreted the organization's mission to fit the concerns and conditions of black girls. Their work relied on using discourses of African American girls' innocence *and* depravity to construct black girlhood as aligned with the leisure opportunities and commitment to citizenship embedded in the Camp Fire program. African American Camp Fire leaders, who confronted the political dimensions of children's play and leisure by galvanizing community resources, and by grappling with segregation and Chicago's collective fears about juvenile delinquency and sexuality, determined that black girls were entitled to childhood experiences. Then I focus on constructions of black girls as bad citizens through an analysis of the interviews conducted by Frazier that contributed to his landmark *The Negro Family in Chicago* (1932). I provide a larger frame for Frazier's conclusions about black girls and families by analyzing the content of black girls' interviews with Frazier and their perspectives on Chicago and their place in the city.

The title of this book refers to Chicago's South Side, where migrants toiled in factories, lived in overcrowded kitchenettes, swayed to the blues on Saturday nights, and shouted gospel praises in storefront churches on Sunday mornings, and to its most beloved and well-known daughter, First Lady Michelle Obama. At the 2008 Democratic National Convention, her mother, Marian Robinson, invited delegates and viewers to learn more about her daughter via a six-minute biopic aptly titled "South Side Girl." The film, which featured Obama's friends, family, and colleagues, highlighted her girlhood in Chicago. The film reinforced the Robinson family's modest beginnings and identity as proud South Siders to the nation. Her early school and family photos highlighted the multiple experiences of the many African American girls and teenage women who grew up on the South Side, whether poor, middle class, or privileged. Ever proud of her connection to the center of Chicago's African American history and life, Mrs. Obama included her neighborhood in her official White House biography. It states that daughters Sasha and Malia were born on the South Side of Chicago, "like their mother."[42]

African Americans considered black girlhood in different ways in their efforts to adjust to and understand the experience of Migration. African American urbanization, for some, did make good on the promises of greater freedom, economic mobility, and rooted families. Yet for most, migration produced ambivalence, disappointment, and confusion about rights, responsibilities, and roles in this new era of black life. African Americans had to respond to the impact of race, gender, and age discrimination in order to make a case that they, too, cared for and supported black girls and that their progress would help articulate the meaning of black girlhood. The girls you will meet in the following pages experienced Chicago in many ways. You will meet girls who realized their dreams in neighborhood schools and improved their families' fortunes in good jobs and girls who grew into women who vowed to never return to the South. You will learn about girls who found a city filled with danger and excitement and, for the first time in their lives, choices about who and what they wanted to become. You will also read stories about girls who could not wait to see the "promised land"; girls whose parents changed in unbearable ways when they arrived at their new homes; and girls whose hopefulness transformed into deep despair that life had not changed at all.

"DO YOU SEE THAT GIRL?"

The Dependent, the Destitute, and

the Delinquent Black Girl

In the September 1916 edition of the *Amanda Smith School News*, principal Adah M. Waters painted a bleak picture of African American girlhood at the dawn of the Great Migration era. Waters asked readers: "Do you see the ragged, unkempt foul-mouthed girl that stands at the street corner pelting those boys with stones for jostling her from the sidewalk?" Founded in 1899 by Christian missionary Amanda Smith as the Amanda Smith Orphanage and Industrial Home for Abandoned Destitute Colored Children, Waters's school had started out as Illinois's first orphanage for African American children. Renamed and reconstituted in 1912 as the Amanda Smith Industrial School for Colored Girls, it relied on Waters's fundraising appeals to stir black Chicagoans to action on behalf of her girls. Waters described a girl with a "face . . . clouded by sullen passion," wearing "soiled motley clothing . . . her scant cover for [her] unwashed body." She warned that this girl's survival and success was important not only in the case of one abandoned child but also for all African Americans at the dawn of a new era. "Nevertheless the young body may imprison a soul destined by the All-Father to say the word, do the deed, think the thought, and live the life that may move or revolutionize a world. Be careful! A soul with mighty potentialities is about to be worse than wasted! That girl . . . needs love, the right environment and training."[1]

The Amanda Smith Industrial School for Colored Girls offered the "right environment and training" for a black girl abandoned by an unwed mother, or for a teenager orphaned by migrant parents whose immune systems had been unable to resist an influenza outbreak. The school bulletin, a key tool for thanking benefactors and attracting potential donors, illustrated the multifaceted concerns about African American girls in Chicago: vulnerability on city streets, harassment from boys, poor or neglectful parents who did not know or care to bathe and properly clothe their daughters, exposure to scrutiny and disdain from onlookers, and worst of all, the lack of a family or community to cultivate a girl's gifts and talents. In one carefully crafted paragraph, Waters invited Chicagoans to consider what they could do to save this girl and other black girls. She also challenged them to think about what girls could ultimately be for their families, communities, and race. The school's brief history demonstrates the enmeshed issues facing African American girls and their advocates from the years immediately preceding the first wave of the Great Migration and extending into the pivotal period when Chicago's black population soared.

The formation of the Amanda Smith Industrial School for Colored Girls and its leaders' tireless efforts to keep it open reveal the complicated ways the first industrial school for orphaned black girls in Chicago made the case for the proper care of black girls by arguing that they were indeed children who were worthy of protection. Paradoxically, the school's advocates did this by emphasizing black girls' future importance: as race mothers, they would lead the crucial work of racial uplift and community rehabilitation. In addition, these advocates established a narrative of black girlhood that was centered on the sanctity and possibilities of the black home and family in an era when poverty and racism severely limited black Chicagoans' ability to fulfill even the smallest parts of the uplift mandate. Fears about girls' sexuality, as well as the suitability of black leaders to manage their own community resources, locked black girls into an impossible position in community battles. Girls' advocates used black girls' moral and social fitness as an indicator of race progress and health in order to compel black Chicagoans to act on behalf of institutions like the Amanda Smith Industrial School for Colored Girls. This chapter uncovers the rhetorical approaches to convincing Chicagoans to care for orphaned black girls and considers the material conditions that created destitution among this population, in order to reveal how black communities highlighted and obscured the impact of the Great Migration on black girls.

In order to better understand the struggles and significance of the Amanda Smith Industrial School for Colored Girls, I look to the organizational strategies of Smith, her successor Waters, and the commitment of the school's board member Ida B. Wells-Barnett in order to present the difficulties of work with girls at the dawn of the Migration. I situate the school in relationship to two important institutional movements in Chicago. The school's founding coincided with the growth of children's social services within a network of orphanages, the Juvenile Court, and girls' homes established and managed by influential white women. As a black institution, the School also contended with the alliances and brokerage politics of the Urban League and other African American organizations led by men. These forces impeded black women's ability to control institutions for girls, and the school's brief history illustrates how shifts in power influenced attitudes and perspectives on black girls' future in Chicago. Through careful examination of cases adjudicated in the city's Court of Domestic Relations and the School's records, a view of the early years of the Migration emerges that shows how black girls and young women entered the foyers, parlors, and admission desks of institutions devoted to their care and other spaces that merely tolerated their presence. The stories in this chapter move beyond the anecdote about the sullen girl longing for the right home and toward the actual girls—some abandoned, some criminalized, some searching for autonomy—who experienced the limits of Chicago's ability to protect and care for them.

This chapter is divided into two sections, the first one devoted to Amanda Smith's journey from slavery into prominence as a figure in the African Methodist Episcopal (AME) Church. Smith's remarkable life, which included close relationships with leaders in an array of social movements and great renown among black and white Methodists, highlights the racial dynamics of women's reform culture in late nineteenth- and early twentieth-century cities. Smith's 1893 autobiography, *The Story of the Lord's Dealings with Mrs. Amanda Smith, the Colored Evangelist: Containing an Account of her Life, Work of Faith, and her Travels in America, England, Ireland, Scotland, India and Africa, as an Independent Missionary*, detailed her visits to orphanages in India and Liberia. She shared with her audience her perspectives on child-rearing, black girlhood, and commitment to the racial uplift beliefs that circulated among her cohort of black institution builders. This section also provides context for understanding Chicago's networks of orphanages, children's homes, and industrial training schools that sought to protect and rehabilitate children, especially those from immigrant and black migrant families.

The second section focuses on the establishment and operations of the Amanda Smith Industrial School for Colored Girls, specifically the racial tensions that hampered its progress and its position in debates about the nature of black girlhood, race, and sexuality. I present a snapshot of girls whom the Juvenile Court and social workers deemed dependent, delinquent, and destitute and the many ways these girls and their families interacted with institutions. Even after its destruction by fire in 1918, the school remained a source of contention and inspiration for black leaders.

THE LORD'S DEALINGS WITH AMANDA SMITH

Nearly a decade before Waters asked if African Americans could truly see the desperate state of their girls, Amanda Smith presided over the institution that she believed was the fulfillment of a great call from God. Smith's journey from her birth into slavery on a plantation in Long Green, Maryland, in 1837 to the morning of June 28, 1899, when she christened the Amanda Smith Orphanage and Industrial Home for Abandoned Destitute Colored Children amid a "wild storm of wind and rain," was a remarkable one.[2] Smith was the eldest girl of Samuel Berry and Miriam Matthews's thirteen children. Berry purchased his family's freedom when Smith was a young girl, and the newly emancipated family settled in Pennsylvania.[3] Smith's early life was filled with tragedies nearly as dismal as her years in bondage. She lost one husband to the Civil War and she endured the deaths of four of her five children by the age of thirty-two.[4] In order to resist bouts of depression and temptations from the secular world, Smith attended lively religious camp meetings and revivals. In 1868, after years of attending invigorating celebrations of faith, Smith committed herself fully to God and became "sanctified"—the pinnacle of human purity in the AME Church. She preached and performed songs at Methodist camp meetings for nine years before she heard the call to go overseas to spread the Word.[5]

In an era when few black women traveled outside their towns and counties, Smith was among a privileged group of black women missionaries who spread Christianity abroad.[6] She set sail for England in 1878, and her next destination, India, proved most valuable to her later work, as she ministered to Christian converts in a church-sponsored orphanage.

Smith concluded her missionary years in Africa, traveling to Liberia and across West Africa, again working in orphanages. She adopted two children while overseas, a boy named Robert and a girl, Frances. Robert later joined the other orphans at the Amanda Smith Orphanage and Industrial Home for Abandoned Destitute Colored Children.

This evangelist's decision to establish an orphanage and later a girls' school drew on her personal experiences as a widowed mother to her own daughter Maizie after the Civil War and as an adoptive mother to Frances, her beloved "Bassa girl" from Liberia, the nation colonized by freed US slaves in the 1820s.[7] After Smith's first husband died, she sent Maizie to board with other families because she lacked the resources to raise her daughter alone. Smith agonized over this decision. "Sometimes she was well taken care of and other times was not. I found that often people do things just for the little money they get out of it." When a family neglected Maizie, and Smith "had to turn around and leave her," she "cried and prayed." Smith remarried in order to create a stable family for Maizie, but that marriage proved unsatisfactory. By the time she embarked on her speaking tour and missions abroad, she had found a school in Baltimore to care for and educate her daughter.[8]

Later, Smith invited her daughter to travel to England and further her education, but Maizie wanted to marry instead. Smith was not initially pleased with her daughter's decision. Citing the fact that few black girls were afforded such a chance to travel, Smith told her daughter: "If you can risk losing the opportunity that not many colored girls have had, and that you will not have again, and think more of the man, and take him in preference after all I have said, I guess the safest plan is that you remain." Smith's affinity for her adopted daughter, Frances, was immediate, and perhaps the girl, who was twelve or thirteen years old when Smith met her, reminded her of the daughter she had had to leave behind in the States. Smith traveled with Frances and Robert to Sierra Leone but when she returned to the United Kingdom, she could not bring Frances with her because of the girl's poor health.[9]

In her autobiography, Smith documented practices toward girls and teenage women that she observed in Africa that upset her. She vividly recounted witnessing a group of men beating a teenage girl, and she used her status as a missionary to retrieve the girl from her attackers and take

FIG 1.1. Amanda Berry Smith established the first orphanage for African American children in Harvey, Illinois. The orphanage later became the Amanda Smith Industrial School for Colored Girls in 1912. "Amanda Smith." Photograph by unknown, 1893.

MANUSCRIPTS, ARCHIVES AND RARE BOOKS DIVISION, SCHOMBURG CENTER FOR RESEARCH IN BLACK CULTURE, THE NEW YORK PUBLIC LIBRARY, ASTOR, LENOX AND TILDEN FOUNDATIONS.

her away from her much older husband. Smith was also critical of Liberia's tolerance of arranged marriages for adolescent girls. "Poor things, they are not consulted; they have no choice in the matter. If they don't like the man, they are obliged to go with him anyway, no matter how illy he may treat them; and sometimes they are cruelly treated. But their own father could not protect them." Smith also criticized the lack of educational opportunities for girls in Africa. "There is so little attention paid to the education of girls; not a single high school for girls in the whole republic of Liberia. It is a great shame and a disgrace to the government." Other Christian missionaries established schools akin to American industrial schools in Liberia, and Smith was impressed by the schools' training models. She was "delighted" with the Episcopal School's "house-keeping department, where in connection with their studies, each girl took her turn in the sweeping, dusting, making bread, biscuit, pie, or cake, and in washing dishes and attending the dining room. This, it seemed to me, was the most essential of all."[10]

With memories of the African and Indian orphanages imprinted on her heart and mind, Smith returned to the United States in 1896. She immediately appealed to her friendships with white reformers to create a home for black children in Illinois. Her friend and colleague Frances Willard, founder of the Women's Christian Temperance Union (WCTU), may have helped her settle in the town of North Harvey, a protemperance community thirty miles north of Chicago. Smith was an avid critic of African Americans who drank alcohol. In an 1886 article for the *Christian Standard Home and Journal,* she wrote: "Oh, how the curse of strong drink has almost ruined us as a church, as a republic, as a race. Africa's greatest need is temperance and holiness. Without these we never can be of any use to our native brethren, nor to ourselves."[11] Willard recruited prominent black Christian women to join the temperance movement and spread the antialcohol message among blacks. Smith and Willard maintained a close relationship throughout Smith's life, despite the fact that many black clubwomen, notably antilynching advocate Ida B. Wells-Barnett, criticized the WCTU president for her apologies for southern lynching. Regardless of her ill feelings toward Willard, Wells-Barnett was among the most dedicated of the Amanda Smith Industrial School for Colored Girls—the later incarnation of Smith's project to help African American children.[12]

BLACK CHILDREN AND INSTITUTIONAL CARE IN CHICAGO

Smith's decision to settle in the Chicago area was a fitting one, considering the city's status as a national model for civic reform and a center of advanced municipal services and child-care institutions in the late nineteenth century. Chicago's first orphanage was established in 1849 in response to a citywide cholera epidemic. Orphanages expanded through the following decades and cared for Protestant and Catholic children separately. Orphans often hailed from homes in which they still had a surviving or remaining parent but the family could not meet the child's needs. Despite the growth of children's institutions into the early twentieth century, few resources were made available to black children.[13] Between 1899 and 1911, the Amanda Smith Orphanage and Industrial Home for Abandoned Destitute Colored Children was the only Protestant institution for the care of African American children in the state of Illinois.

Prior to Smith's opening of her orphanage and later christening of the Amanda Smith Industrial School for Colored Girls, care for black children varied across the state, and black women reformers wondered if the existing institutions provided equal attention and nurturing to black residents. Long before trains deposited scores of black southerners in Chicago, the smattering of blacks in the city and in small Illinois towns had been reading stories of black girls abandoned by the institutions that claimed to save them. On the afternoon of Friday, August 27, 1897, the Geneva State Reformatory for Girls had gathered six of its black residents to serve as pallbearers at the funeral of Annie Lulu Jackson, the first girl to die at the facility. Jackson, a fifteen-year-old resident, had arrived at Geneva in February 1896 in "sickly condition." Under the care of resident physician Doctor Benthol, the young girl had slowly recovered from consumption, or tuberculosis. Mysteriously, her health was improving when she passed away. For concerned black leaders, Jackson's death may have signaled the inability for white-run institutions to provide adequate care for black girls.[14]

Civic and community agencies, such as the Illinois Children's Home and Aid Society (ICHAS), lent support to orphanages and other institutions, and they recognized a need for an organized system to care for black children before the tide of Migration. The ICHAS's 1913 investigation of twenty-two settlement house day nurseries, kindergartens, and orphanages reported that only half of these institutions were willing to accept

African American children and often imposed restrictions on the ones they did admit.[15] For instance, the Chicago Home for Boys claimed that they had tried to admit black children in the past and concluded that integration was a "failure" after one experiment. The Chicago Day Nursery Association admitted that white mothers had objected to their children sharing the nursery with African American children, and nursery heads had swiftly changed their stance on integration in their facility.[16] The Salvation Army Emergency Lodge reported similar backlash because it had allowed integration in all its common areas and only segregated its sleeping quarters. "We found that this close association has caused discontent among the lodgers in a great many instances."[17] The Chicago Foundling Home, established in 1871 to shelter single mothers and their babies, admitted black women and children, but the school's leader felt strongly that black communities were ultimately responsible for their own destitute children. The Home segregated residents in the dining facility, bedrooms, and infirmaries but allowed integration in the nursery and living areas. A 1926 study on similar issues included the opinion of the home's superintendent. "[He] feels very strongly that the Negro people should care for their own dependents, and therefore, preference is given to white cases."[18] These policies and attitudes made black Chicagoans particularly anxious to ensure that the Amanda Smith Industrial School for Colored Girls was on solid footing.

State and city schools devoted to girls did not easily welcome black girls to their institutions. The northwest suburban Park Ridge School for Girls repeatedly deflected questions about its racial policies, allowing it to continue segregating its girls internally or to move black girls off its campus altogether. Founded in 1908, this school sat on forty acres of land, boarded girls in cottages, and provided domestic and practical education for girls who were both delinquent and dependent. Some of the board members and supporters of the Park Ridge School for Girls also sat on the board of the Amanda Smith Orphanage and Industrial Home for Abandoned Destitute Colored Children and the Amanda Smith Industrial School for Colored Girls, and they vehemently defended the segregation practices of the former. In 1911 Ellen Henrotin, civic reformer and early president of the General Federation of Women's Clubs, sat on both organizational boards. She responded to criticism of the racial policies of the Park Ridge School for Girls by Unitarian church minister and activist Celia Parker

Woolley.[19] Woolley asked in an open letter if the school planned to create a segregated cottage for black girls and then launched into a critique of this plan. "Are not your colored wards sure to suffer greatly from delay and loss of that training in domestic science and other branches which your institution was built to supply and which it is already supplying to those residing at this school?" Park Ridge was a well-funded institution for destitute girls, and Woolley emphasized that all eyes were on its leadership. "We hope to learn that your institution, whether under the partial support of state or county or whether private, share[s] our feeling on this point and intend[s] to practice no discrimination against the children in its charges along color or other arbitrary lines."[20] In an open letter published in the *Defender*, Henrotin addressed the claims about Park Ridge, assuring readers that the black girls under its care were sent to Mrs. Covington's Home in Evanston and that the fourteen black girls who had been moved out of the Park Ridge School were allowed to "attend the public school and have the same teacher in domestic science" as the girls living at Park Ridge.[21]

Henrotin's response may have assuaged some fears about the care of black girls—until Mrs. Covington was the subject of an investigation of abuse alleged by her charges. Fourteen-year-old Elizabeth Cain was forced to ride on a policeman's lap while being transported away from Park Ridge. Another girl was not allowed to attend her own mother's funeral and testified that workers kicked and mocked "girls at prayer" at Mrs. Covington's Home. Thirteen-year-old Florence Hagans reported sleeping six to a bed. She also claimed that the matron "whipped one of the girls with a slipper until her arm was black and blue" and threatened to "whip the girls with a rope when they said their prayers." Hagans reported not having enough to eat and testified that the matron told the girls that they could only get more food if they did her laundry. The city's chief probation officer filed charges against the elderly woman.[22] In response to this and other incidents, the West Side Women's Club established a home for black girls aged four to fourteen in 1912. Ida Lewis, the club's president, presided over this home for a year; her sudden death forced the school's closure, and the West Side girls were transferred to the Amanda Smith Industrial School for Colored Girls.[23]

Some of Chicago's Catholic children's homes accepted black children on a limited basis. In 1911 the Sisters of the Good Shepherd opened the South Side's Illinois Technical School for Colored Girls. According to one

FIG 1.2. Few institutions in Chicago opened their doors to African American orphans. Catholic homes sometimes crossed the color line in order to care for black Catholic children. "A Child Shall Lead Them." Photograph by American Baptist Home Missions Society, 1906.

GENERAL RESEARCH AND REFERENCE DIVISION, SCHOMBURG CENTER FOR RESEARCH IN BLACK CULTURE, THE NEW YORK PUBLIC LIBRARY, ASTOR, LENOX AND TILDEN FOUNDATIONS.

historian, the Sisters' initiatives were "met with strong protests from their white neighbors [and] were not encouraged by officials in the Catholic Church."[24] Despite Good Shepherd's promise of providing quality instruction to their girls, many African Americans were not comfortable placing their Protestant children in a Catholic institution. The St. Joseph's Home for the Friendless did not practice segregation, except in its infirmary. Because of this home's commitment to serving Catholics exclusively, "very few Negroes" approached this home for care. The St. Vincent Infant Asylum also shared in this policy.[25]

With few institutional options specifically for orphaned or abandoned black girls, city authorities sometimes sent them to juvenile detention facilities—essentially criminalizing them for being black, without parents, and poor. Sophonisba Breckenridge, University of Chicago political scientist and head of its Department of Household Administration, wrote about this issue after her students visited the Geneva State Reformatory nearly twenty years after Lulu Jackson's mysterious death.[26] In a letter to the ICHAS, Breckinridge wrote: "Some of our students from the University of Chicago who go to Geneva for Psychopathic work have been greatly shocked at finding these dependent girls at this institution for delinquent girls." She continued: "I am wondering... whether the [ICHAS] might look upon the placement of these girls in decent homes even if they are poor, as a better way of caring for them than their commitment to such institutions." An unemployed father in the 1920s learned firsthand about this practice. The girls' parents lived in an abandoned barn, deemed by the Juvenile Court "not fit for children." Desperate and unable to financially provide for his daughters, the father brought them to the Salvation Army shelter. Two months passed and the father failed to retrieve the pair, so the Juvenile Court intervened and placed them in the city's detention home. Eventually, the ICHAS placed the two "nicely behaved" girls with a family, and the father was ordered to pay $2 per month toward their board.[27] The *Defender* had criticized the use of penal institutions for poor black girls in 1913. "That is a most unjust condition of public affairs which gives to a white orphan girl care, education, and training in a school, and then instead of caring for an [African American] orphan girl either farms her out in private homes or sends her to prison."[28]

Black Chicagoans feared that black orphans would fall victim to economic exploitation when they could not find homes. In 1913, the *Chicago Inter-Ocean* reported: "Negro Children Sold into Slavery."[29] A local politician initiated an inquiry into the ICHAS's management of black orphans and accused the charity of "furnishing Negro children to be sold into bondage... on cotton plantations in Southern homes." The ICHAS's primary purpose was to find homes for abandoned and neglected children, so investigators were especially shocked by the discovery that African American children under their care were sent to twenty-six states across the country. When confronted with these accusations, the ICHAS president "admitted some of the charges brought against him." Shortly after the commission shared their findings, the state convened investigations into the state's Juvenile Court and one of its juvenile homes. The city also regularly searched for and raided "baby farms," where parents sold their infants to baby agents, who in turn sold the children. The Juvenile Protective

Association investigated cases of black children at these farms and placed them with Amanda Smith.[30]

Amanda Smith's vision of saving children embraced industrial education for orphaned and dependent children because she believed it could keep them from the idleness she dreaded. Many of the architects of the movement to educate black youth in trades and labor also drew on missionary work.[31] The industrial school movement of the early twentieth century was in accordance with Smith's belief in temperance, self-reliance, thrift, and piety conjoined with lessons in manual labor skills—laundering, basic farm work, and domestic training—to ensure that her orphans would mature into useful, employable citizens. Smith's reputation as a great evangelist and representative of the AME Church attracted the attention of elite blacks, who shared her personal story of triumph over slavery and poverty to establish influential, black-run institutions. Most notably, Tuskegee Institute leader Booker T. Washington and his wife, Margaret Murray Washington, supported Smith's efforts to uplift black orphans through an emphasis on domestic trades. Washington donated $1,000 to Smith, and his wife attended several club meetings to raise funds for the School. In 1909, she traveled to North Harvey, accompanied by black banker Jesse Binga.[32]

Smith was in fine company, as a number of prominent black women and club members supported industrial and boarding schools and girls' homes. Across the country, Smith's counterparts included New York's Victoria Earle Matthews of the White Rose Mission, established in 1897, and Nannie Helen Burroughs of the National Training School for Women and Girls in Washington, DC, established in 1909 under the auspices of the National Baptist Convention's Women's Auxiliary. In an undated essay, "Miss Burroughs Appeals to Parents to Save Their Girls—Now," Burroughs asserted: "Our race will be morally bankrupt if parents do not put first things first in the care and protection of their daughters." Burroughs proposed "Christian boarding schools" as the place to instill "basic training in character ideals."[33]

Like her colleagues across the country, Smith maintained a passion for child protection and ensuring the children received sound moral foundations, but she lacked strong managerial skills and adequate funding to operate the Amanda Smith Orphanage and Industrial Home for Abandoned

Destitute Colored Children. She spent her initial $10,000 purse quickly, although she generated income from her speaking engagements at AME gatherings and the creation of the *Helper*, a newspaper to support the school. Still, her profits did not sufficiently finance the orphanage. African American women's clubs regularly donated and made gifts to Smith, but she could never rely on a consistent source of funding for the orphanage, a problem shared by many other African American self-help institutions.[34] Smith's dependence on charities and her personal income to pay for expenses created constant financial instability. In more flush moments, she regularly purchased plots of land in the hope of expanding the orphanage, but she never had sufficient funds to build on them.[35]

The state made little effort to aid African American children but retained the right to inspect and, if necessary, sanction African-American institutions. The orphanage did not receive significant financial support from the state, but Illinois State Agent for the Visitation of Children and the Illinois Board of Public Charities (IBPC), alongside the orphanage's own board of trustees, regularly scrutinized the Home's practices. Each of the orphanage's monitors took exception to elements of Smith's management style, the home's poor physical condition, and meager rations. Critics raised questions about the amount of time Smith spent traveling, and visitors observed that when Smith was at the home, she preferred to remain in her room to avoid the children and the staff.[36] They speculated that she was depressed and that her advanced age made it difficult for her to keep up with the orphans. The state agent filed multiple reports about the orphanage's problems, noting Smith's absences and the mounting debt she accrued. Despite his reservations, he admitted that he did not revoke the orphanage's charter or recommend its closure because "it was the only institution . . . in the state for the care of the colored children."[37] The IBPC concluded similarly that the orphanage was necessary for maintaining the de facto segregation practices of public and private social services in the city and therefore had to remain open.[38] Cook County not only allowed the crumbling orphanage to continue to exist but also exploited it so as to avoid spending money on African American children altogether.

Eventually, Smith's failing health and the orphanage's needs were too great for her to sustain the enterprise. The 1910 census indicates that she cared for twenty-five children, ranging from a newborn named Margaret to a fifteen-year-old boy named Clarence, with the help of three black matrons and a white teacher.[39] After a newspaper disclosed that Smith was on the verge of a "complete breakdown," she prepared her staff for her departure.[40] Before retiring to Seabring, Florida, she ensured that her legacy would remain by reorganizing the home as an all-girls industrial school. This shift made the school eligible for state funding under the provisions of the 1912 Industrial Act. Cook County's child welfare division would provide a monthly stipend of $15 per girl, and they could then place all African American girls brought to the Juvenile Court in the school.[41] With a new charter as the Amanda Smith Industrial School for Colored Girls, the school staff anticipated the grand reopening with a thorough cleaning of rooms, building renovations, and new decorations pleasing to girls.[42] Boys were relocated to the Louise Manual Training School, established in 1907 on Chicago's West Side by Elizabeth McDonald, an African American volunteer probation officer at the Juvenile Court.[43]

DELINQUENT, DEPENDENT, AND DESTITUTE IN CHICAGO

The reorganization of the brand new Amanda Smith Industrial School for Colored Girls guaranteed that some black girls in need of a home, schooling, and the comfort of knowing that an ever-expanding black community cared about them, could find refuge in the frame house on the corner of 147th and Desplaines Streets. The situations that brought black girls to the school, and to other institutions, complicated the simple labels of "delinquent," "dependent," and "destitute"—the commonplace descriptions for girls under the state's authority. The Juvenile Court routinely classified black girls' condition after collecting information about their families, their own behaviors, and the testimonies of teachers and community members. Regardless of the differences among the three distinct categories, the interplay of race and poverty in Chicago also contributed to how black girls were responded to, discussed, and framed as a problem.[44]

A review of court reports and anecdotes about black girls under institutional care indicates that the three categories do not easily represent the many ways black girls lived with parents, existed in communities, and advocated for themselves. One analysis of dependency among black children summed up their plight as a need for consistent care, suggesting that the way parents approached their new lives in the North as creating instability for their daughters. The researcher's conclusion also demonstrated racially constructed theories about black morality and criticized black people broadly for their inability to care for their girls:

> Frequently relatives live far away in the South and the children of the prisoner or patient are left with neither care nor support. A not uncommon cause for dependency among children is the desertion of a parent because he or she wishes to live with another man or another woman. Such a parent will usually wish to shed the responsibility of the first mate's children. Eleven cases of this type were found among the 75 families studied. A great proportion of illegitimacy was found among these children.... It seems then that the problems presented by the Negro group of children are due to ignorance, poverty, and failure to accept American sex mores.

The indictment that blacks failed to accept "American sex mores" may have resulted from the cases of black girls working in the sex trade or whose parents' jobs in Chicago vice districts rendered them unable to parent to the standards set by the Juvenile Court. Girls and young women also contended with rejection and isolation from their own families. In the case of a nineteen-year-old prostitute who had been arrested multiple times for solicitation, the teenage girl could not rely on her husband to care for her baby girl, whom she had delivered before authorities had placed her in the Lawndale Sanitarium for venereal disease. The husband refused to parent because the child had tested positive for syphilis. Similarly, another prostitution case involved a teenage mother who struggled to care for her baby while working. A landlady testified that this mother "took her baby with her when she went on night expeditions even when she stayed out until two or three in the morning." This teenager's oldest child was already under the care of the Juvenile Court, and eventually she was placed on probation and released to her grandmother's home.[45]

The notion that changes in family lifestyles during the Migration affected girls was not entirely inaccurate. The dissolution of marriages and a parent's occasional wandering eye played a role in girls' experiences in Chicago. Some girls' new living conditions, and their parents' embrace of Migration life, also troubled them. Throughout court records, girls testified that the presence of boarders in households often caused problems — from sexual exploitation to feelings of alienation from their parents when their mother or father became romantically involved with a boarder. One

FIG 1.3. Migrant families struggled to provide for their daughters. African Americans sought assistance from the Urban League, Chicago's Juvenile Court, and local churches. "A Negro Family Just Arrived in Chicago from the Rural South." Photograph by the Chicago Commission for Race Relations, 1922.

GENERAL RESEARCH AND REFERENCE DIVISION, SCHOMBURG CENTER FOR RESEARCH IN BLACK CULTURE, THE NEW YORK PUBLIC LIBRARY, ASTOR, LENOX AND TILDEN FOUNDATIONS.

woman, a divorcee who wanted to remarry a West Indian boarder who lived with her children, pled with the Juvenile Court to allow her to keep them. The woman hoped that marrying the boarder would "provide her and her children stability, but nine months later she was deserted." She was adamant she did not "want the children placed in a Home," so the Court placed the children "on probation" and allowed them to return to their mother.[46] In another case from 1928, twelve-year-old Alondra ran away from home and sought help from the city's Parental School. Alondra claimed that she would not return to her house "while her mother stayed with a man friend in her room." Her mother agreed and "changed her mode of living," but the girl continued to run away from home and was eventually charged with "sexual delinquencies." Juvenile Court records reveal that she was diagnosed with gonorrhea; based on her postal worker stepfather's testimony about her sexual history, she may have contracted the disease from the former boarder. The girl's father asked the court to place her in an institution.[47]

The story of a former Illinois Technical School for Colored Girls student who experienced all three categories of need before the courts, is a sobering illustration of the peripheral issues that kept girls from simply changing their circumstances after leaving institutions. Despite their best efforts, black social workers and school matrons could not address the conditions that kept black girls poor and marginalized in Great Migration Chicago. The daughter of a single mother who died "very young" and the granddaughter of a woman deemed "insane," Lillie's lineage navigated nearly every branch of the city's early twentieth-century social services network. After her time at the Technical School, Lillie was confined to Geneva for two years on account of being "feeble-minded." She was paroled to a private home, where she was sexually abused, and her concerned landlord forced the attacker out of the house because of his "familiarity" with the girl. She then delivered a baby at the Salvation Army Home; her daughter was placed with an adoptive family soon afterward. Lillie, having used many of the city's resources with little success, eventually left Chicago to live with a cousin.[48]

A SCHOOL FOR RACE MOTHERS

Whether her charges were defined by dependency, destitution, or classification as a delinquent, the new principal of the Amanda Smith Industrial School for Colored Girls, Adah Waters, believed she could transform the school from an ordinary industrial school into an outstanding educational institution for Chicago's most marginalized girls. Having attended the Cheyney Institute, Fisk, and Northwestern University, Waters was inspired more by college classrooms than by experiences like Amanda Smith's fiery camp meetings. One of her first major measures at the school was the creation of an academic plan, a proposal so ambitious that it would have provided an unusually high quality of education for the girls. Waters's blueprint required support from school leadership, and she appealed to donors to understand the importance of her school's mission. She stressed the need to develop strong leadership skills in girls and implored donors to help Chicago's "poorer colored girls" to feed "their minds, starving for the better things on which the soul grows." Waters's prescription for this ravenous hunger was industrial training coupled with a "literary foundation."[49] She was hopeful that the school's newly hired faculty—an English teacher and a University of Chicago–trained sewing teacher who agreed to work for free—would help build the cornerstone of a new school with an academically rigorous curriculum.[50] The school would offer "literary training," and "vocations that are of peculiar interest of women, a thorough knowledge of which will make them capable and self-supporting."[51] Waters envisioned offering practical courses in home economics, nursing, hairdressing, and stenography, as well as academic courses in African American history and culture. The most notable component of the measure was the integration of an academic program equivalent to four years of Chicago public high school into the existing industrial plan.[52] At that time, few Americans of any color attended high school regularly, and even fewer African Americans enjoyed such a privilege.

The board did not approve Waters's new school plan, but she was successful in improving the overall quality of instruction. In April 1915, the US Department of the Interior's Education Bureau took notice of Waters's changes, reporting the following year that the Amanda Smith Industrial School for Colored Girls employed three "regular workers and three volunteers" to teach forty-one girls. The report concluded: "The eight elementary grades are well taught. Good work in sewing is done."[53] Undeterred by the rejection of her high school curriculum proposal and the school's poor financial condition, Waters continued to make plans for the future. In 1918 she drafted a second proposal that presented a plan to move the school to Chicago's South Side. She set her sights on a building at the corner of Fiftieth and Indiana Streets, near the Illinois Technical School. Waters asked for funds to purchase "a small factory in which the older girls could work part time and defray their expenses."[54] She presented her ideas to tycoon Julius Rosenwald, owner of Sears, Roebuck, and Company and advocate of southern education, who financed the building of nearly five thousand "Rosenwald Schools" across the South. Rosenwald also supported northern causes like the Amanda Smith Industrial School for Colored Girls and the Phillis Wheatley Clubs—the black working women's boardinghouses.[55] The Amanda Smith Industrial School for Colored Girls housed forty-seven girls that year, and Waters was increasingly willing to compromise her vision of a classical-industrial education in order to provide a high quality education for the girls.[56] The project failed to capture Rosenwald's interest, and the factory-school never materialized. Instead she hired two new employees, a domestic sciences instructor and a social worker.[57]

Waters's leadership and her bold ideas for girls were motivated by a desire to convince both white and black Chicagoans that black girls were indeed worthy of such investments because of their potential for assuming their roles as mothers. She made these arguments while also trying to establish black girls' innocence, vulnerability, and need for community. This strategy was a complicated and, at times, convoluted one because it situated black girls in an impossible ideological place between adulthood and innocence. White girls also played a symbolic function in the nation's imagining of the future that contributed to the southern rape myth and the brutality of lynching. While white girlhood galvanized communities and families to deploy racist violence and policymaking, black girlhood also served to organize and inspire action, as well as buttress claims to racial worthiness and commitment. As Waters and others argued that investing in black girls meant providing future mothers to black people involved in a struggle for progress, the uneasy reference to sex implicit in aligning girls with the ideal state of motherhood limited black women's conversations about actual girls' sexuality when white women opposed integrated institutional care.

Waters supported her arguments by framing African American girls' success as a conduit for African American men to rise above oppression. In a 1918 letter to Rosenwald, she wrote: "It takes the right kind of woman to produce and train a boy into the right kind of man. It takes wonderful love, wisdom and care to build the woman with a harmonious and symmetrical character out of the ill shaped life of a young girl."[58] In another fundraising letter, Waters urged that the investment in girls was a means of strengthening the maternal leadership over, and possibilities for, all African Americans. She wrote that the good fight for African American uplift and social mobility "cannot be done without the right kind of mothers," and she identified girls' social development as serving the "root need" for good "colored mothers among the lowly."[59]

Waters evoked images of the family, and the promises of the Migration, to elicit support for her initiatives. Waters's letters to Rosenwald and other wealthy Chicagoans bring forward dimensions of racial uplift that point to notions of the family in their declarations that black girls are worthy of community care and financial resources. Making a case for girls and for girlhood broadly was rooted in the aspirations of black families to live life free from the imposition of racism and financial restraints. Waters's appeal for support for providing job skills to the poorest and most vulnerable girls was tied to the prescribed roles of African American women in racial uplift projects and the mandates to forge patriarchal leadership in the Migration-era family. Waters made it plain: to help African American girls acquire job skills and become productive citizens was to ultimately guarantee a better life for African American men.

Migration-era discourse on girls and progress was heavily entrenched with the visions of race motherhood and maternalism that created and sustained women's club movements and racial uplift endeavors of the late nineteenth and early twentieth centuries. Maternalism, one of the key strategies used by Gilded Age and Progressive Era white women activists, was a means of securing women's rights to advocate for "women and family" issues, such as mother's pensions, kindergartens, parent-teacher associations, and child health care. Although tied to notions of women's special role as caretakers and nurturers, maternalist rhetoric created spaces for women to exercise considerable social and political power in non-threatening and gender-conforming ways. For African American women activists, who were more likely to actually be mothers than their white colleagues who worked professionally in social outreach, maternalism was also a strategy to gain political voice and power for women and girls.[60]

The call for better black mothers was a direct response to mounting fears about the fate of African American families in Chicago as they struggled to adapt to their new surroundings and exercise their newly found freedoms. As soon as new migrants passed through the exit doors of Chicago's Union Station, community leaders were determining what to make of these strange people, with their homespun clothes and heavy drawls betraying their desire to simply fit into the urban environment. What role could and would girls, and when they grew into women, play in the larger search for a new black expression of self? Waters addressed this question in a speech before the Young People's Lyceum of Grace Presbyterian Church about "the work being accomplished there and the assistance that must be given young girls if they are to make strong women."[61] At the heart of this strategy and ideology was the concept that the race needed strong women and strong mothers to address their needs. Waters's approach rested on positioning black girlhood in ways that accorded with the prevailing notion that black girls were not necessarily children. While she evoked images of vulnerability in suggesting girls needed homes and families, she simultaneously constructed an argument that girls needed to become mothers. Waters intertwined the notions of race motherhood and maternalism to ground her claims about girlhood, creating an incongruous association of black girlhood and black motherhood.

As African American newspapers and club bulletins implored their readers to send their prayers and pennies to the Amanda Smith Industrial School for Colored Girls, white school leaders engaged in a different conversation and raised new questions about the very value of this type of school for black girls. The white members of the school's board, named the Interracial Circle of the Amanda Smith School, lamented the school's dire financial straits and questioned its viability. They wondered if it was in the best hands under African American leadership, and if its mere existence impeded African American progress by allowing Park Ridge, Geneva, and other state-funded institutions to maintain segregation.

Despite the favorable assessment of the new curriculum, Waters's enthusiasm, and the Juvenile Court's financial commitment to the Amanda Smith Industrial School for Colored Girls, white school board members and benefactors concluded that its closure was necessary. In June 1915 a report alerted the board that Judge Merritt W. Pinckney had warned: "Unless radical changes could be brought about the institution . . . it should be closed, in which event the children would be removed to the only one who would receive them, the Illinois Technical School."[62] Pinckney mentioned the school's growing debts and multiple property liens, a legacy of Smith's financial mismanagement. Board member Charles Virden and Judge Pinckney demanded "a financial report and complete accounting of funds used," but Waters's audit was "not furnished in any sort of an intelligent manner." Virden concluded: "The only thing we could ascertain were that numerous debts were outstanding and that funds collected from the county had been paid out, and no satisfactory accounting given."

The judge wanted to dissolve the charter of the Amanda Smith Industrial School for Colored Girls immediately after reviewing the documents, but he changed his mind and agreed to allow it to remain open if he could replace black board members with a roster of white civic leaders. Virden recruited Park Ridge apologist Ellen M. Henrotin and Esther W. S. Brophy, another prominent Chicago clubwoman, to the board, along with two white businessmen. Ida B. Wells-Barnett and three other black members were allowed to retain their seats, but Wells-Barnett's husband, attorney Ferdinand Barnett, was among those removed.[63] The news of his dismissal may have pained Barnett, considering that he had delivered the obituary at Smith's memorial services in Chicago.[64]

Judge Pinckney was not alone in his unfavorable opinion of black leadership. Even the most progressive supporters of the Amanda Smith Industrial School for Colored Girls wondered if African Americans were suited for this undertaking. Edith Abbott, Breckinridge's colleague at the University of Chicago and onetime dean of the university's School of Social Services Administration, remarked to the ICHAS on the shortcomings of the Amanda Smith Industrial School for Colored Girls: "The colored people find it so difficult to raise money for the social enterprises in which they are engaged, that they have a lower standard for such work than the white people have."[65] Abbott proposed the only solution to this was to have whites manage facilities for African American children. Breckinridge agreed and discouraged Rosenwald from supporting the short-lived West Side Woman's Club Home, which would have offered a much-needed second institution for African American girls. "The members of the Club have been talking for a good while about going into this enterprise, and I have been very doubtful about it. I do not feel that they are anywhere near ready to undertake so serious a task. . . . At present, of course, the possibility of any care for dependent colored children is so slight that one is tempted to grasp at a straw."[66] Black institutions often lacked the same financial standing as their white counterparts, but black Chicagoans did establish sound institutions, and black leadership managed under the direst of circumstances. The slow but steady growth of Chicago's Provident Hospital, the Frederick Douglass Settlement House, and the expansion of the Colored Branches of the YMCA proved that black institutions could effectively serve their communities in the face of rampant racial discrimination.[67] But as girls' fates were precarious, so were the institutions that tried to rescue them.

Rosenwald, Abbott, and Breckinridge were also concerned about the role of the Amanda Smith Industrial School for Colored Girls in Chicago's racial politics, and they believed that the time had come for the integration of state-run girls' schools. The mere suggestion of this inflamed resistance among their white colleagues, who argued, on the basis of racialized notions of black girlhood and sexuality, against this challenge to segregation. In the summer of 1915 Edward Wentworth, a successful Chicago realtor and board chair of the Amanda Smith Industrial School for Colored Girls, appealed to Rosenwald for funds to settle $4,000 of the school's debt. Instead Rosenwald offered a suggestion.[68] He proposed that the school devote its energies to compel the Park Ridge School to end its policy of racial segregation and open its doors to black girls.[69] The pro-integration leadership of the Amanda Smith Industrial School for Colored Girls made this recommendation without any acknowledgment of the problems black girls in these institutions would inevitably face. Black girls were regularly met with hostility and substandard care when they were admitted in small numbers at majority-white institutions. Breckinridge, having evaluated the Amanda Smith Industrial School for Colored Girls, wrote to the ICHAS: "I have always felt that it [the school] was a wholly unsuitable place. . . . I am one of those who feel that the Park Ridge Board violates its charter when it refused to accept colored girls."[70] As black leaders wanted black girls to deploy their claim to girlhood as a compelling source of redemption for black people, white leaders believed black girls could easily challenge the color line. White leaders believed that blacks should shutter their institutions and register black girls at resistant institutions. These ideas ignored the implication of this challenge to the safety and well-being of actual girls.

Although Rosenwald and Breckinridge were among the most influential supporters of the Amanda Smith Industrial School for Colored Girls, their ideas were immediately met with rejection, and their colleagues argued against their recommendations by evoking a readily available trope about black sexuality.[71] Newly appointed board member Brophy responded to Rosenwald with a warning that interracial sex was becoming a national problem in all-girls' institutions across the country because "these girls when put with or even near the same class of white girls . . . exercise a very deleterious influence on each other . . . they had [interracial lesbian] love affairs, and act in a way that is demoralizing." She assured Rosenwald that school segregation was preferable because it reduced sexual transgressions, and the Amanda Smith Industrial School for Colored Girls was successful because it reinforced racial isolation by virtue of its supporters within black Chicago. "A woman was just telling me . . . whose sister has been employed at the N.J. State Home for girls, and said it was disgusting. I had heard something of the same nature before, why it should be so I cannot tell. It is bad enough with the white girls. We all want to do the best we can, for these unfortunate girls, and I do think we have excellent influences for them now . . ."[72] Racialized notions of black sexuality broadly worked in concert against African American girls in institutional care across the country, and the literature suggests that these concerns shaped the policies of other homes for girls and of women's prisons. This thinking that black girls sexually manipulated and exploited their white counterparts undergirded the use of separate cottages, jail cells, and reformatory bunks throughout the twentieth century.[73]

Henrotin did not have to look as far as New Jersey's State Home for Girls to buttress her resistance to racial integration. Concerns about interracial sex among girls also circulated around the Geneva reformatory. Between 1900 and 1935—which encompassed the period when Breckinridge and her students discovered dependent black girls among the masses of delinquents—Geneva enrolled approximately four hundred African American girls. The reformatory segregated them in overcrowded cottages; they lived up to fifty girls to a cottage on the reformatory's grounds, while white girls' cottages usually accommodated twenty to twenty-four inmates.[74] Research on Geneva, which is consistent with the literature on sexuality and women's penology, has revealed that criminologists and officers regularly blamed black girls for initiating sex and relationships with their white peers. Whether motivated purely by sexual desire or a need to rebel against the conditions of their confinement, girls, both black and white, devised plots to fight authorities' and administrators' control by leveraging their anxieties about uncontrolled sexuality against them. Girls knew that sharing sleeping quarters in cottages or dancing together during recreation sessions across racial lines was a way to protest segregation as well as other issues, from the reformatory's disciplinary tactics to its dining hall offerings.

Studies of interracial sexual encounters and relationships among incarcerated girls at Geneva squarely located these acts of defiance and resistance among the girls who acted upon their sexual desires within the very nature of black girls. Drawing on ideas about black women's unrestrained and dangerous sexuality, concerned observers tacitly theorized that black girls shared the sexual characteristics of the adults of their race. Reformatory school leaders and politicians used their flawed understanding of black women to shape their approach to black girls. This denial of an acknowledged state of girlhood for black girls was pervasive in the literature and common sense thinking of institutional leadership. In an Illinois Association for Criminal Justice survey, researchers concluded that interracial relationships at Geneva were predicated on a sophisticated system of role-playing among girls. As a result of the supposedly natural sexual inclinations of black girls, researchers determined that black girls played the sexual aggressor, or male, role and seduced white inmates.[75] At Geneva, black girls involved in same-sex pairings with white girls were called "honey girls," and researchers wondered if white girls who paired with them would be influenced thereby to go on to engage in relationships with black men after their release from Geneva.[76]

This research, and other investigations like it, helped segregationists provide a "reasonable" defense for separating girls, because it revolved around seemingly irrefutable facts about black sexuality. The use of social scientific research that explored the dynamics among girls grounded racial separation as a matter of maintaining white girls' sexual and social purity at the expense of the possibility of black girls' sexual innocence. Although many of the white Geneva inmates landed at the institution due to their own criminalized and stigmatized sexual choices, the presence of black girls as "the sexual problem" on the reformatory's campus provided a foil to these girls. The rhetoric surrounding black girls' troubling influence when in such close proximity to their white peers aided in whites' imagining the redemption of "fallen" white girls in contrast to their unsalvageable black schoolmates.[77]

There is no evidence that black board members or teachers of the Amanda Smith Industrial School for Colored Girls addressed their feelings about sexuality-based arguments against integration or against the school's girls. Newspaper articles and women's club notes do tell us that they frequently visited the Geneva campus to encourage black girls to follow the rules and prayed for their well-being at the facility. Black women, on principle, challenged segregation and racial exclusion in public accommodations, among girls' organizations, and in women's clubs, but some may have measured their response to this sexualized racial segregation. In order to reduce any further maligning of black girls' sexual character, they may have quietly accepted the terms of Park Ridge, Geneva, and other facilities and chosen to focus on their own institutions.

BLACK GIRLHOOD AND COMMUNITY RESPONSIBILITY

Unable to fully respond to the claims about black girls' sexuality, black women leaders instead weighed in on the need for black community members to acknowledge the value of black girls and challenged them to prove their commitment to the race by contributing to their causes. The appeals on behalf of "unprotected colored girls" spread throughout black Chicago, and women leaders used support of the girls at the Amanda Smith Industrial School for Colored Girls as a litmus test of Chicagoans' race loyalty and pride. Black women's criticism of the lack of support for black girls mirrored their challenges to black male leadership in the form of clubwomen's organizing "in defense of themselves" when black men failed to respond to attacks on their character and moral fitness.[78] Black clubwomen and civic leaders, experienced in the art of exposing black male leaders' incongruent behavior and asserting their ability to lead, were equally indignant in the defense of black girlhood.

Employees of the Amanda Smith Industrial School for Colored Girls regularly used the pages of black publications like the *Defender*, *Broad Ax*, and the *Fellowship Herald News* to demand community support and accountability. The school's constant state of need led some to accuse black Chicagoans of shirking an important responsibility. One critic believed that black Chicagoans suffered from a distinctly northern "colored problem"—a lack of care for their own girls. Editorials and public comments about the school accused black northerners of failing to understand civic duty and responsibility and spending too many resources on parties and social occasions instead of substantive work. *Broad Ax*, whose editor, Julius Taylor, visited the school, admonished: "This home aims to meet a real and pressing want, as well as cope with a rare opportunity, for be it known this is the only institution of the kind in the Northwest, and is only prevented by a lack of means from enjoying a rapid and substantial progress. In the South, the colored people have learned how to stand together, as witness, Tuskegee, but in the North there is certainly still great room for improvement."[79]

The newspaper reiterated these sentiments when a lecture by a local doctor in support of the school drew a small audience. An editorialist accused: "Dr. Mason's lecturing at Quinn Chapel Monday evening for the benefit of the Amanda Smith Industrial Home [i.e., Amanda Smith Industrial School for Colored Girls], was not well attended and this is laid to the discredit of the Chicago folks who will not turn out in support of their worthy charity institutions."[80] Embedded in these critiques about the community's failures to attend Doctor Mason's event are the stirrings of an ambivalent, yet reflective, response to the question whether Migration could ever transform or even improve black life and black character and to the deployment of the state of black girlhood as proof. A number of black social organizations and individuals did lend support to the Amanda Smith Industrial School for Colored Girls, but the dichotomous pitting of southern loyalty and northern selfishness against each other resonated in future missives about the state of black girls in Chicago.

Waters reasoned that if Chicagoans of means would not be moved by the poverty and destitution of her girls, then she could stir them by forcing them to see their own daughters in the dependent and delinquent girls at the Amanda Smith Industrial School for Colored Girls. Waters recognized the painful reality of race's leveling effect in the lives of black migrants and old settlers alike, and she challenged black Chicagoans to consider the way racism—and the attendant poverty and limits it bore— rendered all black girls in a constant state of precariousness. She wrote in a solicitation pamphlet: "There is a little girl very dear to you. How dreary and cold would this world be should she be taken away? Do you realize that only by the Grace of God her lot is different from that of the little girls from whom I bring your message? An adverse fortune would have made her a dependent girl." She imagined that when readers looked into the eyes of their daughters they would be moved to "help make [the] school a real home for Chicago's unprotected colored girls."[81]

The varying perspectives on the Amanda Smith Industrial School for Colored Girls and its viability came to a head after tragedy struck in the autumn of 1918. Sometime on the night of November 21, a fire swept through the school's boardinghouse. No one was quite sure if the heat of the flames or the cries of two little girls awoke the rest of the students in the upstairs bedrooms. And although help was only two blocks away, the thick black smoke that filled the rooms traveled much faster than the Harvey Fire Department. Black Chicago would soon learn that two little girls, aged three and nine, had suffocated in their bedroom. After the electrical fire was extinguished and the surviving girls were counted, Chicago's black community immediately mourned the demise of the Amanda Smith Industrial School for Colored Girls.

Nine days later, *Defender* readers across the city and country learned of the tragedy on the front page. The headline encapsulated the poignancy of the loss and the state's neglect of its most vulnerable black girls: "Two Girls Perish in Fire at Amanda Smith: Crossed Electric Wires Start Flames Which Destroy Building."[82] Community leaders from the AME Church and the women's clubs worried about what would become of "the most neglected girls in America," who were now left without an institution of their own.[83] The Fire Department's investigation confirmed that faulty electrical wiring had caused the blaze; there was no doubt that state inspectors had overlooked the damaged wires during their annual visits. Advocates of the school immediately placed the blame on the state for allowing the school to operate despite its inadequate and unsafe facilities. They pointed to the state's insistence on maintaining the color line in children's homes and lack of funding for the school as the reasons why the repairs had never been addressed.[84]

The Chicago Urban League—the local branch of the national civil rights organization for African American economic parity and social justice—partnered with the ICHAS in forming a committee to plan for the future of the Amanda Smith Industrial School for Colored Girls, which had been officially closed. This coalition signaled a troubling loss of power for the women who had previously devoted their time and energy to the school's founding and sustenance. Present at the emergency meeting after the blaze were a representative from the Illinois State Council of Defense—a World War I–era organization that had celebrated the end of the war a week before the fire; a minister from the South Park Methodist Church; a *Defender* staff member; and a Juvenile Court worker. This committee stated, rather optimistically in agreement, that from the tragedy "will come another institution, which would typify the modern ideas of caring for the ward of the county, city and state."[85] The committee's inclusion of the term "modern ideas" betrayed the promise of "another institution," as leaders believed that the future of child care rested with home placement, or adoption, as the preferred means of dealing with children under state care by 1918. Wilfred S. Reynolds, as a representative of the ICHAS leadership, did not immediately announce his intentions. Yet two weeks after the fire, he made it clear that a reopened Amanda Smith Industrial School for Colored Girls would have to move toward the national trend. "In the East they are doing away more and more with the institutional care for the normal child and substituting home life."[86]

Reynolds's position originated from a movement initiated decades earlier by white women reformers, many of whom conducted investigations into the draconian and unsanitary conditions of orphanages. These women suggested adoption into private homes as a solution to the problems of child poverty, orphans, and other children deemed victims of circumstance rather than deviants. Formal adoption was a costly proposition for black families, whose financial resources were limited and who already participated in informal care of extended family members and fictive kin. Researchers of Black Belt communities were often impressed by the graciousness of black families toward needy children. When one Chicago widower lost his wife in 1925, he was forced to leave his daughters alone at home while he worked. A child welfare agency investigated the family and found that a "neighbor who has five children of her own" combed the girls' hair and offered to take them in her home. "She is willing to take them and says it will be all right if their father cannot pay her for their care."[87] The agency suggested that children could rely on black kindness, to an extent, to help them. "The generosity of Negroes is quite noticeable, and neighbors and acquaintances are apt to show a great willingness to do all possible for the neglected or abandoned child."[88]

Black community generosity was not a radical discovery for Waters and Wells-Barnett, having spent years fundraising and organizing black women and communities on behalf of girls of the Amanda Smith Industrial School for Colored Girls. Wells-Barnett was uncertain that the ICHAS and the Urban League could easily find good, adoptive homes for black girls. In a move that resembled Judge Pinckney's dismissal of black board members of the school, the committee marginalized black women's position as authorities on what black girls needed most. Wells-Barnett recommended the girls seek shelter at the Frederick Douglass Settlement House, but the Urban League rejected the idea and instead recruited white clubwomen to serve on the new committee for the school. The organizer of several trips to the school and a close personal friend of Amanda Smith herself, Wells-Barnett was so incensed by this experience that she recounted this takeover of the school's management in her autobiography. She pleaded with the participants at a meeting of the City Federation of Colored Women's Clubs to send the girls displaced by the fire to the Douglass Settlement House. "[Urban League head] Mr. T. Arnold Hill very strongly objected to that and called a meeting . . . with the officials of the Children's Home and Aid Society." A later meeting with the ICHAS was the final straw for Wells-Barnett. She recounted that Amelia Sears of the Chicago School of Civics and Philanthropy was given latitude to present her ideas about what should happen to the girls. "[Sears] descanted beautifully on the idea of having no institution."[89] Yet Sears's speech did not recognize the pressing need of the "forty children [who] were made homeless" by the fire. After Sears's presentation, Wells-Barnett remembered having "the privilege of seeing the advice I had given my women disregarded and an enthusiastic acceptance of [Sears's] idea." Wells-Barnett deemed the move ineffective because "very few of the right sort of homes were reached and many people took these children for the money there was in it for themselves. It was a makeshift plan, which has never proved satisfactory."[90]

Years before the fire, a 1912 report on juvenile issues had confirmed Wells-Barnett's fears: "Many people 'adopt' girls from dependent institutions as a cheap solution of the servant girl question—and this phase of child slaving is not child saving. There is investigation before the child is placed, but not enough after."[91] The state's Department of Public Welfare appointed a "visitor for Negro homes" in their Division of Visitation of Children, who reported that in a five-year span in the early 1920s she only removed one child from a private home. Yet community leaders still questioned if this method made children more vulnerable, because they relied on neighbors and family members to tell social workers about "all abuses and neglect."[92]

The extant records of the Amanda Smith Industrial School for Colored Girls provide little detail about what happened to its girls after they received their industrial training or were adopted into families, but some traces of these girls' locations immediately after the fire are recorded at other institutions. The Chicago Home for Girls, also known as the Refuge for Girls, had reluctantly accepted a few African American girls as early as 1899, and they likely boarded some of the girls displaced by the fire. The Refuge's 1918 records indicate an unusually high number of African American girls at the facility: ten. In following years the number declined.[93] Another orphan displaced by the fire, who had become a ward of the state in 1918, spent years in and out of institutional care, having been placed with Waters only months before the fire. After the fire, the ICHAS took custody of this girl, named Sadie, when she was six years old. In the summer of 1922, ICHAS took her under their supervision again. They reported that "she developed behavior problems, refusing to stay in the home in which she was placed and insisting upon living with foster relatives whose homes are not recommended by the Society."[94] The foster relatives may have been a family who boarded her after the fire. The ICHAS assigned nine of the girls, at least three of them teenagers, to private homes within eight days of the fire. The Burgette family, whose social worker daughter, Marie, worked at the Amanda Smith Industrial School for Colored Girls in the spring of 1918, welcomed a little girl.[95] Each family received $3.50 per week for housing the girls; some families boarded up to three girls.[96] The arrangements were often temporary, but some families eagerly adopted the girls. On hearing about the fire, some local families requested a girl to adopt. A Mr. and Mrs. Pierce of Harvey requested a girl of "twelve or thirteen years" to enjoy their family home and neighborhood's "school advantages."[97]

As girls settled into their new living situations, another committee, the Special Committee to Consider Matters Relative to Future Plans Concerning the Care of Colored Girls, assessed how to make home-finding more popular among African Americans. Again, black community leaders who had previously served the Amanda Smith Industrial School for Colored Girls were not selected for this committee. Rosenwald, and other longtime friends and confidantes of both Amanda Smith and Adah

Waters, identified black men and women and suggested that Wells-Barnett serve on the committee, which would ostensibly become the new school's board. In the end, only three African Americans were selected to serve on the nine-person committee. Wells-Barnett was officially out of the advisory circle; Hill, from the Urban League, and a representative from the Federation of Colored Women's Clubs were allowed to stay.[98]

Despite the Special Committee's charge to examine various options for the students of the Amanda Smith Industrial School for Colored Girls, and other black girls without families, the ICHAS's objections to institutionalization stifled any suggestion other than adoption. The ICHAS hired African American women to find suitable homes for girls and mailed notices to churches and community organizations to advertise their availability for adoption. Adoption proved to be an incredibly complicated proposition, for reasons other than financial instability among black Chicagoans. The ICHAS-orchestrated adoption plan confronted black cultural values regarding girls' appearance and their ability to adjust from institutional life to private homes. Social workers of the ICHAS discovered that African American families preferred to adopt girls, and they rarely asked questions about a girl's family or medical history before agreeing to bring her to their homes, but her physical appearance could play a role in a family's decision. Girls with European facial features, light skin, and straight hair were more attractive to potential parents. One study made it clear: "The quality of a child's hair, especially if she is a girl is of utmost importance. The other major consideration is the color of a child. The family does not want the child either lighter or darker than they are, although they will more readily accept a child who is lighter."[99]

The ICHAS reinforced color-conscious practices too. Reynolds sent a note to the president of the Phillis Wheatley Club and a member of the Chicago Federation of Colored Women's Clubs announcing the need for homes for "two mighty fine light brown colored girls, 9 and 7 years of age, full orphans."[100] Under this system, black girls learned a valuable, if painful, lesson about the role their skin tone and appearance would make in shaping their lives, garnering compassion from others, and representing their adoptive families. These mentions of appearance dovetailed with the pleas to ground girls in race motherhood. Both of these approaches to eliciting care for black girls was rooted in adult projections about representations of black people and communities through the images of their girls.

Girls who survived the fire may have been happy to leave their school and live among families, but they did not necessarily adapt easily to their new living arrangements. The general district secretary of Chicago's United Charities found a common problem among black girl adoptees: "Often the children need the discipline of a good institution before they are ready for any private home."[101] The culture of the types of homes that welcomed girls may have been more in line with black middle-class conventions of patriarchal households, with formal mealtimes, constant parental supervision, and a fixation on how the daughter's behavior represented the family for good or bad. Maude Mary Firth, a University of Chicago graduate student, discovered that within a few years of the fire at the Amanda Smith Industrial School for Colored Girls, home-finding was not as successful as the ICHAS had hoped because of these very adjustment problems. Firth wrote in her 1924 thesis: "In a limited number of Cases, the Court places delinquent girls in colored family homes," leaving unprepared families with defiant or emotionally stunted girls.[102] Firth advocated for an institutional setting that could teach black girls how to live in families.

Firth's idea for a transitional home for black orphans came from the Mary Bartelme Clubs, a short-term boarding school for white girls that instructed them on how to assimilate to family life. Established in 1914, the clubs were named for the first woman assistant judge of the Juvenile Court and founder of a special court for delinquent girls. The clubs were open to girls who could not return home after being released from juvenile detention.[103] Local women's clubs supported the initiative and donated clothing and toiletries to the Girls' Court to support the Bartelme Clubs. In 1919, African American women tried to establish a similar program, the Big Sisters Club, to provide "a home for our girls who might be held for juvenile delinquency or improper guardianship."[104] A Big Sisters member claimed that the home was necessary so that African American girls "would not be compelled to associate with criminals" after the Juvenile Court released them. The Big Sisters Club was to serve as a point of "discharge from probation and do social uplift among the Race throughout the city." The state board of charities tabled the Big Sisters Club request because the women had only collected $75 to start the effort.[105]

Eventually, in 1921, a third Bartelme Club was opened for African American girls transitioning out of juvenile facilities.[106] Club founder Etta Shoecraft dedicated the effort to "the underprivileged, unadjusted and needy girls of Chicago."[107] Although some Bartelme Club girls had experience living with their own parents, club leaders did not consider all houses proper homes. Nor did they tolerate bad behavior from their charges. When fourteen-year-old Nancy Bridges came to the club after years of living in orphanages, club staff lamented that they could not sufficiently break her of her "disagreeable, defiant, and impudent" habits and behavior. Nancy had spent a portion of her childhood at the Illinois Soldiers' Orphans Home, then was transferred to the city's Juvenile Detention Home after the Soldiers' Home classified her a "serious problem." In the fall of 1926, after a brief stint at home with her mother, she decided to run away. When Nancy was found and authorities questioned her about her time away, she confessed that "two young men whose names she did not know" had invited her to stay with them in a "vacant house." She admitted to having had sex with one of the men, but a doctor said a medical examination did not corroborate her claim. The club warned the girl that she only had one last chance to stay at the club. After she skipped school one day, club administrators sent her to the Detention Home.[108]

One of Nancy's classmates also frustrated her teachers. After their mother died of pneumonia at the Cook County Hospital in 1919, Janice and Daisy Stephens found themselves living with their father, who began to live "in adultery" with their housekeeper. Mr. Stephens's relationship ended, and he soon began "keeping a disorderly house," such that "white patrons visited it" to solicit prostitutes. A police raid on the house yielded a nineteen-year-old-girl hiding in a closet. The father was sent to prison, and his children were first sent to the Detention Home. The girls' brother was placed in the Chicago Parental School, Janice was sent to the Bartelme Club, and Dhalia, the youngest, was assigned to the Home for the Friendless. Dhalia died of tubercular meningitis shortly after Mr. Stephens was released from prison, and he did not take Janice to the funeral. Janice struggled with behavior problems, and the father hoped that remarrying a "decent woman" could help reunite his family.[109]

While the Big Sisters tried to manage black girls in an institution designed to reduce the very need for institutions, loyalists to the Amanda Smith Industrial School for Colored Girls continued to work toward reopening it. The fire, the ensuing debates over leadership, the ICHAS's and Urban League's marginalization of black women's leadership, and the growing presence of black girls in need of respite from destitution and desperation kept these community leaders engaged in the fight to resist calls to foreclose on their methods and initiatives. Despite the desire to replicate the Amanda Smith Industrial School for Colored Girls, the movement to establish a new school lost momentum with each passing year. For years after the fire, African American organizations held fundraisers for the school, but the shuttered property fell deeper into disrepair. A local pastor was put in charge of the property, but he was unable to keep it secure.[110] In July 1921 burglars vandalized the school, stealing furniture and fixtures. That same year, a local church established a building fund committee and hosted a musical to raise money for the school, and the pastor of St. Monica's Catholic Church in Chicago took up a collection for a new building at a weekend Mass.[111] A Mrs. Holloway, president of the Amanda Smith Home Association and a former employee, planned on selling the Harvey property with hopes of "buying a new site somewhere in the Black Belt." Holloway believed that white residents of Harvey were "hostile to the Home."[112] In March 1922, the still-existing board of the Amanda Smith Industrial School for Colored Girls received "specifications and plans" for a new building, along with the claim that a group of prominent African Americans had "bought a six flat building."[113] The school never reopened and no new modern Amanda Smith Industrial School was ever established. Two years later, Adah Waters settled into a new position as director of the South Side Friendship House for Girls.[114]

CONCLUSION

The story of the Amanda Smith Industrial School for Colored Girls reveals more than the institutional challenges facing African American women leaders in Chicago—it also charts the issues surrounding the emergence of urban, African American girlhood in the Migration period. Records of fundraising efforts for the school and of the questions raised by the challenge of black girls' institutional care highlight the centrality of motherhood, patriarchy, and the uplifting of black families to the efforts to carry out social outreach to girls. The school's goals and method were in line with the framework of racial uplift and the politics of respectability, two dominant ways black women's activism has been understood in the literature of African American women's history. Yet when we look at the Amanda Smith Industrial School for Colored Girls we provide nuance to the analysis of racial uplift as stunting its recipients, exacerbating class tensions, and limiting educated women's ability to articulate their ideas and leadership outside the domestic sphere.

Until a girl reached maturity and fulfilled her role as a mother, her usefulness as a girl was to prepare herself for her future role. Racial uplift projects among girls alert us to the importance of daughters, as well as wives and mothers, to fulfilling the dream of racial respectability, even when racial equality and parity were not within the purview of African Americans. The fantasies that accompanied racial progress were not complete without musings about girls' innocence, vulnerability, and adherence to the patriarch's authority. Girls at the Amanda Smith Industrial School for Colored Girls were surrounded by women whose success was unmatched by the majority of African Americans, but the school's promises of strong womanhood was tied to the possibility of forming outstanding wage earners and mothers, supporting their eventual roles in patriarchal homes. Whether Waters or Wells-Barnett wholeheartedly believed in this ideology is not as important as the fact that they understood the potency and the effectiveness of such arguments to legitimate their work with girls. Yet this framing of girlhood failed to promote the notion that black girls existed as children.

The interactions of the Amanda Smith Industrial School for Colored Girls with white benefactors and community leaders also demonstrate the conflicted role of African American institutions in enabling Jim Crow in the North. Wells-Barnett, Rosenwald, and Breckinridge all viewed the role of African American institutions differently. While supportive and critical whites doubted the ability of African Americans to lead their own institutions, these whites often failed to fully acknowledge the way race impeded African American women's ability to demonstrate the self-sufficiency or high standard of management these whites desired to see. African Americans, regardless of commitment to girlhood, were at times limited not only by material resources but also by the ideological pressures of racial uplift, which ensured that work on behalf of girls rested with sometimes fantastical notions of promoting African American middle-class life and domesticity among girls who were poor, would enter the working class, and would never be able to fully leverage their fathers and brothers to realize the vision of being men in Great Migration family and community life.[115]

The internal battles of the school also point to the sexual nature of the opposition to the educational and social integration of girls' institutions. Research on negative reactions to school integration in the 1950s has traced segregationist protests to fears about race mixing, but rarely is this resistance traced to its roots in early twentieth-century cities in the North, and the way black girls were also marked as sexually threatening to white girls, as well as white boys. Historians of women's incarceration and penology have exposed these tensions, but the case of the Amanda Smith Industrial School for Colored Girls is an interesting one because it was not wholly a reform school and did not share some of the cultural and social aspects of state reformatories and training schools. Despite accommodating a population that the Juvenile Court referred to them, African American supporters of the Amanda Smith Industrial School for Colored Girls did not necessarily construct its girls as criminals or deviants. In the black press and in the school's brochures, its girls were victims of an unjust world that had rendered them alone and in need of the right influences to transcend poverty and discrimination, and ultimately to serve the African American dream of family life. The reluctance on the part of African Americans to support the integration of Park Ridge School may have been a tacit acknowledgment of the sexual anxieties surrounding the racial integration of girls' penal institutions, as well as unwillingness to concede that the girls at the Amanda Smith Industrial School for Colored Girls were anything other than innocent victims of circumstance.

The Amanda Smith Industrial School for Colored Girls is one of the earliest examples of how African American women tried to advocate for girls and the ways girls represented African American hopes and fears. Discussions of the community's insufficient support of the school were a means of critiquing African American race disloyalty, one of the ills of urban life that black leaders challenged migrants and old settlers alike to resist. *Broad Ax*'s and the *Defender*'s upbraiding of communities for leaving girls behind and showing little support for the school simultaneously ignored the real work of black women in order to indict black Chicagoans for an array of problems, from self-hatred to social irresponsibility. The use of girls in this way, as a means of challenging men's concerns about the community while eliding women's active participation, continued throughout the era, as men's political and social work set the tone for African American activism, despite black women's enormous efforts. By partnering with state institutions in the aftermath of the fire, black men were able to take full control of delinquent and dependent girls without having to contend with black women's experiences of or perspectives on what girls needed.

The debates about adoption and institutionalization revolved around three interconnected questions: whether the Amanda Smith Industrial School for Colored Girls helped to maintain the color line in other institutions, whether it was practical to have African American girls try to integrate these institutions, and, if integration was possible, whether African Americans should focus on adoption for their destitute girls. The state of Illinois allowed the school to continue to operate because it was truly the only one of its kind for Protestant African American girls. As in the case of the Amanda Smith Orphanage and Industrial Home for Abandoned Destitute Colored Children, before the fire the Amanda Smith Industrial School for Colored Girls was able to survive because of the state's reluctance to force integration at comparable homes, such as Park Ridge. The African American members of the school's board, supportive neither of a full adoption scheme nor the push toward integration, tried to find temporary institutional solutions for the girls.

As these women focused more and more on the needs and vulnerabilities of Migration-era girls, their actions demonstrated that they believed girls and girlhood were to be protected above all things. The poor treatment of African American girls at Geneva was enough proof for the African American women leading the Amanda Smith Industrial School for Colored Girls to pass on plans to integrate the children. Wells-Barnett made it clear that integration was not her goal, and on the school's opening she told the press that the school "was founded mainly as a protest against the action of Catholic and Protestant institutions in refusing to admit dependent Negro girls."[116] Wells-Barnett argued that adoption did not guarantee the girls a safe or stable home life, and she feared for their safety if sent to private homes.[117] Other black leaders feared this too. A 1913 editorial in the *Defender* claimed: "Our people insist that if our girls are to be 'Jim Crowed' at all we prefer to have them sent to an institution organized, maintained and controlled by our people, who are directly interested in the welfare of these unfortunates."[118]

As more families migrated to the city, African American communities sought spaces where girls could learn the survival skills necessary to care for themselves as well as be inculcated with the values necessary to realize the racial uplift mission of community leaders. By 1918, the year of the fire at the Amanda Smith Industrial School for Colored Girls, Chicago's black population expanded by more than one hundred thousand migrants.[119] Black women's clubs, organized under the umbrella of the Illinois Federation of Colored Women's Clubs, moved quickly to respond to the changing demographics of the city. They continued to take on the plight of migrants and organized makeshift kindergartens in churches, readied boardinghouses for single working women, volunteered to host girls' clubs, and established clearinghouses for those seeking employment.[120] Despite their successes, these women's clubs could not adequately address the numerous needs of the massive waves of men, women, and children who sometimes arrived with little more than hope in their hearts. As the Migration progressed, Chicago's African Americans, both old settlers and newcomers, looked to the network of long-established black churches to rise to the formidable challenge of helping manage the influx. Contentions about sexuality and girlhood would continue to underscore black leaders' meditation on black girls and the Chicago Migration movement.

"MODESTY ON HER CHEEK"

Black Girls and Great Migration Marketplaces

The closing of the Amanda Smith Industrial School for Colored Girls proved devastating to both black girls who needed such an institution and black women reformers who viewed the school as a space for their special brand of leadership and outreach. Although African Americans lost a beloved pillar of black community life, the Great Migration facilitated the growth of other bodies that took the cause of migrant girls seriously. Christian churches in the city, founded by old settlers and prominent black Chicagoans, emerged to welcome migrants and instruct them on how city life was to be lived. For girls and teenage women in particular, churches provided temporary shelter, offered a training course or two to help in the hunt for a decent job, and reinforced that faith was their greatest weapon against loneliness and homesickness.

Churches tried to meet migrant needs, but the sheer volume of newcomers could strain resources and kindness. Migrant girls—who may have been among the most devout in the South—forged new relationships to worship and devotion in the city. Great Migration Chicago provided black southerners with an unprecedented number of options for their social lives, as stores, restaurants, nightclubs, speakeasies, churches, and clubs opened to cater to their specific tastes, as well as dictate them. When girls migrated with their families, they earned wages as they had in the South, but new relationships within families allowed more girls to keep their wages and spend them. Girls enjoyed buying ready-made clothes, records, magazines, and cosmetics. They used their extra earnings to gain

FIG 2.1. The American Red Cross provided provisions to families affected by the 1919 Chicago Race Riot. African American migrants learned that they did not leave racial violence behind when they fled the South. "Provisions supplied by the Red Cross to hundreds of Negro families." Photograph by the Chicago Commission for Race Relations, 1922.

GENERAL RESEARCH AND REFERENCE DIVISION, SCHOMBURG CENTER FOR RESEARCH IN BLACK CULTURE, THE NEW YORK PUBLIC LIBRARY, ASTOR, LENOX AND TILDEN FOUNDATIONS.

admission to movie theatres and dance halls. Black girls, once reliant on church as their entire social world, could now choose how to spend their Wednesday evenings and Sunday mornings.

In this chapter I consider African American girls' interaction with two markets deeply affected by the Great Migration. I use the language of markets to describe the environments in which girls exercised choices about what most captured their imaginations, reflected on what it meant for them to live in the North, and interacted with material goods and spiritual promises. The rise of storefront churches and new church communities, as well as the opening of more shops, boutiques, and five-and-dime stores to cater to black clientele, constituted the Great Migration markets in which girls compared the costs and values of items and ideologies. I explore how black girls interacted with churches and consumer culture, which were two different, but often intersecting, markets that grew as a result of Chicago's black population growth and the presence of so many southerners in the city. I discuss how girls used the popular culture offered in an array of marketplaces, as well as how girls fared among the new markets of religious spaces—from denominations familiar to migrants to movements that challenged mainline Christianity and sprouted from New Negro philosophies. In a climate resplendent with indulgences that spoke to an emerging black urbanism, I argue that black girls navigated these markets as a way of exercising a new-found ability to make choices in their lives. Black girls' participation in, or abstention from, mass culture became essential in how adults discussed the powers and limits of black religious values.

I begin with a discussion of how Christian churches responded to the Migration and how these answers facilitated the emergence of what was known as "New Negro cults"—among them nationalist, political, and religious groups that challenged white supremacy and Christianity explicitly but did not necessarily break free from the paradigm of racial uplift and respectability politics. Using a series of interviews with Great Migration teenage girls and mothers, I examine how Great Migration girls understood their own faith, worship practices, and the utility of church. I then explore the conflicts engendered by girls' participation in Migration-era markets, and how the forces of the sacred (church) and the secular (popular culture) competed in girls' lives. Finally, I turn to the MSTA, a nationalist New Negro religious movement founded in 1925 and credited with being the precursor of the Nation of Islam. I highlight a scandal involving the movement's leader, Noble Drew Ali, and his alleged marriages to child brides to illustrate the importance of girls to the Moorish Science Temple's religious, political, and economic claims and quest for legitimacy among Chicago's migrants and black elites.

Scholars of African American religions agree that the MSTA was a critical precursor to the Nation of Islam and that it helped fill a deep longing among members of the black working class and working poor to gain direction, develop racial self-esteem, and seek out the promises of their new homes. Programs for and ideas on black girlhood, along with other sources, demonstrate that the ideals of the African American nationalist groups, despite their radical calls for separatism and disavowal of whites and their religion and culture, bore a keen likeness to the emphasis on racial uplift in mainstream churches. The MSTA community used girls to illustrate the value and worth of their work among African Americans in Chicago and to make their religious organization more appealing and attractive to migrant families. I connect the ways the MSTA framed black girlhood to the way the Nation of Islam created its girls' programs in the decades following its rise in the 1930s.

THE CHURCH RESPONDS

At a meeting of AME Church bishops in 1917, the year the *Defender* declared would usher in the Migration period, bishops Benjamin Lee and John Hurst prepared a statement on the exodus. While emphasizing that the AME Church should provide "welcome and fellowship" to migrants, Lee and Hurst expressed concern about the vulnerability of this group to fall into urban "haunts of vices." The pair, in language similar to that of educators Booker T. Washington and Carter G. Woodson, encouraged southerners to wait patiently for social change in the South rather than take their chances on a new life in the North. "Those who remain at their homes must cooperate with the sociological movements that are sure to be put into action, to discover the causes of unrest and find a remedy."[1] These two men were surely aware of the struggles facing black southerners, but northern churches were not immediately equipped to handle the influx of migrants. The presence of so many people in material and emotional need caused friction among black church leaders about how to manage the huddled masses of poor, uneducated souls. One report on African Americans and the AME Church from the 1930s observed: "Negro churches in the North, almost grew overnight from memberships of a few hundreds to thousands . . . the northern church especially in great migration centers like Chicago . . . grew by leaps and bounds."[2]

Lee and Hurst's reactions were not representative of all of Chicago's churches. Eventually, as Migration became a fact of life for black northerners across the Midwest and Northeast, churches adopted a greater commitment to the social gospel and heeded the biblical mandate to "welcome the stranger." Churches implemented programs and initiatives to socialize migrants, established employment bureaus, and deployed teams of visitors to ensure migrant homes were as clean and orderly as possible. Some churches saw great potential in the Migration and found strategies to embrace the growth, even if migrants strained nerves and pew capacities. The Olivet Baptist Church's involvement in welcoming migrants is among the strongest examples of an enthusiastic response to the Migration. Founded in 1850, Olivet was one of Chicago's largest and most powerful African

American churches. Olivet took the lead not only in addressing migrant needs but also in encouraging southerners to come north. Olivet expanded its worship services to accommodate the more than four thousand new members it acquired between 1915 and 1919.[3] By 1921 it had grown by a total of 11,144 members.[4]

Olivet's transformation from a church to a vital community resource would have been impossible without the work of its women members. This shift brought deeply committed and often well-educated women into a position to manage the new undertaking, providing them with opportunities to exercise their desired professions when their race and sex limited career opportunities. S. Mattie Fisher, a social worker by training, was one of the most important leaders in Olivet's migrant outreach.[5] Fisher used social science research and social work theory to assist Olivet in responding to migrant appeals for help. She surveyed Black Belt residents in order to assess what migrants most needed from their churches. In addition to collecting basic demographic information from more than five thousand households, Fisher asked people to identify "their church connection" and "their experience as Christian workers in their home church."[6] Armed with vital statistics on the African American families surrounding Olivet's sanctuary, the church successfully helped migrants secure jobs, locate housing, and become part of a community.[7]

GIRLS AND CHURCH

Fisher's research yielded specialized programs for women and girls, and her girls' outreach characterized how mainline African American Christian churches viewed migrant girls. Fisher realized success in welcoming migrant girls into Olivet's programs with the assistance of Jessie Mapp, another Olivet member. On Tuesday nights, between thirty-five and fifty-five girls participated in the Girls Community Guild meetings, which included sewing classes and the reading of devotionals. The guild's focus, like the instruction at the Amanda Smith Industrial School for Colored Girls, was in part on teaching girls how to be good wives and mothers. Fisher was proud that the guild "intended to help them in making the best Christian homes."[8] While their mothers received lessons on home economics, health, and hygiene, daughters received similar messages tailored to their age and level of responsibility in the household.

FIG 2.2. The Olivet Baptist Church organized sewing groups and girls' clubs for recently arrived youth. "The Olivet Baptist Church." Photograph by the Chicago Commission for Race Relations, 1922.

GENERAL RESEARCH AND REFERENCE DIVISION, SCHOMBURG CENTER FOR RESEARCH IN BLACK CULTURE, THE NEW YORK PUBLIC LIBRARY, ASTOR, LENOX AND TILDEN FOUNDATIONS.

Fisher's work was part of the racial uplift culture of black churches that modeled to girls the special mothering role women played in communities. Despite their commitment to helping poor women and girls, churchwomen did not necessarily trust or believe that migrant women could fully take charge of their lives. They put their hopes into the belief that girls, still young and far more impressionable, could adhere to their advice and wisdom. Industrial training school founder Nannie H. Burroughs reported in 1920 to the National Baptist Women's Convention that migrant women "like the children that many of them are . . . satisfy their Wants and forgets [*sic*] their Needs."[9] She claimed that migrant women were "restless, unreliable type[s] whose habit it is to work long enough to get what they want and take many vacations or days off between."[10] Burroughs indicted all migrants when she noted: "The masses of our people are intoxicated."[11]

Smaller churches also provided special girls with programs. In the Lilydale neighborhood, eighty blocks south of Olivet, the local Baptist church also engaged girls in sewing and other activities. University of Chicago student Ruth Pardee studied this lower-middle-class South Side community and reported on the importance of churches to girls' social lives, as well as to adults' control over the girls' movements in the city. The Lilydale Altar Guild was made up of "adolescent girls . . . and a Sunday School teacher" who gathered each week to "decorate the pulpit and rostrum of the church and keep it clean." The Lilydale First Baptist Church Missionary Circle also engaged girls in a sewing group that earned money by "making quilts and other types of fancy work."[12] Lilydale adults, concerned with juvenile delinquency, admitted that church activities were "principally to keep the girls busy and out of mischief."[13] Lilydale was among the more prosperous Black Belt communities, and parents were probably more concerned with keeping girls on a righteous path than with providing them with a useful skill with which to earn money.

Fisher, Mapp, and the Lilydale churchwomen shared their programs' successes with their peers in women's clubs; their reports did not include individual stories of how girls grappled with what their churches communicated to them. Due to the important services that churches like Olivet provided, girls may have been reluctant to express their true feelings about church attendance and programs. Outside the archive of church meeting minutes, and news bulletins that often focused on successes, surveys and studies of Migration life revealed girls' motivations for believing in God, their struggles of faith, and the way urbanizations shifted and reordered their spiritual and social priorities. In a cross-section of interviews and testimonies, girls and teenage women revealed how deeply constitutive their faith was to their identities, and their understanding of the necessity of relying on churches and religious communities to serve their needs, even as they realized church communities' ability to undermine their feelings of self-worth. In interviews conducted at the Chicago Urban League by sociologists, girls also used the topic of church attendance to critique their parents' behavior, including their disappointment that their fathers did not attend church or their surprise at their mothers' shopping for which church best suited their personal needs. These broad and varying conceptions of church and religion provide a fuller perspective on how black girls lived their faith instead of merely complying with what church workers wanted from them.

Migrant girls understood church in the South as a respite from gruel-ing work weeks and one of a few spaces where they could indulge in youth-ful expressions of joy and see friends who also lived-in as domestics. As Elizabeth Clark-Lewis discovered, "although economic necessities forced the employment of every able-bodied person in the rural southern house-hold, white employers did not interfere with African American regular church attendance."[14] Ora Fisher remembered the relief church provided her when she was a girl. "Down North Carolina, you'd get there early for church meetings. For us children it was just a place to play and play. No-body wanted you to do no chores, like at home. And I know it was the only place you could go and not feel somebody was going to make you do something other than sit down and sit still. That was a relief for sure."[15] Mandatory schooling laws and child labor protections did not preclude girls entirely from hard work in Chicago, but the new social arrange-ments of the city lessened the significance of Sunday for black girls and their families. Girls could socialize at school, meet their friends at candy stores, escape chores by stealing away to the back porch of their apartment building, or simply take a walk down one of the wide boulevards of the Black Belt.

For girls hailing from small communities where church was one of the few spaces where black people could express themselves, Chicago pre-sented a dizzying array of new ways of engaging with others and their de-sires. The privileges that accompanied Migration — from purchasing "race" products in stores to enjoying streetcars without degrading Jim Crow signs — also included freedom from restrictive church communities in towns and hamlets where everyone knew and judged one another. Moth-ers, who regularly towed their daughters to church, relaxed their attitudes. Some used church, no longer their only social option, as they saw fit. Mrs. Brannigan, a migrant from New Orleans, had become a Methodist at eigh-teen, but after migrating to Chicago at the age of twenty-seven she found that her thirteen years in Chicago did not bring her closer to a church community. A sporadic attendee of an AME Zion church, she confessed to sociologist E. Franklin Frazier: "I just go 'round different churches.'" Hoping that church would elevate her "despondent" mood, she could not find a satisfactory church home. Yet she did send her "children over to the community Sunday school." Georgia Everly, a teenage girl who had been a committed Baptist in the South, also traveled among Chicago's many churches and found some of the city's new religious groups entertaining, but they did not compel her to convert. "I goes to Sanctified Church every night—33rd and Prairie. I likes to hear them shout and sing. I just go to look at 'em, that's all." Her mother was a member of Ebenezer Church, but only "if she git up in time."

Some black girls were upset by their parents' lax attitude toward church, and they often became the moral voice of their families when their parents failed to maintain a commitment to religious life. Pearl, a teen who attended the Berean Baptist Church at Fifty-Second and Dearborn, offered: "My father don't go to church, he goes to the pool room.... He is a member of the pool room." She added: "My people is so messed up and everything." She inadvertently reflected that she had adopted some of their casual approaches too. When her baby was born, she did not care where the child was baptized. "Ye'ah, some sanctified place down the street there. Mamma took it, I didn't bother to go."[16]

In migrant families where each member kept differing work and school schedules, girls and their family members scattered across the city to attend churches separately. Millie Baker, from Jackson, Mississippi, described her family's church practices and demonstrated how gender shaped expectations about worship in her family.

> My mother and all of us belonged to the Baptist Church [in the South].... I would come home and go to the Methodist church down in Mississippi, that is the only place you can go is church. I would stay in church most all of the time. My mother has prayer meeting every Wednesday morning herself sometimes when we come in. But in Jackson all of us would be there for prayer. Now we hardly ever go. Sometime when we feel sick we go in and let Mamma pray you know. I haven't joined church since I been here. My mother belongs to Pilgrim. But I go to Bethel. She doesn't go any place much. My father goes to church when I carry him. The boys you know how they are, they hardly ever go to church, only when my mother fusses at them and then they will go.[17]

Another motivating factor for spiritual devotion in Chicago was a keen understanding that faith delivered women and their families from sinfulness. Religion was armor against the stage shows, dance halls, and the other vices found in the Black Belt. One young woman, who converted to the Baptist church at age fourteen, recalled: "We all was Baptist ...

God saved me from sin six years ago. You see I was a business manager for some show—or rather carnival, that they used to have on the street."[18] Some girls also regretted their loss of social status in churches in the North. A Tennessee-born migrant longed to return to her role as an "assistant teacher at the Baptist's Sunday School." Chicago was different for her family. She lamented: "We all belonged there . . . my mother been in so many churches [in the North]. Well, I tell you, peoples come up here and git turned around."[19] Girls used the language of being "turned around" or mixed up and confused to describe, critique, and analyze the changes in their families' internal lives. The psychological and existential displacement that accompanied migration, no matter how much it was desired, overwhelmed some girls, and they searched to balance an array of contradictory emotions about Chicago and change. Many girls believed that when they turned to their God for comfort, they could turn themselves right side up and soldier through disappointment and despair. Yet the world around them was so different and could be so chaotic that finding their true north did not seem possible no matter how much they prayed, worshiped, or believed.

GIRLS AT THE MARKET

With unprecedented levels of earning and greater autonomy, girls did not only shop for churches. They also took their power to choose into the commercial spaces of Bronzeville and other business districts in black Chicago. Black girls, along with Chicagoans of every race, gender, and age, enjoyed the popular culture surrounding the metropolis and used consumption to don modern identities, rebel against authority, and mediate tensions about their commitment to the secular and the sacred. In the South, parents collected their daughters' pay from white bosses or expected their girls to release their wages on payday. Ann Brown remembered this vividly in her interview with Lewis: "You knew from the first—you'd give anything you got to her [mother] . . . You'd never see no money! If you saw it you'd not touch it—she'd give you all she had [spanking] if you touched any money."[20]

Girls' access to disposable income created discord within families. The scholarship on rural white families who moved to cities and grappled with their factory worker daughters' indulgence in the city's culture allows us to see the shift in authority and power dynamics in ways that mirrored the conflicts in many black migrant homes. At school and at home, teenage girls used makeup and clothes, popular literature, and social spaces to understand their new city.[21] Younger girls who had yet to discover the power of rouge or the bittersweet joy of sitting through hours of hairdressing enjoyed "E.M.S. colored dolls" and copies of morality books like Mary White Ovington's *Hazel*, about a black girl in Boston sent to visit her family in Alabama.[22]

Wednesday night church meetings and weekends at chaste, clubwomen-sponsored socials could not compete with the Savoy Ballroom and the Regal Theatre for girls looking for a thoroughly urban experience. Dancing at the Savoy was a mark of popularity and a means of celebrating a youthful, cosmopolitan identity. Opened in 1927, it was described as "unquestionably the finest and largest place for dancing that invited colored patronage.... The hall was crowded every night of the week." A year later, the Regal Theatre opened, and patrons found it "even more majestic than the Savoy."[23] One churchgoing girl had to sneak out of the house to go to the Savoy. She disclosed: "I go to shows and the Savoy. I go to the Regal every week and the Metropolitan. Also the little shows around 57th Street . . . I tell you, I like to go on Sunday to the Savoy. Whenever I go I have to slip off and go. You see Mama doesn't want us to go to shows on Sunday, nor play cards or dance."[24]

A night at the Savoy warranted that teenage girls dressed in their finest clothes, painted their faces with cosmetics, and arranged their hair in the latest styles. African American women's beauty culture was a powerful and pervasive force in Chicago during the 1920s because of the multivalent ways it interacted with black life. Teenage girls and young women trained and employed by Annie Malone's Poro School of Hairdressing, Anthony Overton's Hygienic Manufacturing Company, and Madame C. J. Walker's hair treatment empire were given economic freedom while working as beauticians and sales agents.[25] African American girls and women alike tried out new hairstyles using hot combs and straightening treatments. Their hair became canvases with which to display urban identities. African American women's hair, always a topic of social debate and scrutiny, dismayed some of their employers. Among a list of white employers' problems with black domestic workers: "Every Negro servant girl spends at least half of her wages on preparations for taking the kink out of her hair."[26]

FIG 2.3. Some South Side girls used their earnings to enjoy various youth activities, including roller rinks, where they could meet boys. "Crowds watching roller-skating exhibition, Chicago, Illinois." Photograph by Russell Lee for the Farm Security Administration, n.d.

PHOTOGRAPHS AND PRINT DIVISION, SCHOMBURG CENTER FOR RESEARCH IN BLACK CULTURE, THE NEW YORK PUBLIC LIBRARY, ASTOR, LENOX AND TILDEN FOUNDATIONS.

Whether a gross stereotype or a reality, the ability for black working girls and women to "live-out" away from employers, receive real wages instead of a sharecropper's credit, and pay for a hair treatment was a powerful experience that would not end due to a little grumbling from white bosses. Black women's hair and makeup culture, though constructed by a beauty standard that was steeped in Eurocentric ideas of female attractiveness, was still a terrain for expressions of black freedom and sexuality.

Chicago was the center of many cosmetics companies and hair salons, some frequented by their mothers or the first ladies of their churches, but girls sometimes selected styles of adornment and fashion that their elders did not abide. Another migrant girl knew that bobbing her hair—cutting it in a short, flapper style—was considered rebellious by her parents: "My father never wanted me to bob my hair but when I came up here I bobbed it. That was after he was killed."[27] Girls' fascination with adopting northern styles, coupled with the cost of remaining outfitted in the latest fashions, could quickly lead to arguments in black families. Fourteen-year-old Loretta, who earned a salary of $9 per week, purchased clothes with her paycheck instead of surrendering the money to her mother. Angry with her daughter over her spending habits, Loretta's mother beat her, prompting the girl to use a variety of Chicago's resources to escape her home. She wrested her independence from her mother by running away and "through an advertisement in a paper secured work as a domestic servant." Then she appealed to Juvenile Court officers for help. The court empathized with the girl and gladly reported that her condition "improved much while on probation."[28]

Chicago's migrant women, even those in the working class who may have been more open to modern styles of dress, often took exception to the way their daughters succumbed to trends. The case of Lorraine Palmer and her daughter, Johnetta, dramatized the complexities of migrant religious practices, generational culture surrounding popular styles, and the liberties black girls embraced in the city. Mrs. Palmer appeared before the city's Court of Domestic Relations worker at the Urban League to ask for assistance in finding Johnetta. A faithful Baptist woman, she warned the interviewer that in Chicago she was confused on how to assess a woman's worth because of the overwhelming popularity of flapper styles. "You can't tell a decent woman from a bad one. All of 'em wearing skirts about their knees and hair all cut off. So you don't know who you are helping." Johnetta was proof that the city was an unstable space, where girls could be moved to sinful acts in the pursuit of sartorial luxuries.

Mrs. Palmer narrated her troubles with her daughter: "The devil got in her when I came here and my daughter she ran off."[29] On a fateful Easter morning, Johnetta fled her home, and her disappearance was still fresh in her mother's mind when she talked about it a year later.

> I was not able to give her nice things like she wanted. And I whupped my children to keep 'em in their place—for them to go to church instead of dances and shows . . . My daughter asked a girl friend what she was going to get for Easter and the girl said nothing . . . Well, my girl told her that she would have something but that she would not be there to wear it. Well, I noticed how funny she acted that day and so the next

day I carried her to work with me. Well, the next day when I came home she was up under the bed. I told her to come out I wasn't going to whup huh, but that I was just going to put her in the Juvenile home. Well, I went out and while I was sweeping the back stairs, off she went with just her coat and . . . hat.

The battle between the Palmer women illustrated multiple dimensions of how Migration life was lived by girls and their mothers. Johnetta defied her mother's authority and her discipline, resisting both church and corporeal punishments. She had a clear sense of what the Juvenile Home would mean for her—a loss of access to the beautiful things she coveted and a restraint to her independence, so she fled her mother's home and took a chance on the anonymity of the city, where no one would recognize her and report her whereabouts to her mother.

Mrs. Palmer's insistence that Johnetta stay away from dance halls, her belief that church could shield her from sinfulness, and the seriousness with which she took her duty to protect her daughter all signified that she held a traditional view of the city as a polluting influence on girls. Yet this mother's testimony about her own religious choices indicates that she, too, embraced Chicago's new markets, in this case the religious one where new Christian denominations and offshoots welcomed migrants. Her identification as a Baptist was a curious one, because she also acknowledged in the interview that she visited the storefront churches that dotted the thoroughfares of black Chicago. She identified a church at 4021 State Street as her "church home" but said she felt at odds with the church because they "don't 'prove of women preachers." Mrs. Palmer preached at "4001 Federal [and] any place the Law will permit me to preach." Hoping to follow in the footsteps of Chicago's great women pastors, like Lucy Smith and Mary Evans, Mrs. Palmer wanted to establish "a house of prayer where I could call all denominations."[30] She recognized that the city allowed for faithful women to create their own churches, where their leadership and vision could be honored. The Palmer women were more similar than they may have thought on that Easter morning.

Girls who obeyed their disapproving parents and avoided the Savoy, or were not able to spend their wages on new clothes, could still find a way to enjoy the day's popular cultural forms—through black print culture. Migration provided many girls with an opportunity to attend school con-

FIG 2.4. Religious families often prohibited their daughters from going to dances at the Savoy or popular movies at the Regal Theatre. "The movies are popular in the Negro section of Chicago, Illinois, April 1941." Photograph by Russell Lee.

PHOTOGRAPHS AND PRINT DIVISION, SCHOMBURG CENTER FOR RESEARCH IN BLACK CULTURE, THE NEW YORK PUBLIC LIBRARY, ASTOR, LENOX AND TILDEN FOUNDATIONS.

sistently, and black literacy on the whole increased as a result of these new educational opportunities. Girls could read the Billikens section of the *Defender*, with tips on how to be a good citizen, and other publications that wanted to instruct black children in racial uplift values. The *Defender*'s Junior Billiken Club was also a place where black children could articulate their interests and express their creativity. Fourteen-year-old Lillian Turner submitted a poem about "an old lady who arose with the light and was always a-knitting form morning to night." The seventh grader sent in the poem hoping she would also get a "B.B. button and membership card."[31]

Similarly committed to instilling a respectable view of black girlhood was the *Brownies' Book*, a periodical edited by intellectual W. E. B. Du Bois. With short stories by Jessie and Arthur Fauset and other prominent black writers, the *Brownies' Book* presented a vision of what adults wanted children to see, believe, and be perceived as in an era of vicious representations of black children as pickaninnies. These depictions of black children constantly poised to be eaten by alligators or savages showed them as having more animal than human qualities. The cover of the January 1920 edition of *Brownies' Book* featured the epitome of Du Bois's desire for the publication, and black elites' projection of an ideal black girl subject. The magazine features a little girl dressed in a costume, probably for a performance of a fairy tale. Attired in a knee-length white gown, tights, and ballet slippers, the little girl faces the camera with a crown resting atop her head, a forced smile on her face belying the difficulty of remaining *en pointe*. Her arms are stretched up high as if contemplating the possibility of flight. "Designed for all children, but especially ours," wrote Du Bois in dedicating the magazine to the "Children of the Sun." *Brownies' Book* featured many of Du Bois's own ideas about race relations, international brotherhood among the "red, yellow, and black races," and current events for children, from NAACP protests to the accomplishments of black children in predominately white schools.[32]

While some girls enjoyed *Brownies' Book* and the *Defender*'s Billikens column, these uplift prescriptions may have been less appealing to older girls than the story magazines, like *True Story* and later *Negro Romance*. *True Story*, a popular magazine established in 1919, was filled with dramatic stories of sin, love, and redemption. In an interview at the Urban League, teenager Sandy Allen admitted that her family didn't "attend any church" and she preferred to spend her weekends reading copies of *True Story*. She recalled one of her favorite stories, "Quicksands of Life," about a custody battle between two sets of grandparents after the mother "had convulsions when the baby came and died." Sandy also enjoyed the fictions she saw in the movies at the Owl, Regal, and Metropolitan theatres.[33] Another *True Story* reader, Gina Smith, enjoyed the magazine without her mother's approval. "I read *True Story*, *Love Story*, [and] sometime those physical culture books. My mother says it ain't nothing to them love stories, but I like them." Sandy added that she read the magazines, because "colored papers" had "so much robbery in them."[34] Several girls who participated in Urban League interviews complained that the *Defender* only reported sensational crimes and said they believed that these stories exacerbated their fears of city life, so they turned to popular fiction magazines to escape from the world around them.

GIRLS AND THE NEW NEGRO MOVEMENT

As Christian churches set the stage for girls' community involvement and embodied the very values and expectations some girls resisted, new religious and political movements were sweeping across the city to provide migrants with a means of redefining themselves as "New Negroes." The New Negro movement enveloped a broad range of literary, activist, and economic projects of black Americans in the 1920s. The movement called on blacks to use multiple forms of protest to challenge Jim Crow and white supremacy. New Negro artists and intellectuals celebrated their African origins, sought to celebrate race pride in their expressive culture, and asserted the need for black Americans to search for liberation from the prevailing racial order.[35]

Intellectual, cultural, and religious historians have analyzed and assessed the New Negro movement's impact on black life and culture in the early twentieth century. Their insights link New Negro thinking and black nationalism, economic independence, and strategic mobilization. I am most concerned about how New Negro movements influenced the alternate space for migrants seeking spiritual comfort outside of traditional Christian churches and how these movements understood black girlhood's relationship to the religious and commercial marketplaces. In this instance, I will examine the MSTA movement to explore how this religious and political group conceived of black girls, how it mandated how they could participate in these marketplaces, and how the image of the black girl, as well as actual girls, operated to serve the goals of the early MSTA.

Before Ali declared the Moorish Science belief system the true religion of all "Asiatics" (his term for black peoples), Chicagoans were first introduced to notions of black supremacy and self-determination by the Chicago branch of the Universal Negro Improvement Association (UNIA). Jamaican immigrant Marcus Garvey established the UNIA in 1917. The Moorish Science Temple shared many of the organizational and philosophical characteristics of Garvey's UNIA, and an analysis of the UNIA is necessary to understand why Chicagoans embraced the MSTA with its bold declarations about black identity and gender structures.[36] With headquarters in another Migration hub, Harlem, the UNIA spread across the country, appealing to northern migrants as well as southerners in its promises to fortify black masculinity, repatriate black Americans, and restore a lost dignity to a marginalized people. After building an extensive network of UNIA offices, publications, and businesses, Garvey became a notable presence in Chicago.

The *Chicago Whip* endorsed the movement, declaring: "It takes the men and trains them to be manly and lawful, loyal to their race and country."[37] However, the UNIA soon wore out its welcome in Chicago. *Defender* editor Robert Abbott battled with Garvey over the UNIA's sale of their company's stock in the city, and the two race leaders made slanderous charges against each other. By 1919 Abbott and his allies had successfully weakened the movement in Chicago by generating negative news stories about it and reporting its leadership to law enforcement.[38] The movement continued on shaky ground; Chicago's UNIA leaders were able to retain nine thousand members in 1922. By the next year, though, a violent split within the Chicago UNIA group led to its death.[39] Sociologist Allan Spear theorized that the "feud[,] marked by frequent shootings, dissipated whatever strength the movement had retained in Chicago."[40] Meanwhile, the UNIA thrived in New York City: "By 1920, the UNIA claimed a membership of 6 million . . . in addition, the UNIA had several enterprises including laundries, factories, [and] its own ship . . . and newspaper."[41]

A SMALL NEGRO WEARING A FLAMING RED FEZ

Noble Drew Ali, born Timothy Drew, a migrant by way of Newark, New Jersey, took Garvey's place in Chicago. An Illinois Works Progress Administration (WPA) writer described him as a "small Negro wearing a flaming red fez" who was proclaiming "a startling new doctrine." The doctrine captured the attention of black nationalists, those frustrated with Christianity, and other migrants looking to the New Negro religious market for something new.[42] The WPA writer marveled at the way Ali was able to connect with migrants by using his "eloquent tongue, a persuasive, and a native shrewdness, which enabled him to sway the poor and unlettered people who listened to him."[43] In addition to the desire to experience new religious movements, WPA researchers hypothesized that Ali's followers also came to his movement in response to Chicago's 1919 Red Summer race riots. This week-long chaos across the city left twenty-three black and fifteen white Chicagoans dead, 537 people harmed, and nearly a thousand homeless. The riots and other instances of antiblack violence plunged old settlers and newcomers into an existential paradox about the limits of freedom in the North and chastened their hopes that leaving the South would bring them true safety. Memories of the riot, coupled with everyday confrontations with racial discrimination, made them want what "Drew Ali was offering . . . pride and dignity."[44] Ali promised the world to his migrant followers as long as they followed his spiritual and social directives: reject Christianity, commit to black self-help, embrace Moorish identity, and follow the "everlasting gospel of Allah."[45]

Ali incorporated Islam and Eastern philosophies, as well as Christianity, in his Moorish Science holy book, *The Holy Koran of the Moorish Science Temple*, also known as the *Circle Seven Koran*. The *Circle Seven* recast black origins outside North America and Africa and presented an intricate journey of the Asiatic people, with roots in the Middle East, to America and declared Islam their true religion. Ali's new religion presented a curious mélange of ancient African history, studies of the Muslim Koran, and the principles of Garvey's black nationalism. The core of Moorish Temple beliefs revolved around the true identity of black peoples; the Moorish narrative declared that African Americans were in fact "Asiatics" and "Moors." Ali located "Moorish" people in the biblical land of Canaan, in the birthplace of Noah's son, Ham. The Moorish family tree also branched from the people of Moab and West African "Moors." Ali's account of Moorish ancestry proved that African Americans were meant to be Muslims, not Christians. He taught that Jesus was a prophet who was misappropriated by Europeans in order to establish Christianity. The MSTA eschewed the terms "colored" or "black." Ali asserted that African Americans were misnamed "blacks" because Moors had lost their identities in the New World and the reclamation of identity rested in triumph over contemporary racial conditions.[46]

Moorish testimonies of faith centered on the restoration of racial identity. One Temple member, a Louisiana native, disclosed to WPA interviewers: "From the age of seven years he could not believe in Christianity . . . he wanted to be with his own and he never was satisfied until he became a Moslem. Then he learned there was no Negro, black or colored, and he's been happy ever since."[47] The WPA report linked this man's experiences with a larger black freedom struggle. "Many Negroes on the South Side of Chicago flocked to the new teacher . . . a change of status from 'Negro' to 'Asiatic' promised an easy way to salvation."[48]

Frazier referenced the Temple in his study *The Negro Church in America* and classified the MSTA as a "New Negro cult" that offered a "radical secularization" of black religion. He believed that the appeal of the Moorish Science belief system was that it was able to "re-create in the urban environment a type of religious organization in which [southern African Americans] can find warm and sympathetic association and status."[49] Frazier also noticed that by shedding the terms "colored," "black," "Negro," or "Ethiopian" and adopting new identities, a Temple adherent became "a new person . . . with a kind of national identification."[50] In this way the Temple provided what few institutions could—a clear, definable sense that urban life was a true departure from southern violence and Jim Crow—by reconstructing the temporal spaces of religion. The promise of Migration, and of the adoption of New Negro values, offered the possibility that a black citizen could assume a new identity and a new outlook on his or her world.

GENDER AND GIRLHOOD IN THE MOORISH SCIENCE TEMPLE

In addition to the Moorish shift in perspective on black identities, Moorish teachings also claimed to offer its members a means of expressing a more authentic gender identity. As was the case with the UNIA and other black nationalist groups, gender undergirded the construction of Moorish worldviews and practices. The Moorish movement called on men to assert themselves and their commitment to nationalism and to display Moorish masculinity in ways that Christian masculinity and male-headed civil rights organizations did not. The Moorish prescription for men that they rise up for their people was consistent with historian Kevin Gaines's evaluation of the nature of black nationalist groups. "Black nationalism and racial uplift ideology would often phrase both the problem and its solution—representing both black oppression and its remedies—as a question of manhood."[51] In the essay "When the Negro Comes North," a Migration-era writer determined that northern migration allowed men to realize an ideal masculinity because the women and girls in their lives were less susceptible to sexual abuse and exploitation. Echoing the many letters to the *Defender* urging men to migrate so they could realize the full responsibility and articulation of their manhood, the editorial makes the desires of migrant men clear: "We want our women to love and respect us as the protector and not to protect us with their honor and their very souls."[52]

Although focused on how men could experience a new racial-gender order in the North, implicit in this and other statements about Great Migration masculinity was how girls and women would experience and embrace men's protection in radically different ways. Black girls and women would have to not only allow themselves to be protected but also understand protection and the larger claim to fulfillment of black patriarchy as the central goal of remaking their lives in the North. These gendered perspectives of self-efficacy fueled Moorish appeals to renounce Christianity and envelop one's self in Ali's movement. Yet the period's racial realities could not allow for this fully. Arna Bontemps and Jack Conroy, in their 1945 classic *They Seek the City*, reported that Moorish men were "proclaiming in the name of their prophet Noble Drew Ali, that they had been freed of European domination. They flaunted their fezzes on the street and treated the white man with undisguised contempt."[53] The politically savvy Ali, who relied on white and black power brokers to support his businesses, admonished the men for their behavior. Their boldest act was showing whites their Moorish membership cards and yelling "I am a man" on city streets. While his very teachings inspired these actions, Ali redressed aggressors in his newspaper, the *Moorish Voice*: "I hereby inform members that they must end all radical agitating speeches while at work, in their homes or on the streets. We are for peace not destruction. Stop flashing your cards at Europeans, it causes confusion ... our work is to uplift the nation."[54]

Whereas Moorish men expressed their masculinity through antiwhite tirades in public, women and girls could not act so boldly in the name of their new religion. In order to help realize the aims of the MSTA's restorative patriarchy, girls and women were to heed the lessons of the *Circle Seven* for theological guidance and practical matters of conduct, including the appropriate treatment of and behaviors of girls. Through the laws and examples of the *Circle Seven*, Ali called on female Moorish members to take up the work of the Temple as a means of supporting the destiny of Moorish men and to revel in the prophet's (Ali's) directive to be admired by their men and communities.

The MSTA instructed girls on gendered modesty through the *Circle Seven*, and the girls also engaged in MSTA business and social activities.

The MSTA strove to present a respectable presence outside the Temple. Moorish women were equally responsible for developing the qualities of a good spouse in their daughters. The *Circle Seven* celebrated Moorish girls for their purity. The sacred instructions described the ways girls "walketh in maiden sweetness, with innocence in her mind, and modesty on her cheek." Girls were taught that they were the "reasonable companion" to the man rather than the "slave of his passion." Moorish teachings did not vindicate all girls and young women entirely in all matters regarding sexuality and marriage. In the first declaration in the "Holy Instructions and Warning for All Young Men," the *Circle Seven* warned men to keep away from "the harlot" and her "delights," presumably referring to women outside the Temple belief system. In "Marriage Instructions for Man and Wife," the prophet made clear the necessity of Moorish women's participation in men's struggles: "Remember thou art man's reasonable companion . . . to assist him in the toils of life, to soothe his heart with thy tenderness and recompense his care with soft endearments." In the context of marriage, boys were told that girls were "not merely to gratify [the husband] . . . but to assist him in the toils of life." Good Moorish wives learned that "submission and obedience are the lessons of her life." While Moorish women were expected to be toilers, they were also characterized as filled with "luster . . . brighter than the stars of Heaven," with smiles "more delicious than a garden of roses" and a bosom that "transcendeth the lily."[55]

The characterization of Moorish girlhood in this philosophy stood in opposition to the dimmer representations of migrant women and girls in mainline churches and in the rhetoric of middle-class uplift organizations. These uplifters often projected suspicion, if not judgment, on migrant girls and young women. As the Moorish Science community described its woman as having a "mansion of goodness" within her and "virtue . . . at her right hand," churches and their outreach missions emphasized the evil and depravity that resided within the hearts and souls of girls and teenage women. Women like Burroughs advocated for residential industrial schools to train migrant girls, discipline their characters, and use Christian teachings to steer them away from vice. Migrants who desired access to respectability without such castigations found the Temple. The contrast between Moorish conceptions of girlhood and the churched clubwoman's perspective uncovers the class antagonisms that helped to create and sustain new religious movements.

In the realm of representation, Moorish women held an advantage over middle-class Christian women. Although most Moorish converts, regardless of sex, did not possess the social luxuries of respectable middle-class status, they did enjoy some freedoms associated with their social position, particularly when it came to religion. Migrant women could more easily choose their places of worship. The women converts who sought a new beginning in cities were free from the strictures of class, family name, and deep roots in Chicago. They could exercise their options as to whether they would worship, and if so, where and under what terms. Moorish women, and other women in nationalist groups, may have felt that they could choose to be celebrated and admired instead of maligned and judged. They could also make this choice for their daughters.

African American women's historians have determined that part of the appeal of Garveyism—and I would add the Moorish Science Temple to this assessment—for women was its rhetoric on the exaltation and protection of African American womanhood. Barbara Bair notes in her work on the Garvey movement: "Many women embraced these roles and images, including the idea of black women as beautiful and the centrality and worth of motherhood."[56] By embracing their status as symbols of black beauty and motherhood, Moorish women bore significant responsibilities in the Temple to fulfill their goals and represent their faith to the broader public. These perspectives on womanhood had significant impact on how girls served the MSTA mission as well.

Outsiders found the Moorish stance on women and girls remarkable, in light of how Christian women were treated in their home churches. Although essential to the operation and management of churches, most Christian women were rendered invisible outside their specific clubs and projects. Historian of black religion Miles Mark Fisher, writing in 1937, attributed the success of the Temple and other "Negro cults" to their gender dynamics. He argued that their efficacy sprang from the fact that the leaders came from the same humble beginnings as their followers, they appealed to "the unsophisticated churchmen and the forgotten masses," and most remarkably, the "equality for women" that prevailed within the groups.[57] Fisher compared the Temple to mainline Christian churches and may have interpreted the Temple's celebration of black womanhood in its sacred texts and the acknowledgment of women sheikesses in the Temple as equality.

Fisher's impression of the reltive equality between Moorish men and women likely rose from the way women and girls actively participated in the Temple's public culture and philanthropic efforts. Moorish women were named to governorships in temples across the country and were among the recognized leaders of local branches. Within a few years of the MSTA's founding, seamstress Sister Whitehead-Bey, named a "grand sheikess" in the organization, established a second Chicago temple. Whitehead-Bey's leadership helped the movement expand to several northern and southern cities. Ali's wife, Pearl Ali, represented her husband throughout the city. Pearl Ali held high ranks in the national organization, and her leadership was essential to the development of the Temple's appeal to women and its growth in girls and women's programs. She created the Sisters of the Temple. Many of the members of the Sisters, having had contact with African American churches in the past, adopted a model set by Christian women's groups in establishing clubs. The Sisters established a Necessity Fund "to help members in need" and organized a Tag Day, asking members to commit to a "week of sacrifice."[58] On Ali's return from a tour of temples, members were told to "drop as much money as they can spare in a box . . . for fallen humanity." The women's group described their mission: "[Our] paramount object is to uplift fallen humanity and be the right hand of the Prophet by their words, works and deeds."[59] Pearl Ali also was the Temple's national secretary, was treasurer for the Business Men's Club, supervised the Temple's publications (the *Moorish Guide*, under the leadership of editor Sister Juanita Mayo Richardson-Bey, the *Moorish Voice*, and the *Moorish Review*), and worked for the Moorish Manufacturing Company.[60]

Ali recognized the role girls could play in the economic mission of Moorish "uplift of humanity" and declared that the Temple wanted "better positions for our men and women," predicting that "more employment for our boys and girls and bigger unions will follow, and economic security."[61] Pearl Ali established a separate youth group for Moorish girls, with the goals of creating "interest in educational pursuits and to awaken and cultivate an appreciation for the arts, [and] a greater attendance at the literary and trade schools."[62]

The relationship between the sexes in the MSTA was far from equal, although the leadership roles for women in it were notable. Girls and women could serve as temple representatives and figureheads, like the UNIA female presidents, yet Moorish teaching reminded its female members that they must adhere to men's authority. An article in the *Moorish Guide* illustrated that black girls and women needed the Temple in order to suppress their own desires toward white men and that contempt toward black men was contempt for self. A Moorish man opined that when black girls boarded streetcars, they would "prefer to sit next to a Caucasian, or . . . stand up."[63] On one occasion when a white male passenger made a sexual advance toward a black girl, the author, undoubtedly bolstered by his Moorish manhood, intervened. After 'saving her,' he invited her to a Moorish Science Temple "to learn more about herself."[64] These narratives of racial and sexual rescue established an ideological and social process in which black women and girls had to be led toward their true identities, one of the prevailing promises of the MSTA movement. In Moorish society, part of a girl's special role was to respond to her male protector in order to become valuable and useful to the movement. One Moorish Science woman recalled that when she assumed the last name Bey, a "Moorish" surname, she felt: "The Bey on the end of my name made me a woman."[65]

THE MOORISH SCIENCE TEMPLE MARKETPLACE

One key distinction between the UNIA and the MSTA at the time lay in their attitudes toward consumer culture. As Martin Summers posits in his study of masculinity in this period, the UNIA castigated the personal and financial habits of the working class. Summers described Garveyism as "censorious of African Americans and African Caribbeans — particularly black youth — who were absorbed in consumer culture. Thrift and conscientious consumption, along with a solid work ethic, were cornerstones of the respectability preached by the UNIA." The UNIA pleaded with members to "lead ascetic lifestyles by reducing the money they spent on food, fashion, and social activities."[66]

Instead of following the UNIA's precedent in restricting access to consumer goods and commerce, the MSTA embraced a middle path on these issues, capitalizing on black relationships to the market and allowing for some participation. The rise of the Moorish Science movement coincided with an explosion in the creation and advertising of health and beauty aids for African American girls and young women. Perhaps in order to keep girls obedient to the call for modesty when they were outside their family's supervision, the Temple's businesses addressed the lures of the secular world. Moorish girls may have resisted the fashion and hair fads of the 1920s, but the enticements to participate in some form of beauty regime were still strong.

Moorish beauty and appearance standards during the period and the Temple's economic programs shaped Moorish girls' religious and social experiences of Moorish Science identity in ways distinct from the ways other influences shaped other black girls' corresponding experiences. From the remaining documents of the Temple's business practices, the recurring use of the term "Moorish" in advertisements for black beauty products, and the scholarship on the emerging popular and consumer culture borne out of black urbanization, I construct the worlds of girls and teenage women who became members of the Moorish Science Temple in the mid- to late 1920s.

The Temple's first national convention, held during the week of October 15, 1928, exemplified the importance of Moorish girls and women to providing a positive public face for the MSTA. The female members were modestly outfitted in their loosely draped gowns and long scarves, which extended from their covered heads down their backs. The *Defender* and other media outlets observed as thousands of Temple members from across the country gathered to report on their activities, socialize, and participate in a "grand spectacular parade through Chicago's beautiful residential district with all Grand Sheiks . . . in Full Regalia."[67] Delegates from temples across fifteen states converged on Unity Hall and charmed onlookers with a display of fezzes, robes, feathers, other "regalia similar to that worn in eastern countries," and "a camel."

Women populated the formal proceedings; the convention committee secretary, Sister Whitehead-El, presented a report on the West Side's Number Nine Temple; another sister led a "grand musical concert" and updated members on the progress of Detroit's newest temple. Women and girls prepared the "good wholesome meals and the refreshments" offered by the "Moorish Cafeteria Service," one of many Temple businesses staffed by women.[68] The *Defender*, which had initially questioned the appeal and motives of the Temple, praised the convention and especially celebrated the organization's commitment to female modesty, business pursuits, and emphasis on citizenship. "This organization is playing a useful and definite role in advancing the sacred obligations of American citizenship. Indications are the convention will be one of the most interesting ever held in the city."

The Temple's ability to operate its own businesses was lauded as an example of black "collective effort" and a "sound economic program."[69] The Sisters' National Auxiliary organized girls to sew pajamas that were later sold through advertisements in the *Moorish Voice*. The proceeds were used to establish the Moorish National Home for the Aged.[70] The Temple's Unity Hall and The Moorish Lunchroom provided jobs for girls as well as a "respectable" space for working girls to spend time. The hall could be rented out to outsiders as a "hospitable and convenient public gathering place" for "whist parties, balls, and receptions."[71] Staffed by girls and the Sisters of the Temple, the lunchroom prided itself on its cleanliness and excellent customer service. The lunchroom was opened all day, and ladies were allowed to eat there, providing an alternative to Black Belt establishments associated with vice and segregated dining facilities outside black neighborhoods. One Temple historian has noted that Moorish enterprises allowed for "economic independence and the sense of self-worth necessary to overcome racist employment patterns."[72] The economic program relied on Moorish girls and teenage women to work at its businesses and in turn provided a safe work environment for black girls who struggled to find employment in places deemed respectable. Moorish girls could also imagine themselves as an integral force in the Temple's goals by joining the Young Women's Business Club and preparing themselves for more responsibilities in MSTA enterprises. The Temple intervened on girls' behalf by training them within the confines of the organization's enterprises, protecting them from racial discrimination and potential sexual exploitation.

Moorish businesses staffed by girls and teenage women allowed the organization's membership to engage with consumer culture without confronting segregated stores. As Chicago's African American population grew, so did frustrations with inadequate services and concerns over whether African Americans should spend money in places that denied them jobs and decent service. The Moorish grocery store and lunchroom provided blacks with a dignified commercial experience free from poor reception and overcharging.[73] Ali included girls in his larger economic vision, and he encouraged girls and young women to seize on the entrepreneurial spirit of the organization and locate themselves within its mission.

He wrote: "We shall believe in nothing until we have economic power. A beggar people cannot develop the highest in them, nor can they attain to a genius enjoyment of the specialties of life."[74] Ali ensured a steady supply of reliable workers and control over the Temple's girls and young women by allowing the girls to work within the framework of this "economic power" mission.

The mail-order healing products business was popular inside and outside the Temple; one scholar has estimated that Ali's manufacturing company yielded up to $36,000 a year for the Temple.[75] Considering that the Madame C. J. Walker Manufacturing Company estimated their 1931 earnings at approximately $100,000 a couple of years later, the MSTA's industries were quite profitable, without the same sales structure of sales agents as the Walker Company.[76] Instead of participating in a delicate dance to circumvent restrictions on and celebrations of black female beauty in relation to the larger beauty culture market, the MSTA capitalized on it and made it into a profitable arm of its organization, allowing teenage women and girls to indulge in beauty culture on the Temple's terms. The Moorish Manufacturing Company peddled products that promoted holistic healing and black women's beauty. In their advertisements, a single Moorish product claimed to serve nearly a dozen purposes and hinted that it could also aid in sexual vitality. The Moorish Body Builder and Blood Purifier could be used to appear more attractive and claimed to be "beneficial for Rheumatism, lung trouble, rundown constitutions, indigestion and loss of manhood" as well. All of these outcomes could be had for a mere 50 cents. Women and girls used the Moorish antiseptic bath compound as a face wash to combat "skin troubles," and this product also, it was promised, would relieve rheumatism, stiff joints, and sore feet. The Moorish Mineral and Healing Oil also cured many ailments. Yet the testimonial for the product featured a woman who proclaimed that the oil made her "feel like a young girl."[77]

Unlike Adah Waters's desire to see African American girls grow into women in chosen professions, the Temple did not encourage girls to seek wage-earning and regular employment as steps toward a vocation. Rather, girls were to use their training and skills exclusively within the Temple's structures. When girls and women had to work outside the Temple, it was out of economic necessity. Yet Moorish female employment allowed for the Temple to send its best representatives out into the city. Chicago's Moorish girls and women were known to make good domestics. Religious historians have discovered documents that indicate that Moorish maids "quickly gained a reputation for being prompt, efficient, and honest. Because they did not drink, smoke or gamble, their integrity was above reproach."[78]

In the world of the Moorish Temple, the ways a girl appeared in public were as valuable as the quality of her work. Moorish styles of dress ensured that members were easily distinguished by the general public. Moorish teachings stressed modesty and purity, and Moorish girls' clothing reflected the style of dress adopted by Moorish women. Ali mandated that girls not wear short skirts or makeup. Moorish female modesty was framed in contrast to the emerging flapper aesthetic that was causing so much contention among the girls and the families discussed earlier.[79] Alarm about the dangers of the flapper style indicted "carmine cheeks" and "powdered noses," which led "the innocent bystander" to believe that "the female sex have given way to a tendency to overdress their faces."[80] A *Defender* editorialist was less concerned about the flapper craze among African American teenage girls, because "the colored girl is the most modestly dressed member of the female sex." But this writer still cited another critic who decried "a very decided break in the moral level."[81] The flapper panic that characterized the articles on African American girls, Court of Domestic Relations cases, and young women's transgressions centered on the presentation of the face and hair as well as the body. The flapper's rising hemline and stocking-clad leg was complemented by a made-up face and bobbed hair that also represented an embrace of a sexual liberalism that simultaneously terrified and titillated African American observers.

While newspapers reported on flappers showing off their defiant styles at social and community events, Moorish girls appeared in public spaces draped in fabrics from head to toe. The long robes these girls donned while representing their faith was not only a claim to sexual purity but also a reification of the central tenant of Moorish Science identity: the reclamation of a lost heritage and a claim to a self not recognized by whites or black Christians. Moorish girls performed "otherworldliness" and a sexual modesty that was meant to represent the possibility of sacred and chaste black girlhood, but also to contest the racial category of black altogether. Was escaping blackness the only way black girlhood could express itself as sexually chaste? Although the disavowal of the label "Negro" did not render Moorish Science girls without race or racial stigma, the flight from racial and sexual caricatures may have been alluring to women subjected to violence, segregation, and constant sexualization, and those who joined the Temple embraced an opportunity to give this comfort and protection to their daughters.

SCANDAL IN THE MSTA

By the opening days of 1929 the Temple was celebrating economic successes, as its influence moved from the margins of black Chicago to the center of respectability, garnering support from politicians and business interests. Two years earlier, in 1927, the *Defender* had reported on Ali's return from a trip to the South and alerted readers to the Temple's "drive for more members," even providing the Temple's address for "persons desirous of learning of the great work that is being done."[82] In January 1929 Illinois governor Len Small and newly elected black congressman Oscar De Priest, a Republican whose political career had started at Unity Hall, were among the "prominent men, both in business and public life," to attend Ali's birthday celebration.[83] Like Ali, De Priest represented the growing population of African American Chicagoans who constituted an electoral bloc and enthusiastically elected their own "race" representatives.[84]

Within a few months of Ali's birthday celebration, the Temple's problems outpaced its success. As the Temple became divided over Ali's leadership, the beleaguered prophet was accused of murdering a New Orleans Temple leader. He was arrested, and then he disappeared momentarily from police custody. In March 1929, during his disappearance, his former driver and lead rival for control of the Temple, Claude Green, was shot and stabbed several times at Unity Hall. The Chicago police claimed that Ali was the murderer and brought him back to jail, where he was subject to police brutality. While out of jail on bond, Ali died.[85]

In the days following Ali's death, *Defender* readers learned sensational details of a violent struggle between the two men. Their fights over power and money within Ali's Temple, founded only four years earlier, was perhaps not as shocking as the claim that this flamboyant leader had lived with two child brides aged fourteen and sixteen.[86] The news of his marriage to a then-pregnant Mary Lou when she was only twelve years old, coupled with suspicions that Ali had murdered Greene, temporarily destabilized the Temple. Factions fought over Ali's seat of power after his arrest and subsequent death. Religious historians often cite the Moorish Science Temple movement as a critical precursor to the growth of the Nation of Islam in Chicago.[87] Yet few have explored the dynamics surrounding the sexual allegations against Ali and the importance of this movement's perspective on black girlhood.

According to reports from black newspapers, fourteen-year-old Mary Lou and sixteen-year-old Christina were members of the Temple.[88] Mary Lou had become Ali's second wife when she was twelve years old, and when she revealed to authorities that the marriage had no "existence of any legal papers," the authorities determined that Ali had "put one over on this expectant mother" and charged him with statutory rape.[89] Christina had worked as Ali's secretary and shared living quarters with Mary Lou. The girls were held in police custody while authorities conducted an investigation. The *Pittsburgh Courier* suggested that Ali had "ruined a 12-year-old girl."[90] One historian claims that Ali in fact married both girls in "Moorish American ceremonies, but there were no legal records of the marriages," and the state would not have recognized these marriages in addition to his marriage to Pearl Ali.[91] When the *Defender* reported on Ali's polygamy, the newspaper revealed that he had explained his marriage to Christina by claiming that he was "permitted to have more than one wife" and that these marriages could be performed without the authority of a court.[92] Some members of the Temple speculated that the girls' fathers had killed Ali to avenge their daughters' rape. In addition to the murder charges, Ali died before he could appear before the court on charges of contravention under the Mann Act and statutory rape.[93] The *Defender* was one of Ali's harshest critics in the scandal but did not blame him alone for his sexual crimes. The newspaper accused Moorish mothers of giving their underage daughters to him. He had explained that this practice was part of his divine right to girls' bodies, claiming that "it was holy to have their daughters receive the affections of Mohammed's representative here on earth."[94]

This was not the first, or the last, of this type of scandal, which ignited black Chicago's suspicion of urban prophets, condemnation of migrants' perceived susceptibility to trickery, and concerns about the sexual exploitation of black girls. Sociologist Allan Spear documented the "early death" of similar non-Christian religious movements when investigators deemed their leaders false prophets.[95] Black newspapers from the *Pittsburgh Courier* to the *New York Amsterdam News* joined the *Defender* in reporting on the sexual crimes and indiscretions of self-appointed holy men. They chronicled a raid of a New York "cult" that had required the police to "rescue girls in a harem" and published accusations that another prophet had kept a room for "favored virgins" in a farmhouse where he had also sold "comely maidens."[96] The black elites that usually wrote for, edited, and published successful black newspapers looked at the various sects and new religions with contempt, perceiving these groups as exercising a poor influence on migrants and endangering their daughters.

FROM MOORISH SCIENCE GIRLS TO MUSLIM GIRLS' TRAINING

The Moorish Temple's sex scandal led to a loss of the credibility and esteem Chicago's black press and leaders had granted it. The stories of the child brides, coupled with the murder cases, eroded the movement's previously successful recruitment of new followers, but it continued and exists today. Followers of Ali's successor, the Honorable John Givens-El, were loyal to the Moorish Science Temple as Ali created it.[97] The most significant legacy of Ali's death and the erosion of the first Moorish Science Temple in Chicago lay in the establishment and growth of the Nation of Islam. Its founder, Wallace Fard Muhammad, who renounced his early ties to the Moorish Science Temple, emerged under mysterious circumstances similar to Ali's, and his nationality and race were often questioned. Some defectors from the Moorish Science community became members of the Nation of Islam in the 1930s. Just as the fall of the UNIA had created space for the Moorish Science Temple in Chicago, disruption in the MSTA allowed the Nation of Islam to rise. Between 1935 and 1946 the Nation of Islam developed itself as separate from the Moorish Science Temple. Their efforts eventually led to the creation of strong mosque communities across the country and the flourishing of Nation of Islam businesses.[98]

Like the Moorish Science Temple, the Nation of Islam created a sex-segregated social and economic mission for girls. They also reached out to the general population of Chicago's South Side to encourage them to renounce their slave names, embrace authentic racial identities, and obey a strict doctrine of dress, conduct, and diet. As in the Moorish Science Temple of an earlier period, women and girls in the Nation of Islam prepared themselves to be useful to their families and communities and to represent black femininity and beauty borne out of modesty and purity. The Muslim Girls Training program, a prominent feature of the Nation of Islam's Lost-Found mosques from Harlem to Chicago to Detroit and Los Angeles, provided black girls with what the Moorish Science Temple did not fully realize under Ali's leadership—a fully formed educational and social program that reified the purity and girlhood denied to them in the larger world. The Muslim Girls Training and the General Civilization Class defined the terms of black girlhood clearly and forcefully. Muslim Girls Training students were required to dress modestly and cover their hair. The Nation of Islam conceived of the Muslim Girls Training as a substitute for going to public schools, and academic instruction sometimes lasted only three hours a day, allowing girls to work in Nation of Islam businesses.

The Nation also used the girls in the Muslim Girls Training program to make products, such as lace, clothing, and foodstuffs, to be sold at mosques and stores.[99] Boys and girls were taught the same academic courses, but girls were required to take special courses in "basic domestic skills—housekeeping, child-rearing and hygiene."[100] The girls' programs were segregated by age at each stage, and the girls were able to access higher levels of training, as well as more instruction toward marriage. The junior girls' program, developed for teenage girls and known as the General Civilization Class, instructed girls on the philosophical aspects of their faith and the rules they were to follow. Girls were told: "Do not use lipstick or make up, do not wear hair up unless wearing a long dress, do not smoke or drink alcohol, do not commit adultery, do not use pork in any form . . . do not wear heels over 1.5 inches." Girls were also instructed to "not dance with anyone except one's husband."[101] By the 1940s the Civilization Class was expanded to offer "gymnastics, cooking, sewing, and household management as well as child rearing."[102]

The Moorish Temple's sex scandals may have alerted Nation of Islam leaders in the 1930s to the way their treatment of black girls and the public presentation of their black girl membership could shape their success in Chicago, especially with the power brokers of the Black Metropolis. The Nation of Islam supported the racial uplift values of right appearance and right behavior for black girls and young women. They did this not to impress on whites their potential for equality and acceptance but to uplift their own race, support the demands of masculinity, and bolster the race pride implicit in the Nation's message. With the slowing of the Moor-ish Science Temple movement, the Black Muslim community interpreted its role as "training" black girls for Muslim womanhood in even more carefully guarded terms. One scholar described Nation of Islam girls and women as "jealously guarded" and prohibited from "shaking hands with men or intermingling with the opposite sex as the Christians do." Despite these gestures of social elevation toward girls and women, he also found them "clearly secondary" to the male leadership.[103]

As the Nation of Islam grew into a strong political and economic voice in Chicago, observers in the midst of grappling with the city's growing rates of Black Belt poverty, unplanned teenage pregnancy, and youth vio-lence would point with admiration to the way the Nation of Islam trained girls and young women and look to their formulation of girlhood for an-swers for all black girls. Yet, as was the case with the MSTA, placing black girls on a pedestal, using rhetoric about their beauty and modesty, and uti-lizing ideas about girls to reify black nationalism could never adequately protect girls from racism, violence, and sexual exploitation.

CONCLUSION

Black migration to Chicago transformed the city's religious and com-mercial spaces. Mainline black, Christian churches clamored to reach out to southerners to ameliorate the poverty, joblessness, and alienation they encountered in their new homes. When churchwomen undertook Chris-tian outreach, they often carried judgmental and demeaning perceptions of the people they claimed to see as brothers and sisters in faith. They also perceived work with girls as an opportunity to redirect their poor habits and channel their youthful energies toward socially acceptable be-haviors. Christian churches may have embraced this change more if the newcomers were of the same social class; yet migrants often embodied the very characteristics that African American northerners hoped to keep at a distance. Racial uplift projects that originated from black churches not only were concerned with migrant living and social conditions but also wanted to reduce any negative associations with "backward" southerners. Although women's leadership helped to reform the culture of churches to fulfill a greater servant role for migrants, the simple fact that migrant women and girls participated in organized church outreach did not mean they were entirely sold on the values and messages espoused.[104] Migrant women did not achieve social status at the same level as their instructors in their betterment classes, but church membership and activity was one way these women could move one step closer toward respectability.

Girls were involved in a wide range of activities at churches, but Chicago presented many alluring and sometimes competing pursuits that reduced the social significance of churches. With earnings from better paying jobs and more freedom to explore the city, black girls began to relate differently to the authority of their parents. They expressed this break from parental obligations by not attending church or not fully investing in one church. Black girls followed in their parents' footsteps when they did not take church attendance as seriously as they had in the South, or when they explored different church groups and decided which one most suited their tastes and interests.

While deciding how they would relate to religion and faith in the North, girls also created new identities through the embrace of the city's popular culture outlets. From shopping in clothing stores to reading periodicals to dancing in ballrooms, black teenage girls created urban personas and adapted to new styles as a way to indulge in pleasure, confront parental pressures and expectations, and enjoy city life. Chicago's cosmetics and beauty industries could provide vital portals to self-articulation through a compact case filled with blushing power or a seat in a hot comb emporium. The prevalence of spaces of leisure electrified black youth culture and emboldened girls to seek independence from their families.

The values of two markets—one religious, the other commercial—coincided in New Negro religions. When Chicago's Christian churches failed to capture the hearts and minds of black Chicagoans, they investigated the possibilities in religious and political groups that seemingly offered a different message to migrants. The Moorish Science Temple's founding and early history is an illustrative example of the relationship between the emergence of these Migration-era markets and the "use" of black girlhood to support an array of ideas about black life in a period of change. Historian Evelyn Brooks Higginbotham's scholarship on black women in the Baptist church concluded that racial uplift "stood at odds with the daily practices . . . aesthetic tastes" and "expressive culture" of black southerners.[105] Yet one of the outstanding features of the Moorish Science Temple was that its resonance with black migrants rested in its rejection of these very elements of folk culture and in its ideas about black girls' and women's modesty as a cornerstone of their identity. The work of the MSTA reminds us that racial uplift projects targeted toward girls occurred in varying political, social, and religious sites. Although scholars tend to situate racial uplift within the purview of Chicago's middle-class, old-settler, and Black Metropolis elites, these elites were not the exclusive owners of the complex emotions and ideals that inspired the morals-and-manners strain of black politics and social activism.[106]

Women in the MSTA, like their sisters from the UNIA, articulated a space for themselves through what Ula Taylor has described as community feminism, "a territory that allowed [women] to join feminism and nationalism in a single, coherent, consistent framework."[107] For women and girls in particular, the MSTA provided opportunities for leadership and institution building outside the framework of elite women's church organizing, allowing illiterate and working-class women a chance to exercise power and gain new skills. Within the Temple, women were given an opportunity to manage and direct major projects and to occupy positions unavailable to them in the outside world. A Moorish woman who may have been a maid in her secular life could be a supervisor or newspaper editor in the Moorish community.

The Moorish Science Temple defined and understood black girlhood in relationship to its religious ideologies on race and gender, as well as the economic and commercial developments of Chicago's Migration period. The Temple's rapid expansion and recruitment of members from the South was the result of a compelling and attractive alternative to Chicago's all-too-often bleak working conditions and segregated markets and restaurants and the tensions among mainstream African American churches. Gradually, through its participation in business and Chicago's civic life, the Moorish Science Temple became a recognized organization among black Chicago's leadership elite through its economic success, and it capitalized on its ability to use girls and teenage women to represent its values and progress in the midst of growing concerns about the impact urbanization had on girls and teenage women. The MSTA established its legitimacy among Chicago's black press, politicians, and businesses in part by impressing them with the sartorial demands and obedience it required of its girls and young women, who were poised to appear in public spaces as models of virtue.

The MSTA embodied contradictions in realizing its goals of re
ity through radicalism. The MSTA embraced racial uplift whi'
mainstream religious groups and empowered girls and young w⌣
understand themselves outside the purview of white supremacy. At the
same time, it created a fetish of Moorish girls' modesty and purity and
capitalized on the marketplace desires of girls and women. The Moorish
world created a marketplace of ideologies and experiences that did not
jeopardize their exalted status. Despite the call for Moorish girls to conform to standards far more restrictive than girls in Christian establishments, the surrounding culture around Moorish girls sexualized them as
much as it aimed to repress their sexuality.

The child bride scandal involving the MSTA, the Temple's successes between 1925 and 1929, and its viability after Ali's public censure and death
invites scholars to examine the many dimensions of the belief system in
the context of Great Migration Chicago and gender and sexuality. In most
narratives about the Temple's struggles after Ali's arrest, scholars have focused on the infighting and the murder case, ignoring the scandal altogether. Some MSTA adherents deny the story, suggesting that the black
press fabricated the tale to discredit Ali. Regardless of the veracity of the
claim, it is important to examine why such an allegation contributed to
the unraveling of an organization that was gaining the respect of Chicago's
Black Belt politicians and elites. Although not a part of the middle-class
reform culture that explicitly reached out to girls in the early Migration
years, the Moorish Science Temple, as with Chicago's other religious institutions, also engaged in vital conversations on black girls and sexuality in
the city. For women who fled the South to protect their daughters from
the southern climate of sexual exploitation, violence, and degradation,
these hyperbolic expressions of love for black women may have been appealing and appeared safer for their girls. For girls, the MSTA experience
allowed them to see poor African American women engaging in highly
regarded forms of leadership and labor while still living within the param-
eters of an exalted Moorish life. Religious institutions were not immune
to the complications that accompanied mass migration. As the Black Belt
expanded and more black girls entered schools, community centers, and
new jobs, the question of black girlhood and racial progress would continue to challenge Migration communities across the city.

"THE POSSIBILITIES OF THE NEGRO GIRL"

Black Girls and the Great Depression

When families planned on migrating, they might never have anticipated the ability to select places of leisure or worship so easily, but even the most casual reader of the *Defender* knew that there were far more educational opportunities for their girls in Chicago than in the South. Black migrant girls encountered unprecedented options to attend elementary and high schools as well as to pursue special training programs that prepared them for clerical work, nursing, and hairdressing. In addition, the state's great colleges and universities—the University of Chicago, the University of Illinois at Urbana-Champaign, and the Illinois Normal College—educated a generation of black women who were committed to seeing the brightest migrant girls attain the highest educational levels. Even so, the opportunity to pursue a quality education in Chicago was not without barriers. This chapter examines the way schools reacted to migrant girls and treated them within the confines of Black Belt schools and of schools with few black children. I also discuss the way economic instability in families affected girls' ability to pursue the education they desired, with particular attention to the economic calamities that fell upon black Chicagoans during the Great Depression.

Scholarship on the impact of the Great Depression on African American communities has focused on the ways blacks were economically marginalized long before the fateful market crash, the struggles for male employment during the Depression, and the exclusion of blacks from the New Deal economic recovery. Yet by examining the educational and occupational realities of black girls' lives during this period, as well as the way black leaders responded to the impact of the Depression on girls, we become able to see another dimension to how black girlhood operated in the rhetoric about race progress, economic mobility, and the value of the Migration to individuals and communities. This chapter makes clear how black girls in Chicago experienced the Great Depression and the ways various movements used images and ideas of black girlhood to mobilize communities, to critique the binds of race and gender in black professional life, and to demonstrate the possibility for racial integration.

After providing girls' perspectives and feelings about attending school in Chicago, I look at three distinct responses to the educational hopes and professional limitations faced by black girls in the North. First, I interrogate the history, methods, and approach of the Alpha Kappa Alpha (AKA) sorority's vocational guidance program, established as the group's national project in 1926. Although the Depression hampered some of the sorority's goals, AKA women remained committed to bringing black girls to higher education and white-collar careers. Then I focus on the figure of black girls in the city's "Don't Buy Where You Can't Work" campaign, an initiative devoted to pressuring white-owned businesses to hire teenaged girls and young black women to work as clerks and shopgirls. The final section of the chapter focuses on black girls' participation in the New Deal–sponsored National Youth Administration Resident School for Girls, an interracial training school designed to train teenage girls for community and recreational leadership positions. Although the origins of these programs differed, they all believed that black girls' successes transcended individual attainment and could serve a wide array of social and political agendas.

BLACK GIRLS AT SCHOOL

Many migrant parents were motivated to move to Chicago after hearing of the greater educational opportunities for African American girls. Chicago's public schools were open to African American children as early as 1849, when a state law mandated that children five years of age and older attend school.[1] By the middle of the Civil War, Illinois was long established as a portal to freedom for runaway slaves, but few black children used the public school system in critical numbers. In 1863 Chicago established five night schools, with one designated for "Negroes [to receive] the rudiments of a thorough English education." Over the next thirty years, night schools began to be integrated, and the Illinois General Assembly made public school a right for all children, warning that school boards would be fined if they did not comply with the law.[2]

The disparity in educational opportunities between the North and the South was quite stark. In 1910 approximately 315,000 black teenagers and young adults up to age twenty-one attended some type of school in northern cities. Only twenty-five thousand black children in the South attended one of the sixty-four high schools that served the entire region's black population. In Chicago, 90 percent of black southern-born students were considered "overage elementary pupils," a source of embarrassment for many migrant youth when they tried to enroll in school.[3] By 1912 Chicago's Third and Fourteenth Wards had more than one thousand students in public schools, and the Second Ward had nearly three thousand African American pupils.[4] By 1920 Chicago's public schools had absorbed thirteen thousand migrant children into its system over the course of ten years, and more than 90 percent of African American children between the ages of seven and thirteen attended school regularly.[5]

The opening of more schools to African American children also helped working parents adapt to northern jobs. Parents in the South often brought children to work alongside them or keep them company in the workplace, particularly in fields and on farms. Children in the cities could be cared for by schools while parents worked in private homes or in factories that only employed adults.[6] All children were required to attend school in Chicago until age sixteen under the state's mandatory school attendance policy. The Juvenile Court hired African American clubwomen, social workers, and truancy officers to ensure that black children attended school.[7]

The schools available to migrant children were not Chicago's very best, and the poor conditions of Black Belt schools could easily endanger girls' safety. One Migration scholar discovered that "relative to schools in other parts of the city, schools in Chicago's black neighborhoods tended to be old, poorly equipped, and by 1918, overcrowded."[8] Some schools were especially unsafe for girls. When University of Chicago AKA member Maudelle Bousfield became the principal of the Keith School in 1927, she was concerned about the building's lack of security and sparse facilities. She recalled in an interview: "It was run-down like I don't know what . . . Somebody was needed . . . to prevent tramps from coming into the school and getting girls when they went to the toilet."[9] The city's school board rarely provided funds to renovate or upgrade black elementary and high schools, and they fell into deep disrepair as the Migration progressed. Yet most migrants still took advantage of Chicago's schools, no matter how dilapidated they were, because they were usually better than the dusty, one-room schoolhouses of their southern towns.

The girls featured throughout this chapter were mostly teenagers, and some were able to enroll in junior high and high schools, including the famed Wendell Phillips High School, as well as Englewood, Hyde Park, and Lucy Flower on the city's South and West Sides. By 1918, Phillips was 56 percent black, Flower 20 percent, and Englewood and Hyde Park each 6 percent. These girls were particularly remarkable, in light of James Grossman's finding that migrant parents often realized that "few had children with sufficient education to attend a Chicago high school immediately upon arrival."[10] Some students and parents may have become discouraged by the obstacles to entering school and elected to bypass school attendance. Southern-born children were sometimes isolated from both their white and northern-born black peers because of their manner of speaking, dress, and academic deficiencies. Sociologist Allan Spear reported that southern children's "inferior educational and cultural background retarded their scholastic achievement and frequently created disciplinary problems."[11]

Disciplinary issues were frequently cited in reports of the poor performance of southern migrant girls, who experienced a varied set of confrontations in public high schools. These girls dealt with outright contempt from white teachers and classmates and derision from middle-class black classmates. Yet they also appreciated the optimism of patient instructors who argued that with a little time, migrant girls could indeed succeed academically. A 1922 survey of Chicago schools included teachers' reflections on "the progress of the Southern Negro." At one school, a thirteen-year-old girl tried to mask her literacy problems. A teacher quickly noticed and made sure to help her. The teacher remembered that the girl had "pretended to read with her book upside down, but in a little more than a year, she was doing sixth-grade work."[12] Another thirteen-year-old girl from Alabama attended school for the first time after she moved to Chicago; the local school in her southern town did not have enough seats to accommodate her. The teacher disclosed that she was "confident that she could put her through several grades" in a year and added that girls "who have been deprived in the South of their rights educationally are very eager. At first they are timid, but they learn very quickly."[13]

Ione Margaret Mack's qualitative interviews with thirty-one Chicago educators corroborated claims of girls' academic and disciplinary struggles in schools. Mack did not identify any of the Chicago institutions, but her descriptors throughout the text hint that the survey participants included administrators at the Illinois Technical School for Girls; Annabell Prescott, an AKA alumna and dean of girls at Wendell Phillips; and various deans of girls at Chicago public schools with black populations ranging from less than 1 percent to all black. Mack also spoke with teachers of topics ranging from domestic arts to civics to Latin, settlement house workers, and YWCA Girls Reserves secretaries. Mack noted a list of disciplinary charges common among black girls. These "misdemeanors" ranged from the benign and expected, such as "talking" and "impudence" to transgressions that raised alarms because they confirmed racialized stereotypes of black girls' unrestrained sexuality, such as "undue freedom with boys" and "charlestoning." As was the case with their white counterparts, girls' interactions with boys were heavily monitored, and parents could receive a note from school if their girls were engaged in "dirty talk," "dirty notes," or "buying valentines in [the] store across from school."[14]

Administrators who were uncertain about the fitness of southern black girls for northern schools were apt to assign a racialized lens to black girls who had problems at their schools. Discipline problems among the fourteen high schools studied illustrated how black girls' poverty contributed to their problems at a school. Girls were cited for "stealing apples from cooking room," "inadequate clothing," and "unclean personal appearance." Black girls' clothing choices and engagement with popular culture were also subject to scrutiny and school punishment. Deans expressed frustration over black girls' "powdering nose, painting lips, and combing hair in class," or "refusing to remove hair ornament," "wearing sweater even in heated room," "wearing ear rings," and "taking coat off reluctantly when requested."

Another root cause of black girls' problems was that some of the administrative staff and teachers in the Chicago public schools were not entirely convinced that black girls belonged in their schools. The dean of girls at a school located in a community where few blacks lived reported that black girls, particularly migrant girls, were "unable to do the fine adjustment work in sewing," but on account of their "fondness for eating" could be "efficient in cooking." A teacher in a vocational school echoed the dean's claims about the kinds of domestic arts black girls could perform. She claimed that black girls often dropped out of school after one year to work in lampshade factories, and she noted that black girls lacked the "fine muscular adjustments necessary for Domestic Art work." She continued: "They are not able to manage with skill even a scrubbing brush."[15] Although not representative of all teachers, these perspectives on black girls' ability made the challenge to seek meaningful education, commit to it, and search for a skill or vocation much more difficult.

Southern children were markedly different from their northern peers, and sometimes school was the site of their embarrassment and shaming about the ways they carried themselves and dressed. In the spring of 1934, a girl with the initials G.W. sent Eleanor Roosevelt a letter about her life in Chicago. G.W. was among the scores of girls who sent requests to the First Lady for school clothes and shoes so they could attend school or apply for jobs at respectable places. This seventeen-year-old Phillips High School student confided in Roosevelt, whom many black girls saw as a white ally: "I am behind but I would like to finish if it is possible." Her sixty-six-year-old grandmother took care of her, her brother, and two other grandchildren. "I wont [sic] to ask you to send me a winter coat . . . a pair of stockings . . . a dress . . . a pair of shoes." The girl wanted the clothes so she could fit in with her classmates. "I come in contack [sic] with so many school girls and boys of my own age. They all look so nice and I want to look nice too of course."[16]

Opal Mantel would have been able to relate to G.W.'s feelings. A sophomore at Bowen High School, she noticed differences between her peers and the more "sophisticated" teens living downtown whose parents were either Chicago natives or early migrants who had ascended Chicago's social ladder. "These kids out here think they can't ever be anything or do anything, you see that what their folks tell them. Now, my mother is different, she says that just because we are colored is no sign that we can do things that are worthwhile." Her family's support allowed Opal to have aspirations of higher education and a career.

I hope to go to University some day, I don't know how . . . you see my mother will help me . . . most of these kids mother's think that you shouldn't go to school a lot . . . because you are colored and colored folks never did amount to much . . . and that there's nothing so bad as an educated fool . . . why they think that education makes you a fool . . . I don't see. My mother says that if the education makes a fool out of you . . . you were a fool to begin with.[17]

Mack argued that social structure, not biology or cultural inferiority, were responsible for black girls' academic shortcomings, and she castigated the racism of school administrators, namely girls' deans and principals, for making racial arguments for why black girls grappled with behavioral problems. "The process of selection," she wrote in the introduction to her thesis, "has worked against the girl of black color with an almost brutal power. . . . Relatively few are high school girls. To the privileged few will be committed the task of leadership. It will be literally a burden of leadership of the many uneducated who will not know the way."[18] Mack acknowledged the pressures put on black girls to excel at school, and her declaration that black girls felt the weight of their position among the Talented Tenth—W. E. B. Du Bois's term for the black elite responsible for their race's uplift—is rare in the body of research on migrant girls and northern schools.[19] Mack cast the problems faced by black girls sympathetically, questioned the stress placed on black girlhood, and in turn challenged black and white adults to consider black girls as children who psychically could not fully carry the load of race leadership. Her research suggested the limitations of using black girls in the service of the agenda of race progress. She offered a solution through religious education, which could respond to the troubled state of black girlhood and ease the tensions racial oppression engendered.

With better schools to attend and greater educational levels to attain, black girls in Chicago had to balance their economic obligations to their families with an expanding sense of their educational possibilities. Some migrant mothers enlisted their daughters in "home work," assembling items at home instead of traveling to factories, so they could make time for school. Home work allowed for more personal autonomy than domestic work, but the need to meet employer minimums could prove stressful. When social worker Myra Colson undertook a study of the home work system, she noted that migrant women lost significant professional status when they came north. "It is not uncommon to find women who were

FIG 3.1. Migrant girls were sometimes ashamed of their humble backgrounds in the South. Chicago-born teens sometimes ridiculed them, and teachers doubted their ability to succeed in northern schools. "Typical Plantation Homes in the South of Migrants to Chicago." Photograph by the Chicago Commission for Race Relations, 1922.

PHOTOGRAPHS AND PRINT DIVISION, SCHOMBURG CENTER FOR RESEARCH IN BLACK CULTURE, THE NEW YORK PUBLIC LIBRARY, ASTOR, LENOX AND TILDEN FOUNDATIONS.

teachers in the south reduced to factory work in a northern city. In many localities in the South, an unbelievable minimum of training is required for a Negro teacher, so that it is not surprising to find her less effective in securing work in a big city than some of the other migrants." At the same time, wages on the whole were far better in home work. Colson noted: "one school teacher is a forelady in a flower and novelty shop at a salary beyond what she enjoyed as a teacher in the South." Some women saw home work as the price they had to pay for migrating and the many ways they could enjoy their lives outside the South. Colson reported: "Another former teacher, a college graduate, and a member of one of the 'first families' of the South prefers the freedom and glamour of city life and industrial employment to her former limited life in a small city."[20]

For girls, the home work system encapsulated the opportunities and obstacles of Migration. Colson profiled Millie May, a Mississippi migrant, who came to Chicago at age twelve in 1926. She completed junior high school by age fourteen and soon began financially supporting herself. She discovered home work was a viable option and that "she would rather work at home than in the factory" because it maximized her work hours, but it left little time for school. At the height of the assembly season, Millie worked from 8:30 in the morning until 10:00 at night, allowing only two hours per day for meals. When work slowed down, she ventured into the city and earned less money, working at a laundry for $15 a week.

Winnie Lord managed to stay in school while doing home work. She enrolled in the state normal school after finishing Crane Junior College in hopes of becoming a teacher. Her brother also attended school while working, and the family pooled their earnings to pay his costs at the University of Chicago.[21] In another family studied, a mother relied on her fifteen- and eighteen-year-old daughters to help her reach her work quotas. One of her girls took the "business course" at Hyde Park High School and then came home at 5:00 each day and worked until 11:00 at night, earning $2 for her family. She managed to study for school in the mornings. Even when girls did not live with parents, they still upheld financial responsibilities to people "back home." Mary Carter, from Athens, Alabama, arrived in Chicago at age four after both of her parents died. Despite her parents' death, when she became a teenager and found work, she still supported family in the South.[22]

ALPHA KAPPA ALPHA AND THE VOCATIONAL GUIDANCE MOVEMENT

The complicated world that black girls navigated in helping their families in their daily struggles in the city, as well as building a meaningful future, concerned Chicago's black women educators. As Chicago's schools and neighborhoods grew increasingly segregated, black education professionals assumed the leadership of the schools, training programs, and research institutes that were devoted to understanding how to reach the masses of black children and teenagers who enrolled in school. Members of AKA, many of whom were University of Chicago alumnae, surveyed the state of black female students in Chicago and formulated plans to help girls attend high school, enroll in college, and focus on career goals.

From housing to educational support and leadership training to friendship, sororities provided critical support to the small cohort of African American college women on campuses across the country in the early twentieth century. In the fall of 1913, six of the University of Chicago's black women students elected to establish AKA's second, or Beta, chapter. Unlike their sisters at the historically black Howard University, where AKA was founded, the Beta women were not fully integrated into their college's life.[23] Although the University of Chicago admitted black students as early as 1870, conferring nine undergraduate degrees to black students between 1900 and 1910, the majority of black students were graduate-level candidates. Between 1870 and 1945, the University of Chicago awarded forty-five doctorates to black scholars; the majority of these students graduated from what was known as the modern University of Chicago, which emerged from a series of reforms after 1890. Open to both women and men, the University of Chicago led the world in research in education and the social sciences—particularly sociology, anthropology, and economics—and trained an influential cohort of black social scientists and educators.[24] Despite the enrollment of black students, segregation in dormitories and student activities reigned.[25]

Given the lack of housing and the dearth of social options for African American students, black women students gladly welcomed the national AKA officer who traveled to the Hyde Park campus in May 1914.[26] Zelma Watson George, a native of Kansas who enrolled at the university in 1920, credited the sorority with making her years at the university bearable after being excluded from housing and athletics.[27] She was rejected from the university choir because she was deemed "too good" and was often harassed at university facilities. While swimming at the university pool, she heard a fellow student complain "I'm not accustomed to swimming with niggers."[28] A month after the women at the University of Chicago pledged their oath to AKA at the inaugural initiation ceremony, eight women at the University of Illinois established the Gamma chapter of AKA. In 1922, Beta chapter alumnae members formed the Theta Omega chapter for college graduates in Chicago.[29]

After AKA women graduated from college, they often entered social service fields, integrating their academic work into their sorority-sponsored philanthropic and community action. Alumna Adelaide Turner worked for the Phillis Wheatley Home in Muncie, Indiana, later establishing the first African American girls' camp in the area.[30] Her sorority sister Annabell Prescott earned the highest score on the Chicago Board of Education's special exam for the position of dean of girls. In 1927, Prescott, at the age of twenty-five, was the "youngest dean of girls in the Chicago high schools and perhaps the youngest in the country." She worked at Wendell Phillips, where she taught French and Spanish before her promotion. The *Defender* praised her work with Phillips High girls, noting that "those who know her best declare that she puts most of herself into her school work, as she enjoys the big and varied opportunities it gives for work with young girls, influencing them, encouraging them, shaping their lives a bit, sometimes lending a vision where there is none."[31]

Sorority women had a clear vision of their responsibility toward uplifting the black girls and teenage women around them. As the sorority grew on campuses across the country, local AKA chapters and leadership looked to its informal brother fraternity, Alpha Phi Alpha, for ideas on determining and crafting sorority projects. In the early 1920s the fraternity established the "Go to High School, Go to College" program to "encourage Negro youths to continue their education."[32] In 1923 President Warren G. Harding lauded the Alphas' efforts in addressing "the need for effective work to reduce illiteracy among the Colored people . . . through the equipment of members of the Colored Race to do educational work."[33] As the Alphas gained more visibility for their program, national AKA officers began to seek ways to institutionalize a similar program. In 1924, AKA formally adopted the "observances of a vocational guidance week as a part of its national program."[34]

Prior to black Greek-letter societies' interventions in vocational guidance, the field was well established among northern schools serving white students. The first school-based vocational guidance program began at Central High School in Detroit. Between 1898 and 1907, Jesse B. Davis, recognized as the founder of school guidance, provided career counseling to eleventh graders. As a school principal in Grand Rapids, Michigan, he required the school's seventh graders to write an essay on a career interest each week. In 1913 he established the National Vocational Guidance Association, with the goal of "assisting the individual to choose an occupation, prepare for it, enter upon and progress in it."[35] Public schools across the country instituted vocational counseling programs at various grade levels to ensure that young people could make thoughtful decisions about their life's work.

Chicago's AKA women engaged in a wide range of activities to support vocational guidance efforts. They made speeches about it at their meetings, held Vocational Guidance Weeks at schools, and hosted elegant social events to support scholarship funds for girls. In 1923 the sorority awarded Dorothy Clark Jackson a scholarship to fund her studies at the University of Chicago. She was one of the youngest recipients of the award at fifteen years old, yet "she maintained the highest average of the girl graduates of the various Chicago high schools."[36] The AKA's 1925 dance at the Renaissance Casino was expected to "open the season with a bang," and the proceeds of the dance would help "the worthy young women of our Race who are clamoring for an education and deserving of the help."[37] At the conclusion of the 1926 Vocational Guidance Week, the Chicago chapters produced a play to raise funds and celebrate the event. The annual week was described in the press as working to "assist the coming generation of college youth to even greater achievement" and "eliminating the wasted energy that goes with blundering into wrong careers . . . [and] occupations."[38]

In May 1928 the Beta chapter began to take their message out of their guidance planning meetings and into the larger city to raise awareness about how the movement could work for the business community. They ended the year's Vocational Guidance Week with tours of various Chicago businesses, including the *Defender*'s main printing plant, where editor Robert Abbott personally greeted the girls.[39] In June 1929 the Gamma chapter announced that Emma Henrine Herndon had won their annual essay contest with her paper, "My Plans for the Future." She was a graduate of Champaign High School and served as an occasional contributor to the *Defender*.[40] The next year, the Beta chapter awarded the prize to Ruth Marian Jackson, who was active in a wide array of extracurricular activities. She was a member of the Women's Athletic Association, played on the senior basketball team, and was a YWCA Girl Reserves honor member. She also used the scholarship to attend the University of Chicago, where she developed an interest in "social service work, especially the medical feature of it."[41] A few years later, Chicago's renowned beauty school, Poro College, hosted a six-week vocational guidance series, with the sorority hosting a conference and "get-acquainted" tea party there.[42]

Earlier generations of clubwomen, many of whom had not attended white colleges and universities like the University of Chicago, used the language of race motherhood and argued for women's special role in communities; AKA women instead incorporated "scientific" (meaning qualitative) and largely academic arguments for work with girls. As college-educated women, many of them trained in education, sociology, and child development, AKA members viewed African American girls as struggling with distinct problems that only they could solve, as well-read and experienced practitioners of social outreach rather than as simply mother-citizens. One sorority member declared: "The problems peculiar to girls are no longer those of right or wrong, but they are such problems as call for scientific solution."[43] Instead of relying solely on traditional racial uplift rhetoric about the relationship between work and moral elevation, the first "scientists" of this early program hoped that by providing uniform standards on advising girls and teenage women on careers, they could devise a formula to evaluate fitness and appropriateness for careers. The sorority also enlisted other bodies to help them assess the effectiveness of the effort; AKA commissioned a "detailed study of Vocational Guidance" and committed to giving their reports to the United Negro Youth of America organization, where files were "made for follow-up work so as to tabulate and ascertain results."[44]

The women of AKA connected the science of choosing the right career to the alleviation of social problems in African American communities, girls' personal feelings of fulfillment, and the development of sound mental and emotional health. The sorority's president, Pauline Sims-Puryear, prefaced the national office's instructions on vocational guidance with a warning about the gravity of the consequences when girls entered the wrong line of work. She asserted that vocational missteps led to the "failure of adjustment, failure to realize that the environment can be modified to meet one's needs and capacities, in short, failure to recognize . . . possibilities."[45] In another address to the membership about the importance of guidance, she again framed the issue in terms of the greater good, and she reiterated how careers could serve as a vehicle for ensuring that African American girls developed into normal, productive members of society. "It has been repeatedly stated that the tragedy of our present-day life is the misfit. Some Scullery Maid may have become a Madame Curie . . . had they had scientific advice on the matter of choosing a vocation.[46] Sims-

Puryear concluded that vocational guidance would "make a unique contribution to hundreds of young girls facing the necessity of making decisions regarding their life's work."[47] The language of "misfit" and "scullery maid" and the reference to scientist Marie Curie illustrate the way AKA women collapsed social class distinctions among girls in order to suggest that all girls had the potential to use professions to uplift the race.

One AKA president advocated entry into such esoteric fields as "bacteriology, creative writing and forestry."[48] The women of AKA knew what they were up against when they adopted vocational guidance as the sorority's national program. The organization consisted mostly of educators and social workers, so they were aware of the problems and pitfalls of African American girls' education and career counseling. Yet they also knew how powerful representations of exceptional girl achievers could be for the larger race's sense of pride and to combat white critiques of black, female youth. Instead of contributing to the notion that the struggle of Migration was only about men's achieving dominion over families and communities, AKA implicitly challenged this vision and saw black girlhood as serving a very different, but still valuable, role.

Keith School principal Bousfield, a Beta chapter founder who served as an AKA national president, studied education and advocated for reform in Chicago's public schools.[49] The first black woman graduate of the University of Illinois, Bousfield completed her doctoral training at the University of Chicago, which prepared her to serve as the city's first black school principal at an elementary school and later at Phillips High in the 1940s.[50] While a teacher at Phillips, she encouraged vocational guidance clubs. As early as 1923, the Phillips High yearbook described the club as proof that "girls are beginning to realize their responsibility to themselves in the matter of choosing the right vocation."[51] Club members' activities included trips to local companies, writing letters of introduction to more than 350 businesses, and studying materials from the US Department of the Interior and other guidance literature to learn about potential careers. By 1927 these clubs were reaching beyond the high school community to spread the message of guidance to younger students, encouraging "junior high and elementary school graduates to go into high school."[52] In Phillips High yearbooks from 1924 to 1928, several high school girls listed the Vocational Guidance Club and the Vocational Guidance Boosters among their extracurricular activities. Club members and boosters went on to attend the University of Chicago, the Chicago Normal School, and the University of Illinois.[53]

One of the major goals of vocational guidance was to expose girls to the possibility of working in fields where African American women were underrepresented in order to signal to the world the gains of all African Americans. Baltimore sorority member Vivian J. Cooke argued that vocational guidance emerged as a result of the changes in African American life due to the Migration. African American girls were no longer "rural" and naive: they understood "the opportunity to see the fundamental work of the world in progress." Cooke emphasized that vocational guidance was about "specialization," not just skill acquisition. Cooke, unlike most of her colleagues who wrote about guidance, valued black women's work in the home and workplace equally. "Along with other fundamental changes came a new day for women imposing upon them a double duty that of home life and the likelihood of employment before and after marriage," she once wrote. "She must meet both situations in her choice of occupation." Cooke's discussion of the urbanization of African American women indicated that the modern girl would never fret over how paid labor would compromise the gendered expectations of marriage and family life. Cooke lessened any perceived threat of African American women gaining too much power by assuring that most women's professional growth occurred within the women's sphere of work. "Statistics of vocational life show that women are engaged in practically all of the nine divisions of gainful occupations" and in the "ever growing callings" of "library work, social service and various phases of the teaching profession."[54]

The AKA strategy required that advocates offer incredible optimism in the face of the bleak job prospects for girls and young women across the country. Nationally, African Americans made up less than 5 percent of all high school students between 1920 and 1930, reflecting the lack of high schools for African Americans in the rural South, where the majority of African Americans still lived. Chicago's high school attendance rate was much higher than the national statistic but did not yield greater educational gains for girls.[55] By 1940, 50 percent of white and African American girls in Chicago attended high school. Despite this parity, 60 percent of white girls could expect to gain white-collar positions after their schooling was complete; only 10 percent of African American girls would have that same chance.

In an article, "Possibilities of the Negro Girl," for the sorority's national magazine, *The Ivy Leaf*, Millie E. Hale advised: "Girls have faith in your own ability to win. Color of skin or texture of hair are no handicaps to winning the game. A diamond encased in a brown velvet box has the same brilliancy as one encased in a white velvet box." Hale's example of a diamond in a brown jewelry box was Lydia Mason, a Fisk University graduate. After completing Fisk, Mason was awarded a $1,000 scholarship to Juilliard. Using Mason's accomplishment as a model, Hale summed up the moral of the young woman's story: "Had Lydia Mason become despondent over color, she would not have had courage to enter the contest. She had faith in self, however and won. There are many Lydia Masons, who need encouragement and an awakening of their possibilities, who need the courage and conviction of their ability to win."[56] Hale believed that girls dwelling among society's lowest rungs were merely in need of AKA women to extend their hands downward and give them the right values—not necessarily the right opportunities.

NOTHING BUT HOUSEWORK AND CLEANING

For African American girls and teenagers, imagining a dream career was doubly poignant because of educational barriers coupled with a paucity of occupational choices. For girls who remained committed to school in light of racial prejudice and financial instability, life after school was not easy, considering the race and gender barriers to what St. Clair Drake and Horace Cayton termed "clean occupations." The majority of Chicago's African American girls rarely had avenues to pursue work outside of the realm of domestic service when they were ready to enter the workforce. One African American girl reflected on this problem: "Teacher said not to take a commercial course because there were no jobs opening up for a colored. So there's nothing but housework and cleaning left for you to do."[57]

African American activists and organizations promoted programs that dignified domestic work by professionalizing its practice and redefining the potential of domestic work to contribute to the larger project of racial equality. Chicago activist Fannie Barrier Williams implored African Americans to change their perceptions of domestic work in order to encourage girls to capitalize on wage earning, maximize their access to jobs as household help during the Migration period, and give them a role within racial uplift movements. Williams believed that if domestic workers were good at their jobs, they could then give whites a favorable impression of black people as a group. In the *Voice of the Negro*, Williams hypothesized: "When intelligence takes the place of ignorance, and good manners, efficiency, and self-respect take the place of shiftlessness and irresponsibility in American homes, one of the chief causes of race prejudice will be removed."[58] Fellow contributor Katherine Davis Chapman Tillman, a white supporter of black youth employment, in her *Voice of the Negro* piece "Paying Professions for Colored Girls," advised: "It is wise for them to consider what work is open to them and what their chances of success are in their chosen field."[59] Tillman supported nursing as a means of providing opportunities for individual young women while also creating ways for them to represent the entire race; lifesaving work could demonstrate black girls' intelligence and skill level to whites.[60]

No matter how much emphasis was placed on dignifying domestic work, it was still difficult, dirty, and often degrading. Domestic workers in Chicago knew the strains of the work on their own physical and emotional well-being, and they hoped that their daughters would have better chances for other types of employment. Unfortunately, the web of poverty, racism, and sexism ensnared girls and trapped them in low-wage domestic work. One survey found that "domestic workers often expressed the hope that their children would be able to find other types of work."[61] A maid described her oldest daughter as "quite bitter against what she calls the American social system and our financial insecurity," and she hoped that her daughter, who also worked as a housekeeper, could "escape a life as a [life-long] domestic worker, for I know too well the things that make a girl desperate on these jobs."[62] The woman did not elaborate on "the things," but the literature on black domestic work in the North and South suggest that girls sometimes sought work in the sex trade to escape the degradation involved in cleaning and tending to other people's homes. Private homes were spaces where employers physically and sexually abused black women and girl workers, and some young women believed that prostitution and stage dancing allowed them far more power over their own sexuality in the workplace.[63]

Advocates of domestic training often failed to acknowledge that girls and teenage women articulated their desire for academic training, even those who may have known little else in the South. A collection on migrant attitudes toward education discovered that "a preference of Negro children for academic work was reported by the principals and teachers at two high schools." Fully aware of the intraracial social dynamics that formed migrant and old-settler relationships, the report concluded: "Negro children took academic work because they thought it gave them better social standing." Another school principal shared that black girls wanted to "know nothing about industrial training" and didn't care for "sewing and cooking."[64]

Girls perceived education in the North as more than an avenue to a career: it was a means of freedom from racism and white rule. Two sisters from Arkansas, aged eighteen and fourteen, migrated to Chicago because they believed that they could finally "do something and not have to work for these white people." The younger sister told an interviewer: "[Chicago] was said to be a place where colored people had a chance . . . I want to be a teacher." She added: "You know the world is calling for knowledge. I want to study so I can get out from under the foot of these white people." Another migrant girl, whose parents were farmers, moved to Chicago after completing the fourth grade in the South. On arriving in the city, the girl had to work in a laundry to help support her family. The family was described as "timid and self-conscious," and it was said that they "avoided contacts" and "helpful suggestions"; the daughter identified an academic path as the only way to elevate her parents' "community status." The girl admitted that she was "ashamed of the manners" of her parents, and she eventually enrolled at Phillips High's night school.[65]

Longings aside, researchers of African American employment issues discovered that one of the tragic ironies of the northern color line was that highly educated girls were also represented among the toiling masses of domestic workers. One study concluded: "Colored girls are often bitter in their comments about a society which condemns them to "the white folks kitchen." They also reported that "girls who have had high school training, especially, look upon domestic service as the most undesirable form of employment."[66] The Chicago Commission on Race Relations inquiry into black girls' and young women's work found that "young-women college graduates are frequently forced to work as ushers in theaters and as ladies' maids. This condition helps to account for the ease with which 1,500 Negro girls with more than average schooling were recruited in less than two months for the mail-order houses."[67] No amount of exposure to

FIG 3.2. Mothers sometimes enlisted their daughters' help with home work, a system that allowed them to assemble products such as hats, lampshades, and silk flowers at home instead of working in factories. Girls could attend school and help their mothers at night. "Negro Women and Girls in a Large Hat-Making Concern." Photograph by the Chicago Commission for Race Relations, 1922.

GENERAL RESEARCH AND REFERENCE DIVISION, SCHOMBURG CENTER FOR RESEARCH IN BLACK CULTURE, THE NEW YORK PUBLIC LIBRARY, ASTOR, LENOX AND TILDEN FOUNDATIONS.

professional women or vocational guidance tea parties with AKA members could protect the throngs of overqualified African American high school and college graduates who needed work from the fate of low-level employment. The demands and financial strains of girls' labor are echoed in Richard Wright's *Twelve Million Negro Voices*. One part folk poem and one part ode to southern farmers and Migration families, Wright's lyrical meditation on the Migration spoke of women's exploitation and girls' necessary, but equally exploited, labor. "As a whole, they must go to work at an earlier age than any other section of the nation's population," Wright commented. "For every five white girls between the ages of ten and fifteen who must work, twenty-five of our black girls must work; for every five white mothers who must leave their children unattended at home in order to work, twenty-five of our black mothers must leave their children unattended at home in order to work."[68]

GIRLS AND GREAT DEPRESSION REALITIES

Considering the enormous factors that competed with the efficacy of the vocational guidance movement, the sorority enjoyed modest success in educating girls about careers, funding college scholarships, and hosting social events to raise awareness about girls' opportunities after high school. Yet the momentum for greater vocational guidance programs was stopped abruptly by the Great Depression, a period of economic chaos that swept the United States beginning in the autumn of 1929 and reverberated for more than a decade afterward. The national leaders of the AKA addressed the Great Depression by adding employment services for African Americans to its annual convention. Sorority head Maude E. Brown announced at the 1932 convention in Cincinnati that AKA had "established a clearinghouse for the unemployed." She acknowledged the destructive tolls of the Depression and noted that "no country, no people, no race, no class is safe from the great crisis."[69]

Chicago, like Cincinnati, was a hub of African American job opportunities during World War I, and the Depression single-handedly obliterated many of the positions that had attracted migrants to the area. By 1932, 50 percent of African American Chicagoans were unemployed, with 130,000 of the city's black residents on relief or governmental financial assistance. Chicago's major industries, which had once offered an array of jobs in manufacturing and commerce, lost seven hundred thousand jobs.[70] African American men, women, and youth were often the first to lose jobs or were removed from positions to accommodate white job seekers. Black women workers became the greatest casualty in the reshaping of household budgets and the cutting back on family expenditures such as laundry service, live-in and live-out maids, and child care. Job-seeking African American girls could no longer rely on white families for a steady supply of employment.

Labor historians have examined the racialized and gendered ways that black women experienced the Great Depression and have emphasized that the Depression did not radically change black women's lives, as they often had to "get by with little in the way of material resources."[71] The Depression definitely hampered the employment prospects for black girls and teenage women, due to a decrease in demand for their services, as well as a drastic decrease in wages, but sociologist Oliver Cromwell Cox dated changes in the employment of domestic servants nearly a decade before the Great Crash.[72] In his study "The Negroes' Use of Their Buying Power in Chicago as a Means of Securing Employment," he estimated a loss of sixty-five thousand "Negro domestic personal service workers" between 1910 and 1920, reported that seventy-eight thousand laundress positions were also eliminated, and noted a reduction of "cooks and servants" by ten thousand.[73] Yet the Depression may have effectively shaped the way elite black women, like those in the AKA, understood the role young women could play in black economic prosperity. For black youth, the Depression muted the educational gains of those who migrated from the South, and attempts to equalize opportunities across the color line highlighted the gross disparities in school resources. In 1930, less than a year after the start of the crisis, slightly more than 10 percent of black youth attended high school in the South. Hundreds of counties in fourteen southern states had no black high schools, and the schools that were open were available to students less than half of the calendar year. Funding for schools was grossly unequal across regions throughout the 1930s. For example, Mississippi spent an average of $20.13 per black child on education; New York State spent $134.12 during the 1935–1936 school year.[74]

For Chicago's African American teachers, the Depression altered their ability to work with girls. Marry Herrick, a civics teacher at the Jean Baptiste Point DuSable High School and past president of the Federation of Women High School Teachers, was concerned about programmatic cuts after the Depression, especially "supervisory service and vocational guidance." Teachers endured what she called "payless pay days," and the schools were "8½ months behind" on paychecks. For nearly a decade after the market crash, African American schools still endured the closure of junior high schools and the end of manual training, domestic science, and physical education classes.[75]

DON'T BUY WHERE YOU CAN'T WORK

With employment in private homes dwindling, AKA hoped to increase employment in small businesses and stores that populated Black Belt neighborhoods but rarely employed black girls and teenage women. The sorority partnered with black civil rights organizations and threatened to boycott white-owned businesses in African American neighborhoods unless they hired African American girls and young women. Sorority and fraternity members joined "Don't Buy Where You Can't Work" campaigns across the Midwest and East Coast, from Chicago to Harlem. Chicago AKAs joined the fight that called on Black Belt residents to "spend your money where you can work."[76] In this section I consider the way black girls figured in the rhetoric and imaginings in the black boycotts to add a broader perspective on how African Americans understood girls' potential to mediate racial and economic injustice, as well as to resuscitate black girls' presence in this critical period before the rise of mass movements during the civil rights era. These campaigns targeted South Side stores almost exclusively. This measure proved helpful, if not entirely redemptive, for African American girls seeking jobs.

The radical *Chicago Whip* and its editor, attorney Joseph Bibb, wholeheartedly championed the cause. Bibb and a cadre of black labor leaders and political leftists implored Black Belt businesses, such as the Woolworth's and Walgreens variety stores, to hire black teenage women who reflected the racially homogenous community they served. The boycott used two strategies. First, they asked merchants to reconsider their racially exclusionary hiring practices and tried to negotiate an employment strategy that would secure positions in stores opening in Black Belt locations. Second, if employers refused, leaders organized mass meetings to inform black consumers that resisting these businesses was sound social and economic policy because a boycott proved the power of the black dollar. Then organizers mobilized picketers to obstruct store entryways, pass out leaflets, and if necessary shame buyers away from targeted stores.

Employers rebutted that they refused to hire black clerks because their white employees could not adapt to working with blacks on equal footing. This had been a long-running issue in the city: in 1918, the Chicago Mercantile Company had lost six of its African American workers due to a battle over the use of restrooms in the offices. After a group of white women complained about sharing the facilities with black women, the southern-born manager implemented a Jim Crow mandate, instructing: "All colored girls will use toilet and wash room in the basement. White girls on the fourth floor." The black employees appealed to the company's president, to no avail. With their demands unheard, the women collected their final pay and never returned to the office again.[77] One owner responded to the boycott by blaming his employees. "If we ever tried using Negroes as clerks the white workers would make trouble, I am sure of that. Our customers would object. A good many are from South and would make trouble even if Chicago people did not."[78] The Chicago Telephone Company deployed the same logic of needing to protect worker relations in its refusal to hire young black women as operators.

Within a year of the economy's crash, the movement began to see some small progress in realizing its demands. In October 1930 the first signs of the end of the Woolworth's boycott appeared when "five colored girls were engaged to assist in readying the new [store] for its opening, and in learning the stock." When this new South Side location officially opened on October 4, twenty-one black girls were hired to work alongside white girls as clerks—a first for the chain.[79] Boycott leader Eugene Mann effectively called an end to the Woolworth's action when he "called the people to witness this change of policy, and recommended that they restore their patronage to these stores as soon as colored girls appeared in them." In total, Bibb and his associates secured more than fifteen thousand jobs for black Chicagoans.[80] Among those jobs were small victories for black girls and teenage women, including the hiring of African American girls at a grocery store, a Sears, a Walgreens, and a Woolworth's.[81] Eventually a quarter of Walgreens clerks were young black women.[82] Albion Holsey of the National Negro Business League expressed his gratitude to Bibb. "The entire Negro race owes a debt of gratitude for the courageous fight with its happy conclusion."[83]

Throughout the boycott literature, news articles, and appeals to businesses, leaders constructed an image of an attractive, well-kempt black girl—actually a single, older teenage girl—as the solution to the problem of employment discrimination. Depression-era activism around private employment often focused on men returning to work in order to provide for their families, but this was not the only way black Chicagoans envisioned economic relief. By casting the ideal black worker as a teenage girl, the campaign built on decades of black girls' economic contributions to their families and communities and acknowledged that Chicago was home to many talented and well-educated girls who might never realize their full intellectual abilities and professional dreams.

As for the girls who went to work after the boycott expanded their hiring opportunities, they brought to their cashier stands and stockrooms mixed emotions about what this victory meant for them. Work as clerks in department stores was "cleaner" than working inside homes, but the highly skilled and intelligent black girl clerk could not be convinced that such work was entirely edifying or interesting. A. C. Thayer, head of the Chicago Urban League Industrial Department, admitted that the move to secure black girls jobs as clerks "disillusioned colored girls about the excellence of work as clerks in stores." Before the boycott, the Chicago Urban League had routinely lobbied retailer Sears, Roebuck and Company for positions for girls. The retailer hired six hundred African Americans as temporary shopgirls during the Christmas season of 1918. Later, Sears employed an additional fourteen hundred African Americans in a "special division suitable for females."[84] The clerk positions paid between $10 and $20 per week, with most averaging $14. Clerks soon discovered that the work was "more tedious and monotonous than they expected," and the wages were "low for the high average degree of training" the girls often possessed.

These clerk wages were exponentially greater than what the most desperate girls earned in Chicago's "slave markets" on the city's West Side. During the toughest years of the Depression, girls and women congregated at the corners of Halsted and Twelfth Streets: "a large number of girls [would go] there daily and hire themselves by the day to the highest bidder. The more enterprising would solicit—others would wait to be approached." One domestic testified: "Many days I worked for 50 cents a day and no carfare—one meal was given. I then applied for relief." The woman was not eligible for government assistance because the state bureau determined that she could always find employment at that market.[85] Girls continued to apply for clerk positions because they were keenly aware of Thayer's conclusion: "The consensus of opinion is that a position, such as clerk in a store, is infinitely more acceptable to a colored graduate than work as a domestic servant, dish washer, or porter.[86]

For girls looking to enjoy the social aspects of working outside a household, clerking at a store could provide some privileges. Cayton and Drake observed: "clerical and sales positions . . . [can keep] girls temporarily employed until they find a husband." Stories in the *Defender* and dime store novels may have given young women the impression that entering the labor market was the same as enlisting in the marriage market. "Such positions, even when the pay is low, have been glamorized and are surrounded with an aura of folklore." Cayton and Drake also found that the chosen few who worked in clerical and sales fields formed their own social groups and participated in "the sharing of gossip about boyfriends and a sort of ritualized primping and mutual admiration of clothes and physical attractiveness." The sociologists blamed girls for introducing these sexual dynamics into the workplace, but the powerful way a girl's attractiveness shaped her ability to secure these jobs could not be ignored. Cayton and Drake faulted girls for believing "the myths surrounding secretary and boss and the popular stories of the intimate activities of traveling salesmen" and for perceiving their work with "overtones of sexual as well as economic competition." But black girls seeking work with the public often knew that managers preferred to hire attractive women, as well as those who had light skin and European features. White employers justified color discrimination by arguing that they could not jeopardize "goodwill and profits by experimenting with types of workers with whom they feel the [white] public is not familiar."[87]

THE NATIONAL YOUTH ADMINISTRATION RESIDENT SCHOOL FOR GIRLS

While Chicago activists were using boycotts and brokering agreements with retailers on the local level, the federal government was crafting its national response to the Depression with a series of initiatives to create jobs, provide worker training, and galvanize citizens to imagine a secure future. African Americans were largely excluded from the benefits of the New Deal era, but black political insiders and activists were able to convince President Franklin D. Roosevelt and his brain trust to include black citizens in New Deal programs. Among the new agencies and offices created by the New Deal, the National Youth Administration (NYA) was most relevant to how black girls benefited from the federal government's attempt to revive the nation. Established in 1935 under the auspices of the WPA, the NYA employed high school and college students in various work-study programs, provided part-time jobs for youth whose parents were on relief, and supplied stipends to college students."[88] In 1936, President Roosevelt appointed black educator Mary McLeod Bethune, founder of what would become Bethune-Cookman University in Florida, director of the Division of Negro Affairs for the NYA. In a 1938 NYA pamphlet she explained that her agency would "take thousands of youth, idle in farm and city, becoming dependent upon others, and give them a chance of earning their own way in school or on a job.[89]

The NYA's most important work with black girls in Chicago was the NYA Resident School for Girls, one of dozens of short-term training programs sponsored by the agency. The NYA School represented a middle ground between the AKA's call for black girls to focus their hopes on attending college and becoming pioneers in their fields and the boycott movement's actions to secure practical clerk positions. The most notable features of this school's seven-year history included its decision to enroll both black and white girls in a residential school, its focus on girls' leadership development, and its integrated teaching and administrative staff. From the moment the NYA came to Illinois, it was applauded and criticized across the color line. While the *Defender* praised Bethune for advocating for black youth via the NYA, the *Chicago Tribune* regularly referred to NYA programs as boondoggles.[90] Anti–Roosevelt politicians mounted vicious attacks on the NYA, which was among the most liberal of New Deal programs. For black girls, their NYA experiences epitomized the challenges they faced in education, labor, and the culture at large.

The planners of the NYA Resident School for Girls harnessed federal resources to fund, staff, and organize it and from its inception knew that it could offer a powerful social experiment in race relations. In the fall of 1935, national NYA leader Hilda Smith, a specialist in workers' education, approved a payment of $25,000 to W. S. Reynolds, who had moved from the leadership of the ICHAS to the role of executive secretary of the Illinois Emergency Relief Committee.[91] By the following winter the school's planners had decided to hire teachers in dramatics, handicrafts, physical education, and American folklore. The curriculum consisted of twelve weeks of leadership training, with four classes and a mandatory session on folklore. Organizers deemed folklore "essential because its sociological viewpoint" was "helpful in making happy living arrangements." At the time of the school's opening, few girls in the city, state, or nation experienced interracial learning, let alone living. The coordinators of the NYA believed that they could use the school's training to expand girls' ability to relate to others and, in turn, to be a positive influence on the community programs they would be qualified to lead after graduation.

While school organizers hoped to promote a harmonious school com-

FIG 3.3. The National Youth Administration provided training courses to African American girls during the New Deal. These girls worked at the South Parkway Branch YWCA. "NYA youth assisting in South Parkway Branch, Y.W.C.A. in Chicago; Mame Mason Higgins is Executive Secretary." Photograph by the National Youth Administration, n.d.

PHOTOGRAPHS AND PRINT DIVISION, SCHOMBURG CENTER FOR RESEARCH IN BLACK CULTURE, THE NEW YORK PUBLIC LIBRARY, ASTOR, LENOX AND TILDEN FOUNDATIONS.

munity by teaching girls to form interracial friendships and close other social divides, staff members struggled to get along with each other and resist external pressures from red-baiting critics. In a letter to NYA leader Marguerite Gilmore, an Illinois field worker named Jane complained of NYA director William Campbell's attempts to undermine her and her colleagues' vision for a sound education for girls. "The chief obstacle is the NYA director . . . who is really pretty awful," wrote Jane in November 1935. After Campbell criticized the program for being "a bit heavier, from a trade union standpoint," he called an emergency meeting to tell the teachers they "had no right to teach social sciences." He asked: "Why would these little girls be interested in that, for they get enough sadness at home.

Give them lightness and cheer, food, recreation, a little home economics alone!" One teacher wrote: "We had been advised to keep any "peace indoctrination" out of the curriculum, along with mention of trade unionism, etc." The same opinion held over the next day, when Campbell made a special trip to an NYA supported camp in southern Illinois to see whether "Communism" was rampant there. Gilmore and her co-workers took exception to his recommending "sweetness, light, and nothing remotely suggesting . . . economic disorders" to shape the school's blueprint. "It makes me furious, except for the fact that any normal school when provided with current magazines and papers will discuss such things informally." Jane concluded: "To run a camp with Campbell holding the position of authority would be like trying to deal with a red-baiting vigilante committee."[92] The insinuation that the school should not engage in discourse on current events irritated the women leaders because it deemed the NYA inferior to traditional educational institutions. Campbell's preoccupation with the political implications of the curriculum may have evolved from his awareness about how an interracial program would be perceived by the public, as well as his own sexist ideas about what girls could handle.

The school provided valuable employment for the female staff, as well as students, allowing highly educated white and black women a strong salary during the Depression. Katherine Knight of Rockford, Illinois, was appointed director in the winter of 1935 at a salary of $175 per month. Having attended Northwestern, the University of Chicago, the University of Wisconsin, Rockford College, and Columbia University, Knight had studied statistics, education, and sociology. Her work experience included stints at NYA camps in New York and Illinois and the human resources office of Western Electric Company. Associate director Julia Dalrymple, a Chicago native, had spent three years at the University of Chicago and enrolled in a normal course to prepare herself before she spent thirteen years working at the residence halls of Kendall College. Among the small group of black teachers at the school was Virginia Sutton, from the city's South Side, who earned the same $94 per month as her white counterparts; she was also trained at the University of Chicago, where she was working on a master's degree in "personnel procedure" with Sophonisba Breckinridge. A graduate of Alabama Normal School, Sutton was the folklore teacher with the special responsibility of using the class to "assist in cooperation of mixed groups." Mathilda Bunton, another black teacher, was a recreation assistant. She completed three years of education courses at Northwestern University, worked with the Douglas Smith Fund, and assisted with crafts and music at the YWCA and the city's Union Park.[93]

The NYA organizers required potential students "be from relief or WPA families," at least sixteen years old, and "in good physical health." They also mandated that the girls have completed "two years of high school work," but they soon discovered "that the group of selected applicants" included "about 85% who have graduated from high school." Most of the girls were unemployed, and the few who did "part-time or scattered work" had mostly been "domestic help." Some had completed "commercial training in high school, but had never found a job."[94] Even with the partial high school requirement, the NYA was flooded with applications. Officials were "overwhelmed with the response to this program," including receiving "over four hundred applications ... already selective in nature," in 1936. One sixteen-year-old girl "hitch-hiked sixty miles and spent some hard-come-by cash on a tourist room overnight" to make it to her 9 AM interview with an NYA selection committee.[95]

After months of contentious arguments and debates about the nature of the NYA Resident School for Girls, it finally opened in January 1936. Among the class were "twenty race girls" selected from across the state. Housed in a former orphanage and settlement house, a few blocks east of the University of Chicago campus, students embarked on their three-month training experience.[96] An average day at the NYA School began with one of the four required classes, followed by a lunch break, and then electives ranging from puppetry to tap dancing and cooking. On Wednesday afternoons the schedule deviated from the four-class formula with educational tours of the city. After dinner, girls returned to classes for more electives. Girls could earn certification in "community leadership and health education."[97]

The *Defender* praised the NYA's "larger social commitment to improve race relations."[98] They described the school as a place where "girls of both races live and work together with no distinction as to color or creed."[99] Helen St. James, a black student, was elected chairman of her NYA class's student council, and she delivered the commencement address in the spring of 1936.[100] The *Defender*, and other NYA supporters, believed that the very best black girls were utilizing the school in preparation for serv-

FIG 3.4. The National Youth Administration Resident School for Girls was held at the Good Shepherd Community Center in Chicago's Hyde Park neighborhood. Photograph by Russell Lee for Farm Security Administration, n.d.

PHOTOGRAPHS AND PRINT DIVISION, SCHOMBURG CENTER FOR RESEARCH IN BLACK CULTURE, THE NEW YORK PUBLIC LIBRARY, ASTOR, LENOX AND TILDEN FOUNDATIONS.

ing as positive representatives of their race. In turn, black girls, who were often isolated from their white peers, could foster interracial understanding by excelling at the school's programs. The newspaper mused: "White girls, whose opinions of their darker sisters have been warped by the prejudices of their community, are given the opportunity of learning the truth for themselves. Similarly, race girls, who have had faulty opinions of their white sisters, have discovered through the intimacy of their new relationship that the only difference after all is the color of the skin and that is of no consequence. The mixed faculty of the school has likewise done much to make better citizens of the girls."[101] In this school, and other interracial programs, black girls were reliable surrogates for black communities and represented their strivings, ambitions, and suitability to be equal participants in not only the national recovery but also the democratic project itself.

Programs of the NYA, like the AKA vocational guidance effort and the fight for clerk positions, could only do so much to insulate black girls from racism and sexism in searching for employment. Although many girls enjoyed the NYA courses and activities, some black girls found that the program yielded very little in results. Georgia Washington, nominated best student at Chicago's Medill High School, took courses at the NYA school in the spring of 1941. An accomplished musician and athlete, Washington wondered "what good her record will do her," because of the lack of meaningful work for black girls after high school. Washington shared that she "was very happy to live in a democracy" and appreciated "all her freedoms" but longed to live in a world where jobs were given on the basis of "ability instead of . . . color." She was tired of her teacher telling her "clerical jobs are not for colored folk."[102] Some NYA graduates fared better and went on to fulfill the group's mission immediately after leaving the school. By the summer of 1936, two black alumnae of the school were "conducting special programs in recreation" for African American children in the southern Illinois towns of Cairo and Harrisburg.[103]

NYA officials were not naïve to the employment issues faced by black girls and teenage women. During a 1941 field visit to Illinois, Leah K. Dickinson, an NYA Regional Supervisor of Service Projects, noted that a Work Center in downtown Chicago had done little more than provide "hot lunches for youth." She noticed that, "Almost all of the girls on this unit are Negro and yet I am told that there is almost no placement of Negro girls in restaurant or hotel service in Chicago." She advised that the program focus on boys instead and find something else for girls to do. "Some real thought [must] be given to the matter of employment outlets for the Negro girls on this project. If it would seem that there is more chance for the Negro boys to get employment in restaurants and hotels, perhaps we should be giving them this opportunity and find another project for the girls."[104] Despite the concerns about job placements, NYA evaluators were hopeful that Illinois's commitment to interracial projects could benefit youth in the long run. Field Investigator Ora B. Stokes reported that during her visit to the same work site Dickinson evaluated, she was glad to see "in the sewing unit for girls . . . the power machines were being operated by all girls without distinction as to race. This was really democracy in action." She also found that "democracy was in action" at a site dedicated to teaching girls about radio production, "without regard to race or creed and [with a] spirit of friendliness."[105]

The NYA Resident School for Girls, and similar projects, constantly negotiated its position and argued that it was a crucial service to the nation, and it outlasted many New Deal initiatives, but its demise alerted black Chicagoans to the limits of racial progress as the nation entered World War II. From their inception, the NYA schools and programs were targets of criticism, and politicians regularly ordered investigations of its federal administrators. Amid growing criticism of the program for promoting idleness, interfering with private business, and internal mismanagement, the NYA ceased its activities in 1943.[106] The NYA schools, in particular, were attacked because of their goal of fostering positive race relations. The *Defender* characterized the end of the NYA as a death at the hands of a "race-baiting GOP and southern Dems." New York Republican congressman John Taber led the charge against the NYA with a speech in 1943 about the school's promotion of race mixing: "In my territory, out of their private boarding school, we see a white boy, and a black girl come out . . . the entire program is demoralizing."[107] In the debates and subsequent death of the NYA, black girls were victims of devastating characterizations about their sexuality. Although powerful black voices among AKA, the economic boycott movement, and the NYA all aligned to buttress the notion that black girls would play a key role in the future of their race, the mere mention of a white boy and black girl as classmates and potential sexual partners was too powerful to overcome. References to race mixing, sexual impropriety, and the assumption of racial equality among girls all served to dismantle an expansive, New Deal program. For AKA women and devoted NYA teachers "of the race," this moment reminded them that black girlhood could not be so easily redefined to highlight what black girls could do for an ailing people or nation. No matter how strenuous the efforts to bring them into spaces where they could showcase the very best of the race or represent how much they fulfilled the nation's ideals of citizenship and hard work, the specter of racialized, sexualized stereotypes followed them. The NYA school had done what Bethune had mandated: "Lift the fallen to their feet so that they can again walk or run for themselves. . . . Give them a chance to learn to 'do for themselves.'" Yet black girls were reminded that this was not always so simple.

CONCLUSION

Gradually, as the nation slowly recovered under the New Deal and prepared for its involvement with Word War II efforts, each of the three movements evolved and grew into new approaches to secure opportunities for girls and promote racial equality. Assessing the impact of the Depression on black girls, and the way black leaders configured their responses with notions of the ability of black girls to represent their race, sheds light on the future social movements in the South and North.

The AKA's vocational guidance movement was the first of many projects led by black sorority women after the Depression, when traditional black women's clubs began to decline in size, power, and influence. The ability for AKA to leverage its message about black girls and black women's importance in the midst of chaos would grow into savvy political maneuvering and leadership in the decades after they shifted their focus away from vocational guidance and into other arenas of social equality and economic justice. In 1934, AKAs began to turn their attention to public health initiatives in the South. During the summer, groups of sorority members organized mobile clinics and education programs as part of the AKA Mississippi Health Project.[108] Although as late as 1939 the *Defender*'s society page noted that the launch of the annual vocational guidance program was "stronger this year than ever," and named more than a dozen women who served on the program's committee, vocational guidance began to fade into the annals of the sorority's history.[109] By 1939, when the health project's director, Dr. Dorothy Boulding Ferebee, was elected the sorority's president, AKA changed its primary focus to health activism.[110] The sorority remained committed to girls' and women's education, but the health project eclipsed vocational guidance as the sorority's main focus.[111] Vocational guidance became a tertiary agenda item for the membership, and its gradual fading away from the national sorority platform may have been an acknowledgment of the limits of the message and the era.

The activism surrounding "Don't Buy Where You Can't Work" campaigns continued and grew into the civil rights movement's demands for desegregated public accommodations and greater hiring among black communities, no doubt arguing the success of the Depression-era campaigns and of individual black girls who obtained clerk positions. The growth of wartime industries and the need for female labor to replace men away at war reordered demands for black employment in Chicago, and black girls no longer figured prominently in boycott campaigns. National civil rights organizations capitalized on black men's military service and jobs in the war industries to highlight black men's patriotism and commitment to the charge of preserving democracy abroad. The World War II era led more migrant youth to Chicago, and increasingly city leaders were concerned about juvenile delinquency and keeping black children in segregated communities where they could not cause trouble to whites. In the next chapter, I examine World War II–era approaches to black girls' patriotism and to their problems.

The NYA's demise was not an end of all experiments in interracial cooperation, but the agency's abrupt closure did foreclose on an avenue to girls' training and employment. Black girls would continue to elicit sympathy and suspicion in schools and settlement houses. In other spaces, they faced racial-sexual stereotypes that influenced how adults perceived them, and how they saw themselves. The NYA's experiment with interracial education, and the black leadership that hoped it would translate into a greater push to desegregate other schools and youth programs, would resonate in the years following the landmark *Brown v. Board of Education* Supreme Court decision.

These three seemingly disparate movements and approaches to the Depression are all connected by the incredible value black girls brought to developing the agenda of black leaders during the Migration's most difficult days. By maintaining the focus on black girls and girlhood, a new story of black urbanization appears—one fraught with perils and possibilities.

"DID I DO RIGHT?"

The Black Girl Citizen

The Great Depression deflated black hopes of economic stability in Chicago, but southerners still continued to take a chance on going up North throughout the 1930s and 1940s. As was the case before the economic crash, black girls in Chicago continued their search for ways to address their needs and quell their fears about city life. For girls born into the restrictive and threatening culture of the Jim Crow South, Chicago was at the very least a place that allowed for comparatively more access to pieces of a childhood experience. Yet racial barriers within children's organizations and black anxieties about urbanization truncated black girls' ability to claim a fully carefree girlhood.

In this chapter I delve into the way black girls appeared in discourses on urbanization in the post–Depression Migration period through a consideration of black girls' roles as representative citizens. I examine black girls' encounters with a quintessential childhood activity—camping—in order to theorize the period's representational strategies surrounding black girlhood. I introduce the concept of the politics of play, which encompassed the way black leaders and civic organizations used advocacy for black girls' participation in children's organizations to make claims about blacks' fitness for citizenship and social equality. Adults not only promoted black children's participation in the Boy Scouts, Girl Scouts, and Camp Fire Girls to signal their right to full citizenship, but also did so to argue a case for a protected black childhood.

The politics of play rely on two seemingly contradictory notions: that black children are inherently innocent and that they are sophisticated and capable of fighting the virulent forces of racism and white supremacy. Like the respectability politics that framed black women's advocacy and self-defense, the politics of play required the construction of a dichotomy between good and bad race representatives.[1] I consider the way black women adopted, promoted, and interpreted the Camp Fire Girls program as a way to mark and foreground a good black girl citizen. The African American women who brought Camp Fire Girls to the South Side capitalized on the program's values of patriotism, community involvement, and elevation of women's work. Yet the key way Camp Fire Girls instilled these values, through camping, was limited, due to segregation policies and lack of financial resources to build campsites exclusively for black girls. Chicago's black Camp Fire community reinterpreted this organization to provide black girls with experiences that resonated with them as racialized subjects and social beings.

I then focus on black girls excluded from the role of representative girl citizen: teenage mothers, juvenile delinquents, and poor girls who did not elicit much support from Camp Fire councils and other children's organizations. Using the transcripts of E. Franklin Frazier's interviews for his landmark study *The Negro Family in Chicago* and the research of his white graduate advisor, the University of Chicago's Ernest W. Burgess, I uncover the way ostracized girls understood their roles in black communities. In their interviews and essays, they talk about sex, dating, family dynamics, and their impressions of Chicago. Although they did not appear in laudatory *Defender* columns as models of their race, instead appearing on police blotter updates and in condemning articles, their legacies are not small. Their testimonies, which were sometimes distorted and manipulated by researchers, shaped critical discourses about black families, urbanization, and social policy.

These disparate groups of girls were both targets of programs that were based on the belief that exposure to the outdoors through camping and hiking could prevent or reduce their propensity for juvenile delinquency. Delinquent girls represented the race's problems, and they served as the evidence as to why black girls needed access to camping. The appeals to establish campgrounds, challenge racial segregation at community camps, and provide greater recreational spaces for girls highlighted black girls' success stories and referred to the black girls who existed on the outer margins of racial respectability. Scholars have effectively and convincingly chronicled the moral panics that contributed to the way adults framed their work with the girls they labeled delinquents; my concern is to highlight how these girls claimed their own rights as child citizens. In telling their stories, they expressed the way they reasoned and understood their choices, dealt with their marginalization, and critiqued the failure of adults to parent and guide them.

A SENSE OF FREEDOM, A SEPARATION FROM CROWDS

Organized summer camps are rooted in nineteenth-century recreation activities originally designed for elite and middle-class white boys. Gradually, summer camps were made available to children of both sexes. Settlement houses and churches made summer camps available to poor, immigrant, and working-class children. Camp Fire Girls and the Girl Scouts legitimated camping for girls, and by the time African Americans organized to participate in national children's organizations, camping was an unquestionable pleasure of childhood in the United States. Summer camps, as historian Leslie Paris has shown, "provided many American children's first experience of community beyond their immediate family and home neighborhoods."[2] Black chapters of Camp Fire, Boy Scouts, and Girl Scouts worked to provide their own camping facilities for African American children. Paris sums up summer camps as working to "consolidate the notion of childhood as a time apart, at once protected and playful."[3]

The forces of racial terror and the realities of economic demands limited black girls' ability to feel protected and encouraged to play. Girl domestics did not count days until summer, because the change in seasons only ushered in more responsibilities. One migrant woman remembered how much she "hated to see summer coming" because it often meant being sent away from home to work full-time in a white family's home. "When I was eight, I went there for a month to care for the children . . . Never been away from home when they sent me and you cried all the time . . . You felt so bad, and cried. But I never went home a summer from eight years 'til I was twelve years old."[4] She did not know a summer break until she migrated to Washington, DC. Mathilene Anderson also dreaded summers. "You'd help the white missus all summer and . . . all summer you worked like a dog! They didn't care that you were a child. They saw you as a worker. And they worked you so bad."[5]

Even girls who never toiled as domestics and grew up mostly in Chicago were also disappointed by their options for enjoying their summers. In the fall of 1940, eighth grader Gina Winters completed a section of the Human Relations Scale entitled "What Do I Like to Do?" University of Chicago researchers created the scale to learn more about American children's living conditions, relationships, and aptitudes, and they presented their findings to the annual White House Conference on Child Health and Protection. Under the heading of the things she "wanted the very most," in neat cursive writing Gina listed a new coat, to become a nurse, and to "go to camps."[6] Gina's options were limited by her race. She could have competed for a coveted spot in a *Defender*-sponsored contest that awarded a trip to camp. She could have asked her mother to investigate options at Hull House, only a few blocks from her apartment on Clybourne Avenue. Gina's best option was joining the Camp Fire Girls, but as a black member there was still no guarantee she would ever get to camp.

In order to understand why Gina could become a Camp Fire Girl but not be able to go to summer camp, it is important to outline the racial roots of the founding and growth of the organization. The Camp Fire Girls program, fittingly, was born on a camping trip, in a place very different from Chicago's South Side. Founders Dr. Luther Gulick and his wife, Charlotte, may have never imagined African American girls when they embarked on the creation of a group that would inspire and ignite "the out-of-doors habit and the out-of-doors spirit" in girls.[7] In the summer of 1910, while the Gulicks enjoyed their annual camping expedition with their six children at the edge of Lake Sebago, Maine, the parents decided to add new elements to their camping routine. They devised a system of recognition to reward their children for completing their chores; these honors provided a rough sketch of the bead and badge system later used in Camp Fire ceremonies.[8] The Gulicks wanted to cultivate an "essentially . . . feminine program" that "stimulates the imagination, guides it into channels of beauty, inspires ideals through its simple ritual, encourage healthful activities and an appreciation of the feminine role."[9] These social reformers also wanted girls, who increasingly were living in urban hubs, to enjoy "a sense of freedom" and a "separation from crowds."[10]

The Gulicks' vision of a "feminine role" was as much about race as about gender. Other than a desire to create a special group for their daughters after learning about the Boy Scouts of America, the Camp Fire Girls' creation was motivated by racial anxiety. The Gulicks were among a cohort of white, educated Progressive Movement members who grappled both with the changing demographics of the United States and with emerging challenges to long-held gender roles that determined women's place in society, and they clamored for a remedy to the impacts of these changes on children.[11] Comparatively higher birth rates among African Americans and newly arrived immigrants frightened some middle-class whites, and these whites conceived of work with children as a means of resolving a crisis of white femininity and masculinity as well as of racial superiority. The white patriarch's loss of masculinity, in his fear of being characterized as weak and unable to defend his family, also endangered the social power of the members of his household. Panicked men created children's organizations that could prepare their children for a new world by reinforcing notions of racial superiority and physical vitality.[12]

Luther Gulick looked around him and saw women's agitation for suffrage, the modernization of the middle-class family's lifestyle, and girls' greater independence from their families through wage earning as detrimental to white domination. The Gulicks feared that their daughters would grow up in a world that did not recognize their proper gender roles or the special gifts white women brought to the home and, through raising sons, society at large. In a 1915 issue of the *Journal of Heredity*, a pro-eugenics journal, an article declared: "fitness for motherhood is a happy by-product of Camp Fire activities, which makes for splendid physique and intelligent control of one's own body and mind."[13] For white middle-class Americans, taking their daughters camping was one step toward developing a stronger race by enabling girls to become strong mothers, producing "sturdy, healthy, and happy" babies for the nation.[14] Ultimately, by directing modern girls toward the work of the home, the Gulicks contributed to the preservation of the white nation, a nation that they and other eugenicists believed was in deep peril. Yet Camp Fire's desire to reify whiteness did not preclude its uses in other contexts and communities. Along with Girl Scouts, Camp Fire councils were used to assimilate the daughters of ethnic whites and encouraged them to learn American history, adopt national customs, and exclusively use the English language in order to "become white."[15]

Camp Fire's welcome to non-native-born white girls revealed their belief that immigrants could benefit from Americanization, but the logic of assimilation could not answer the question of black girls' participation in the burgeoning group. The leaders did not establish any rules about race during the critical period between 1910 and 1914, when they drafted policies, created ceremonies and honors systems, designed uniforms and accessories, and selected their governing board. The Gulicks made no mention of race or ethnicity in their membership protocols and requirements, but as Camp Fire expanded in the South, the executive board was forced to confront race and the future of the program.

In 1914 a group of white Camp Fire advisors in Nashville—called sponsors and guardians—alerted the national Camp Fire office to rumors that Bethlehem Settlement House worker Lizzie Smith had not only created a Camp Fire group but also had boasted that her girls had "the same privileges as white girls." In an era when the slightest suggestion of social equality could ignite racist violence and retribution, the sponsors were certain that no white girl would join an organization that counted African Americans among its roster.[16] The complaint forced the Camp Fire leadership to wonder if rejecting Jim Crow would hamper its institutional progress. By 1914 Camp Fire Girls numbered more than sixty thousand, and the organization was involved in a heated competition with the Girl Scouts. Based in Savannah, Georgia, Girl Scouts was gaining ground in the South, and Camp Fire leaders reasoned that an equivocal stance on anything resembling racial equality would undoubtedly undermine expansion in the region.

Gulick took the Nashville matter to his board of directors. Board member James McCulloh, of the American Interchurch Council, perceived Smith's actions as a politically motivated stunt and asserted that Camp Fire was not formally involved with African American girls in the South. McCulloh advised Gulick to order Smith to reorganize the group under the name of the Girls of the Forward Quest, an African American girls club that predated Camp Fire. African American girls groups often employed this tactic to coexist with white groups. The YWCA used this strategy when African American girls sought membership in their girls' programs and clubs. White girls joined the Y's Girls Reserves, while black girls became members of Blue Triangle League Clubs.[17] The Nashville controversy was never quite resolved. Smith's group disbanded the same year they were reported for violating the racial rules of the South. Camp Fire eventually decided only to accept African American groups as long as they organized

FIG 4.1. The YWCA Girls Reserves provided African American girls with opportunities to enjoy the outdoors and go camping. Photograph from *The Work of Colored Women*, compiled by Jane Olcott, 1919.

GENERAL RESEARCH AND REFERENCE DIVISION, SCHOMBURG CENTER FOR RESEARCH IN BLACK CULTURE, THE NEW YORK PUBLIC LIBRARY, ASTOR, LENOX AND TILDEN FOUNDATIONS.

in areas where whites were able to establish Camp Fire first.[18] Girls learned racial rules from an early age. When black girls' organizations encountered these types of problems, it reinforced the racial hierarchies of Jim Crow in the minds of children of all colors.[19]

The "whites first" policy may account for the significant numbers of black Camp Fire Girls councils across Illinois as early as the 1910s. The Gulicks headquartered Camp Fire in New York City, but Chicago became a major center of Camp Fire activity, in part due to Jane Addams's early appointment to the Camp Fire board. Addams brought Camp Fire to settlement houses, and workers used the program to Americanize eastern European, Irish, and Italian immigrant girls.[20] Meanwhile, African American girls attended Camp Fire events at settlement houses that tried to "northernize" southern black girls and instill values similar to the ones taught to girls whose parents were born overseas.

Settlement houses were important to Camp Fire's African American population because black churches were often unable to sustain youth groups. A black Camp Fire council met regularly at Hyde Park's Clotee Scott Settlement in 1915.[21] There is no evidence of the group in the official histories of the Chicago Area Camp Fire District, yet the *Defender* posted notices of its meetings and events weekly.[22] White girls could rely on schools and churches to aid in providing recreational opportunities, but African American places of worship were often overtaxed and could not provide adequate support. The 1933 report *The Negro's Church* found that "formal recreational work is not well developed in the Negroes [*sic*] churches. In many instances where churches have advertised recreational work as part of the program, the actual promotion of this work has been short-lived."[23]

Black Camp Fire councils grew stronger during World War I and the following years due to the creation of an offshoot program called the Minute Girls. Gulick devised the Minute Girls "to help those who wish to prepare quickly and specifically for service in time of war or public calamity."[24] Unlike the larger Camp Fire body, Minute Girls were to demonstrate toughness above a nurturing demeanor. Minute Girls were charged with abolishing their "nerves and softness." Gulick explained that Minute Girls was "founded on the belief that in war as in peace the largest power of woman lies in the protection and development of the home and its ideals, the care of children, of the sick and injured—all in the relation to this largest needs of the community.[25] Gulick mandated thirteen requirements for Minute Girls, including wearing a special uniform, "five minutes of callisthenic exercises daily," "walking forty miles over the course of four days," learning first aid, donating $1 to a relief organization, and, most important, demonstrating patriotism.[26]

The Minute Girls, coupled with Migration population increases, provided an important channel for black girls' participation in the politics of play and contribution in response to black calls for equal rights through patriotism. Since the Revolutionary War, African Americans have participated in military initiatives to make claims to their freedom, suitability for citizenship, and to highlight the depth of racial hatred, from slavery to Jim Crow. In the literature on black military participation, black girls are rarely considered in conversations about patriotism and civil rights. When we shift the focus to black girls in the Great Migration period, we can observe girls' position in these critical campaigns, such as the Double V effort for victory abroad and at home, before the civil rights movement propelled children onto the stage of conflict over public schools and public accommodations. In the world of children's organizations, black girls presented the face of the community's desire for equality. The Migration period, which encompassed the end of World War I and the entirety of World War II, provided pivotal moments for black citizens to use their patriotism to combat racism.[27] Clubwoman and Republican Party activist Irene McCoy Gaines spearheaded bringing Minute Girls to the South Side, knowing that it met the needs of black girls who were seeking activities, as well as supporting racial progress. She described the introduction of Minute Girls as the day when "a great hope was born in the heart of the colored girl."[28]

After World War I ended the Minute Girls dissolved, but the values of patriotism and community engagement continued to elicit greater black participation in Camp Fire. The Loma Council formed and gathered weekly at the Frederick Douglass Center between 1918 and the early 1930s. Chicago suffragist Irene Goins led the Loma and made it a priority to publicize its good works. In March 1918, four months after the end of World War I, the *Defender* announced that the "club recently organized [and] is making rapid progress . . . doing charity work and many a heart has been filled with joy by a deed done by this club."[29] Loma girls participated in patriotic activities, and the newspaper described them as "a new organization in this locality . . . pledged to aid in war relief work."[30] They hosted a "grand patriotic pageant and council fire" at the Unity Club House, which later became the Moorish Science Temple's entertainment venue.[31] During World War II another council staged a program at the Colored Young Women's Christian Association titled "Our Men in Service," which also featured a speech by local Republican George B. McKibbin.[32] Black Camp Fire Girls activities and membership growth coincided with the expansion of black social spaces like the Unity Club, the colored YWCAs, and storefront churches. These spaces allowed girls to organize public events and appearances. At events ranging from the annual *Defender*-sponsored Bud Billiken Day Parade to church fundraisers, black Camp Fire girls donned their uniforms and alerted all observers, white and black, that they too embodied the highest of American ideals values.

In addition to the focus on patriotism, Camp Fire's emphasis on girls' special responsibilities and promise as a way to build better women resonated with African American leaders. In a 1916 *Defender* report, the newspaper praised Camp Fire for being "an organization of girls and women to develop the home spirit and make it dominate the entire community." The article applauded Camp Fire's desire to uplift women's work by "organizing a girl's daily home life; and to show that the daily drudgery may be made to contribute to the beauty of living."[33] Gulick believed Camp Fire's curriculum converted menial and laborious tasks into artful and enjoyable experiences for girls, all of which were rewarded by Camp Fire beads and badges. Included in Gulick's listing of potentially transformative activities were learning to make "ten standard soups," sleeping with "windows open," and "planning the family expenditures for food at $2 a week."[34] Gulick himself recognized these activities as "everyday drudgery," yet he placed housework in the context of a merit-based system and stressed how important preparation for perfect womanhood and motherhood were to home and nation. Camp Fire Girls created its own world of exciting chores and scientific standards for housework. According to the *Defender* article, Camp Fire also helped reduce bad behavior among girls by promoting a "happy social life," because "the girls must know how to work as well as play."[35]

Camp Fire's promotion of women's "daily drudgery" and the exaltation of the hidden "beauty of living" in these activities mirrored the ways African American pragmatists attempted to mediate the strain of domestic work and the economic realities of so many black girls and teenage women. For African American girls, who may have looked toward the bleak and often inevitable future of working as a domestic as their only occupational possibility, Camp Fire dignified these acts. Camp Fire made work patriotic and a celebration of the historical forces that built the nation. Camp Fire's appeal to African American circles resembled the rhetoric of domestic training and industrial programs that elevated black women's work to the levels of science and precision to generate more respect for their labor. Most important, unlike school, Camp Fire was a voluntary activity designed to make girls feel both special and useful to the larger community.

After Minute Girls ceased its activities, Oececa Camp Fire Girls became the most organized of Chicago's black Camp Fire councils. Although the girls were organized by 1931, they may have adopted the name Oececa later, around 1937.[36] The *Defender* regularly covered their activities, supporters, and attempts to establish black camping opportunities for girls. Oececa girls mainly hailed from Chicago's Second Ward, which enveloped some of the poorest areas in the Black Belt, but Camp Fire's guardians and sponsors were often elite African American women with political ties. They provided a platform for promoting Camp Fire among their equally influential friends. One of the longest serving Oececa guardians, Blanche E. King, was credited with "bringing the Camp Fire Girls to the South Side for the inhabitants of the Second Ward," in order "to help the girls in the district who need it the most."[37] As the wife of attorney and Illinois state representative William King, she was able to join forces with her husband to raise the profile of Camp Fire. Representative King's rise from humble beginnings in Louisiana to fourteen years of service in the Illinois House and Senate between 1925 and 1939 made the Kings a symbol of African American progress. The couple regularly opened up their home to Camp Fire Girls, including an "annual installation" to award badges and beads and to name new sponsors and guardians.[38]

Although the Camp Fire organization did not mandate it, in 1931 the Kings endowed a scholarship program for local girls. They selected Ruth Reese, a Phillips High School alumna and University of Illinois undergraduate, for the first award. The Kings selected her because William King related to her background. He was touched by her family's particular struggle "of the mother trying to care for a family of ten children without any support."[39] Reese later became a member of AKA and a teacher at the city's Madden Park Field House, one of the few public, recreational clubs available to African American girls.[40]

The Kings, Irene Gaines, and Irene Goins enlisted their most prominent friends in helping with the effort to publicize and build on Camp Fire work.[41] They found allies: singer Ethel Waters, Ida B. Wells-Barnett's daughter and biographer Alfreda Duster, distinguished librarian Vivian Harsh, and boxer Joe Louis and his family presented guest lectures and made appearances at Oececa events. Camp Fire volunteers enjoyed a special camaraderie, and this network of women created a social group centered on how to form black girls into model citizens. They hosted meet-

FIG 4.2. Founded in 1910, Camp Fire Girls believed that girls needed contact with nature in order to develop the skills to become good mothers. "Camp Fire Girls canoeing." Photograph from *Evergirls Magazine*, c. 1923.

PHOTOGRAPHY COLLECTION, MIRIAM AND IRA D. WALLACH DIVISION OF ART, PRINTS AND PHOTOGRAPHS, THE NEW YORK PUBLIC LIBRARY, ASTOR, LENOX AND TILDEN FOUNDATIONS. USED BY PERMISSION OF CAMP FIRE.

ings, retreats, and book groups with each other, discussing race-conscious works, such as W. E. B. Du Bois's 1920 collection *Darkwater: Voices from Within the Veil.*

Black Camp Fire women organizers placed their work in a larger dialogue about African American life and cultural values. In the summer of 1940, black Camp Fire sponsors and guardians gathered to "collaborate on the state of the program." Camp Fire Girls prepared a skit about "the thought of Camp Fire" at the historic 1940 Negro Exposition.[42] The Negro Exposition, which celebrated the seventy-fifth anniversary of the end of slavery, beckoned black Americans from across the country to Chicago. The event prompted black leaders to reflect on the ways African American people understood themselves in relationship to freedom and progress, as well as their frustration with the slow pace of securing greater racial justice and equality. Camp Fire sponsors and guardians contributed to the Negro Exposition's women's week celebration. The inclusion of Camp Fire Girls and supporters at the Exposition revealed how much Camp Fire women valued girls' participation in leisure and civic activity by selecting them to represent African American success after Emancipation.[43]

BLACK GIRLS AND JUVENILE DELINQUENCY

Access to camping was not just a reward for or expression of "good citizenship." Camping was also a part of the agenda of many of the city's civic organizations as they developed a greater overall interest in eradicating juvenile delinquency. Black Chicagoans concerned with juvenile delinquency included an array of antisocial behaviors in the category. Delinquency ranged from loitering to petty theft to disobedience and sexual experimentation. Chicago's reform culture shaped the definition of delinquency. Reformers tried to prevent delinquency by intervening in domestic disputes between parents and children, promoting stable families through social welfare programs, and establishing special penal institutions for youth. In 1899 Chicago's Juvenile Court codified the notion that children and adults should be treated differently before the law, and Progressive women reformers and social scientists joined forces to focus on the nature of juvenile offenders in order to make them into productive adult citizens. By the beginning of the Great Migration period, juvenile delinquency researchers and crusaders, who had studied delinquent behavior among Chicago's immigrant youth, pointed to racial theories, poverty, and community influences to explain why some children repeatedly defied their parents or broke the law.

From the early days of the Migration onward, African American girls appeared before the Juvenile Court, but in low numbers, due to the sparse black population in Chicago in 1899. Prior to 1917, black girls' appearances before the court did not elicit widespread concern from community leaders. In a report on the first decade of the court, researchers found that black girls represented approximately 6.2 percent of all cases.[44] Juvenile officers charged girls with "desertion of home, ungovernable ways and wayward contact," which encompassed defiant behavior against parents, especially fathers. Scholars have examined how turn-of-the-century parents used the juvenile courts as an extension of their parental authority, and girls especially could find themselves brought before a judge for selecting the wrong boyfriend, staying out too late, or challenging family rules.[45] The superintendent at the Geneva Reformatory for Girls claimed that African American girls demonstrated a "tendency on the part of colored inmates toward violence," but they were not overrepresented in the juvenile population in the 1910s, and there were no noticeable differences in "conduct on probation and parole."[46]

Eventually, disparities in juvenile delinquency rates between white and black girls became more pronounced. Between 1920 and 1930, girls represented about 40 percent of all cases involving African American youth and about half of all dependency cases.[47] The trend continued to rise after the Great Depression. Horace Cayton and St. Clair Drake's 1945 *Black Metropolis* linked economic depression to rises in black juvenile delinquency rates. The sociologists found that in 1930, the Juvenile Court classified 20 percent of its boy delinquents as Negro; the rates for black girls were almost as high.[48] The study also reported that by 1944, African American girls made up 36 percent of the girls at the Illinois State Reformatory, the institution that had once alarmed Sophonisba Breckinridge because it housed girls who were merely orphaned and not criminals.[49]

Black civic leaders feared that black youth were more susceptible to delinquency after the Great Depression because they were more desperate to provide for themselves and their families. They also believed that the Depression destabilized black families, leading to a lack of parental supervision. In 1936, the Reverend Richard Keller reported a "startling increase" of African American children in the juvenile courts and highlighted that younger and younger children were being brought into Chicago's juvenile detention centers and training schools. He connected this rise in youth crime to "the pressing problem of providing a livelihood" during the post-Depression years. Keller determined that if Chicagoans were to reduce "gangsterism" and "the disintegration of family life," blacks had to give "boys and girls the opportunity for constructive activity to fill their leisure time." Keller characterized black families as "hard hit during the past five years by the depression" and "not . . . able to provide their progeny with adequate facilities for recreation and development."[50] Cayton and Drake's *Black Metropolis* also revealed that the Depression had spawned an increase in the number of youth offenders in the Juvenile Court. The report claimed that in 1930, twenty of every one hundred boys called before the Juvenile Court were African American; the rates for girls were almost as high.[51] Cayton and Drake, like Keller, emphasized the importance of opening recreation to black children so as to curb further delinquency problems.

On the whole, youth advocates and researchers framed the issue of juvenile delinquency in terms of familial poverty and the lack of opportunities for alternatives to crime. Yet some observers were concerned that poor children were disproportionately and sometimes unjustifiably implicated in juvenile delinquency. In a 1940 letter to the editor of the *Defender*, A. L. Foster, executive secretary of the Chicago Urban League, expressed concern that poor youth were being unfairly accused of the rise in juvenile delinquency. "The present wave of lawlessness among youth may partly be explained by the present economic situation, bad housing, over-crowded conditions, etc. but it is significant that there is no greater increase in juvenile delinquency among boys and girls who are on relief than among those young people who have . . . economic advantage."[52] Due to the widespread devastation of the Depression, African Americans who had once enjoyed some of the trappings of a middle-class life may have found themselves in closer proximity to the African American youth targeted by truancy and police officers.

Perspectives on why camping was valuable reflected some of the same undertones as racial uplift discourses: children needed contact with the right influences in order to change their demeanor and learn right behavior. Chicago's Central YMCA president Dr. T. H. Nelson called summer camp one of "the most effective types of educational enterprises" because "the whole . . . girl [is] dealt with." Nelson asserted: "Girls at camp become acquainted with new beauties through lessons on insects, flowers, bird, wood, lore, fields, and streams. . . . Nature is always an excellent teacher."[53] Just as mixing with the "better classes" helped influence the underclass, nature served a civilizing function similar to that of the middle class. The YWCA also lent support to these measures. Crystal Bird, a representative of the YWCA Negro Girl Reserves, characterized the Black Belt girls she worked with as "very simple," but their camping trips were "crude attempts" at bringing to them "for the first time in their lives, a knowledge of the joy of living in a tent, of cooking a meal in the open on a hillside, of splashing about in a cool-running stream; and also of bringing to them a real gain in physical fitness."[54] Southside Community Committee director Golden B. Darby agreed with Nelson and Bird, declaring that "the value of a week in camp is immeasurable as the contacts and experiences the children receive do more for them than like experiences in the city for a month or more." Darby's assessment that nature was inherently more valuable to children than city life represented the prevailing notion among juvenile delinquency experts that the outdoors had a rehabilitative impact on youth. All of these promotions of camping led the Southside Community Committee's initiative on camping to find "interest in camp so great" that more and more girls applied to camps to "seek to be among the fortunate."[55]

CAMPING AND THE COLOR LINE

Black Camp Fire Girls groups focused on public acts of patriotism and community involvement because opportunities for girls to camp consistently were difficult to organize. The color line in camping was reinforced by the potent forces of segregation: the "local customs" of rural areas that refused integration and the dangers that befell black children when they did participate in interracial camping. Parents and community leaders, including those who detested Jim Crow the most, found themselves confronted with accommodating it in order to allow their children to enjoy childhood experiences. Historians have documented the efforts to bring quality education to children as part of the long struggle to improve African American life, but the parallel fight to bring recreational activities to children has not been as well captured outside of civil rights movement challenges to segregation at public pools and amusement parks. Camping activism involved many of the same aspects of parent protest for integrated schools: fundraising and institution building, determining whether integration or accommodation was more favorable, and selecting representative young people to secure victories in racially mixed settings.

Black clubwomen and Camp Fire leaders spent considerable time and effort on expanding the camp experience so as to include black girls. African American groups throughout Illinois prioritized fundraising for camps. In 1930 the Galesburg chapter of the National Association of Colored Women's Clubs (NACW) shared plans for a girls' camp in the district.[56] The 1935 platform of the Illinois state branch of this association included girls' camping, and the Illinois Federation of Colored Women's

Clubs operated a camp in central Illinois. An East St. Louis clubwoman, Annette Officer, secured the lot, and her colleague Carrie Horton, state president of the National Association of Colored Women's Clubs, "developed it and provided tents, cots, and arrangements for cooking and a caretaker."[57] The National Association of Colored Girls (NACG), an offshoot of the National Association of Colored Women's Clubs organized in 1930, included camping among its primary aims. The National Association of Colored Girls created a camp at Lake Storey, Illinois, where girls' clubs could attend and invite guests.[58]

Some women of means were able to establish private camps. Sarah L. Coleman opened a camp for African American children in conjunction with the Chicago Park District, which may indicate that the parks were in no hurry to integrate existing camps. A member of the Central Northern District Association of Colored Women's clubs, Coleman established the Camp in 1935 in the Illinois Forest Preserves. She opened the camp because "girls of the Race were limited for such recreational activities." Coleman wanted "to give the same program that other camps offer."[59] She raised funds for the project through pretty baby competitions and popularity contests. The desire to "give the same" to African American girls indicates that camping was more than an activity to occupy children over the course of a long, hot summer or a means of keeping girls away from danger or trouble. Providing a camp experience was a clear marker that black girls deserved all the privileges other girls enjoyed.

When black girls crossed the color line in camps and recreational clubs, they confronted rejection, lukewarm acceptance, and sometimes surprising friendships. But no matter how these experiences unfolded, girls were constantly burdened to speak for and represent their race. In the early 1940s, the Chicago Commons Settlement House experimented with interracial clubs and camping, and staff members made careful observations about the experiences. From the diaries and logs of camp personnel, it is clear that black girls felt the weight of their role when dealing with white authority figures and fellow campers. These interracial groups were limited in their activities because of the discriminatory policies of many of Chicago's leisure spaces. In a 1944 report about the Chicago Commons day camp, a disappointed worker recorded: "Trips were not planned to the Forest Preserves because the swimming pools were not open to both Negro and white children."[60]

The following year the Commons tried to promote integration within the confines of the settlement's facilities, avoiding the racial barriers to public accommodations altogether. This strategy still proved difficult because they relied on girls to manage the process. A worker filed a statement on the situation: "Last year one white group invited a negro girl to join them after the staff had asked them to consider it, pointing out that she was the only coloured girl of her age in the community. The Negro girl had a rather hard time of it. It was better than nothing, but not being too well adjusted herself socially, the added strain of an alien group did not make for real happiness."[61] When another African American girl wandered into the all-white Jack and Jill Club at the Commons, the club's members protested to the dance committee. "This is our club . . . we don't want her at the dance," they complained. The girls refused to dance with the girl, so she left, and she never returned to the settlement house.[62] Sometimes African American girls rejected white peers. A worker noted: "We have trouble with one group of Negro girls who consistently refuse to accept different groups of white girls in the class."[63]

Despite the problems at the settlement house, the Chicago Commons embarked on interracial camping trips, hoping that by isolating the children in a new environment they could become more open to children of other races. For girls at these summer camps, the experience could also prove unsatisfying. In a 1944 log about a camping trip, a counselor remarked that white and black campers socialized at "crafts, woodshop, and cooking" but maintained segregated sleeping quarters. White parents and children insisted on this arrangement, and organizers complied. Problems at interracial camping sites may have also arisen from the pressure black girls felt to represent all African American children at the risk of standing out or jeopardizing already delicate race relations. When one African American camper stole items from the camp's craft room, two African American girls reported the misdeed. A camp official reminded the other black children present of the "terrific repercussion" that the incident "might have on the other negro children."[64]

When black girls expressed discomfort over their treatment by white campers, white adults held them responsible for changing their outlook. Ten-year-old Janie White was one of only three African American girls in her cabin at a Chicago Commons camp in the summer of 1950; camp counselors closely watched the girl, and they recorded a racial incident in her cabin. The tensions between Janie and white campers started after "she made a remark about her being Negro and having to live as others (meaning whites) want you to." Camp counselors interpreted Janie's frustration as positive, possibly misreading the girl's anger. The counselors concluded that Janie eventually "accepted her race and never did once complain about not being white."[65] The counselors reasoned that accepting one's own racial identity was necessary for children to properly integrate in these settings. They hoped that Janie would follow nine-year-old Jean Kyle's examples because she did not express "any particular racial or cultural attitudes" and also accepted "the fact that she was a Negro." Jean may have also kept quiet about her feelings about race, and she could have avoided white campers; her counselor noted that she spent most of her time with the third black camper, Essie Mae Height, despite being in a "group... [with] a fairly equal balance of Negro and white girls."[66]

The mere presence of black girls in the camp setting sparked conversation about race and social dynamics, which counselors believed was a crucial step in reducing racial conflict. Adults encouraged black girls to argue for their position on race, in hopes of transforming white perceptions. One frank discussion between white girls and black girls about "the Negro problem" led a white camper to conclude that "the negro was equal and should be given a chance," but she maintained that she "did not believe in intermarriage." The counselors used facts about black history to reform white girls' attitudes toward blacks. "We mentioned G. W. Carver and other great Negroes and . . . contributions they'd made to civilization." At the camp's conclusion, the children even danced with each other without "a tension or forced situation."[67] Counselors deemed the children jitterbugging with each other a success, but the racial climate of Chicago in 1945 may have kept this incident buried in Commons notes and largely unpublicized. The children, safe to traverse racial boundaries at camp, sometimes failed to maintain those relationships when they returned home. In 1949, an interracial group called the Jesters disbanded after one month, even though they had all roomed at camp together the previous summer. Young people would need more than a few weeks of camp to surmount deeply embedded racial attitudes, and black girls could only do so much to eradicate racism.

A CAMP OF THEIR OWN

The Chicago Commons camps, and other experiments in interracial friendship, could not accommodate all the black girls who hoped to go to camp. So Chicago Camp Fire focused their energies on establishing their own camps. Camp Fire sponsors discussed dormitories for Sunset Hills, near the Illinois and Missouri border, as early as a November 1940 meeting. In 1944 the Camp Fire revue "Sentimental Moods" was dedicated to a building fund for more dorms at Sunset Hills. In the fall of 1947 the Oececa Girls finally got the news that they had waited decades to hear. National Association of Negro Musicians member Annette B. White donated twenty-five lots of land in Idlewild, Michigan, in the northwestern section of the state's Lower Peninsula, to the girls to establish a camp.[68] Idlewild, known as Michigan's Black Eden, was the Midwest's most welcoming vacation spot for African Americans.[69] Gaines, and other members of the Idlewild Lot Owners Association, had tried to establish some form of children's camp at Idlewild for years, with little success. The property was appraised at $20,000, and it was a major donation to the group, considering the barriers to African American camping. The gift was made as a tribute to White's sister, Fannie Henry, "a musician and one of the first sponsors of the Camp Fire Girl movement in the state."[70] White, a member of the Ida B. Wells Woman's Club, and her sister Fannie were prolific local musicians; White often performed at society luncheons and garden parties.[71] White's musical activities also helped raise funds for the "race Kiddies under the care of the Illinois Children's Home and Aid Society."[72]

Oececa's board then moved to raise $5,000 to supply the camp with buildings. In the fall, the Oececa honored White with an "autumn soiree" to raise funds to pay for cabins on the donated land.[73] White's allocation to the Oececa Girls was an important moment for those who worked for African American girls in the late 1940s. White was a representative race woman, and her ability to donate a significant amount of land to the organization represented some of the gains in the clout and financial status of African American women in the North. The Oececa Girls celebrated and enjoyed their new camp facilities in Idlewild, and the Camp Fire community continued to grow.

Throughout the 1950s other Camp Fire councils accommodated more African American girls. By 1954 the new council of Tep Pwe Tanda Camp

Fire Girls was established and participated in a "spring vacation tour" of the *Defender*'s offices.[74] The following year, perhaps prompted by a national call to recruit more members, Chicago councils began a membership drive. In 1956 a new council named the We-Ce-Ko-Co formed to organize girls in the far South Side.[75] In 1958 a young girls' group named the Bluebirds met at Bronzeville's Wentworth Gardens public housing community.[76] Eventually, in the 1960s, Camp Fire nationally took a clear stance on integration, and the councils worked to ensure that campsites were open to all Camp Fire Girls regardless of race.

DELINQUENT GIRLS AND CITIZENSHIP

Black Camp Fire Girls, Girl Scouts, and campers at settlement house programs were the race's best representatives, but they were not the only representations of black girls that circulated in Migration Chicago. This section focuses on the research about the girls and teenage women who appeared in sociological studies of the problems of ghettoization and who were talked about by court officers and teachers. These girls and women would have never been sent to camp at Idlewild or with Chicago Commons girls. Their choices—to pursue boyfriends, drink alcohol, have premarital sex, expose abuse in their homes, and refuse forced marriage proposals—made the case for camping programs and settlement house activities. Camping and recreational advocates pointed to these girls as proof of what happens when girls are not adequately saved from the city. These girls' social conditions and stories exacerbated black and white adults' shared anxieties about the negative impacts of urbanization. Although these girls did not elevate the case for black moral fitness or preparation for the responsibilities of society, their perspectives and insights regarding Chicago indicate that they held their own visions relating to their rights as citizens and the limits of citizenship in Chicago.

One of the most important studies on girls and Great Migration delinquency was Frazier's *The Negro Family in Chicago*, published in 1932. Frazier used his interviews with teenage mothers participating in a special school program to prove his ideas about the crisis of fathers and family in Chicago. Frazier argued that the problems of African Americans in the city were rooted in the dissolution of close, black family life after migration.[77] In the nearly seventy years spanning Emancipation to his writing of *Negro Family*, Frazier declared, "nearly all that the Negro had achieved in the way of stable and organized family life went to pieces."[78] Frazier believed that black families did not easily adjust to life in the North and that blacks were in the middle of a long readjustment period, which would require social and community resources in order to reach equilibrium. He pointed to the degradation of fathers' influence as a key element in why juvenile delinquency, poverty, and stagnation had taken over Chicago's "zones," his terminology for the parts of the Black Belt he studied. "The widespread family disorganization among Negroes has resulted from the failure of the father to play the role in family life required by American society." Frazier advocated for a "society, which will enable the Negro father to play the role."[79] The society Frazier imagined would ultimately require greater economic resources to be allocated for black men, women to abdicate the authority they gained from wage earning, and parents to exercise greater control over their children.[80] This expansive study yielded his controversial theories of black familial disorganization and the disintegration of patriarchal homes during the Migration and served as the basis of his ideas on black matriarchy.[81]

Frazier and his research team asked the teenage mothers questions about their religious, social, and sexual lives, and their responses were consolidated into a few passages in his published text. Frazier made clear the importance of girls' sexual choices in evaluating their family and community worth. Frazier deemed middle-class black girls more socially stable because they upheld mandates against premarital sex more than working-class and poor girls, who were deemed bad and disordered. Although he never used the word "citizen" to refer to black girls, he did prove his arguments about the problems black girls faced by highlighting their appearances before the Juvenile Court, profiling a teenage girl arrested for murder, their admission to the maternity ward at the Cook County Hospital, and the appeal for services for the indigent. Frazier's framing of how girls interacted with Chicago's institutions suggested that they too were representing their race's worst citizens.

Frazier's study concluded that the girls he interviewed reflected a loss in black sexual morality and that their pregnant bodies epitomized black personal and community failure, but the content of their interviews suggests a diversity of thoughtful and nuanced perspectives on the city and their role as citizens. Within the extant archive of *Negro Family* are fuller narratives on girls and Great Migration Chicago that provide greater depth of insight into how girls understood their lives. When one examines the original transcripts of the girls' interviews, differentiating this mass of girls labeled "bad citizens," it becomes clear that black migrant girls fit themselves into their own moral schema. Frazier's transcripts, paired with the teenage girls' assignments at the school, provide a window into the feelings Migration engendered, the dangers that followed girls around the city, and the way the most maligned girls fortified their sense of self.

I also include the testimonies of teenagers in sociologist Ernest W. Burgess's study of South Chicago, a predominately Mexican section of the city ten miles south of downtown. Burgess's study included stories of girls who experienced sexual exploitation, unplanned pregnancy, and jealousy among peers.[82] Frazier's and Burgess's interviews encompass girls' Great Migration stories from the late 1920s into the 1940s. These interviews, taken as a whole, reveal that this group of migrant girls held their own ideas about citizenship. They asserted their right to be protected, forgiven, and cared for in their families, schools, and communities. Despite the problems they faced with their pregnancies or their lack of education, they believed that migrating was their best option for improving their lives. When parents, social workers, and friends failed them, they felt entitled to their anger, disappointment, and search for alternative means to get their needs met.

The consistent themes throughout the interviews include disillusionment and disappointment about migration, especially with Chicago's working conditions and slums. After discussing how girls presented their frustrations with the city's color line and nefarious employment practices, I discuss girls' sexual experiences. Some girls held their communities responsible for not adequately educating them about sex, shielding them from abuse and violence, or simply misunderstanding their views on sexual morality. Although these girls were never brought into the spheres of race representatives, they acknowledged their own value and sense of purpose without the help of a Camp Fire guidebook or an invitation to a spring formal.

"I SAW TOO MUCH DOWN THERE"

When some girls migrated with their families to Chicago, they could not imagine the urban landscape they would call home. Descriptive stories in the *Defender* and exaggerated accounts from family members who had returned home to tell tales of the big city could not fully capture what the city was like. Adjectives could not do justice to the height of the Loop skyscrapers, the smell of the Armour stockyards, or the spectacular scenes of fashionably attired patrons at Chicago's most elegant theatres to an excited southern girl. Nor did some girls believe the warnings and alarms about how tough city life could be despite higher wages and longer school terms. In Frazier's many interviews with teenage women who migrated as little girls is a sense that Chicago had let them down. The city was not as pristine, racially open, or charitable as they had hoped. Their responses to interviews made clear to whoever was listening that they had had expectations for the city that were not met. "I don't think Chicago is so progressive," remarked one girl. "It is on the decrease. I just heard wonders of Chicago but things have certainly changed here."[83] The girl may have absorbed more of the economic and social realities of the city rather than measured any real change.

A fifteen-year-old from West Point, Georgia, who had arrived in Chicago prepared to fall in love with her adopted city, expressed only regret about migration. "I am very sorry that I came to Chicago. I saw too much—the elevated—everything. Some things I had never seen before." She believed Chicago changed her and wondered if she could ever return to the South. She also believed that she had been betrayed because the promises of better jobs and working conditions did not materialize. She had avoided working for white people in the South, and found in Chicago a tragic irony: in a more racially equitable city, she was abused at work. "My mother wouldn't even let me work for any white people there. I know the first white woman I worked for here. I never will forget, because she worked me most nigh to death and didn't pay me anything."[84]

A migrant from downstate Illinois was shocked by her experiences working at the Pompei Hotel, a known location for solicitation. Desperate to support herself after her husband deserted her, the woman soon discovered the hotel was "not a fit place" for girls and young women. A fellow maid was actually a prostitute and "would drink with [guests] and do anything else, while she worked. She was also alarmed by the stream of teen girls soliciting at the Pompei. "Girls from 15, 16, and 18 come up there with those men and lay around with them. I told the boss it was terrible. And the language they use is terrible."[85]

In these and other stories, girls levied a strong critique against their families for bringing them north, as well as against employers for tricking them into working at prostitution dens, lying about wages, and mistreating them. Although they were upset by these conditions, it is revelatory that they knew they could—and should—expect better from people in positions of authority. In light of the triple binds of sex, race, and age, migrant girls knew that injustice was intolerable and unacceptable. If these girls were not necessarily involved in the citizenship courses or the patriotic displays that circulated in Camp Fire or Girl Scouts, how did they develop a sense of these expectations? The experience of Migration, and the articulation of its possibilities, remained deeply with these girls. The hopes of a better life in the North not only fueled their optimism, but it reshaped their ideas about what life could be, and they were able to voice the sources and consequences of the shortcomings of their experience.

JAZZING WITH BOYS

After struggles to find decent employment and good wages, romantic and sexual relationships with boys and men shaped a number of girls' Migration experience. Frazier asserted that migrant girls' sexual choices were animated by "precociousness" and their "knowledge of sexual matters and other forms of vice" were acted out in "the demoralized behavior that was characteristic of" the Black Belt girl and her family, "who defined sex for her." In his collection of life stories of "youthful mothers," Frazier concluded, the girls demonstrated "stimulation of an interest in sex at an early age." He added: "In some cases their first experience as unmarried mothers was a prelude to the more sophisticated modes of behavior that were common in this area." This characterization represented some of the stories he collected, but their sexual experiences also revealed different states of mind—naivete, curiosity, loneliness, and ignorance.

Sixteen-year-old Sandy Allen did not know why she chose to have sex with a boyfriend, admitting she was not very interested in sex; rather, she wanted to keep up with her friends. The interviewer asked her if she enjoyed her first sexual experience; she replied: "I don't know." She was then asked if she had "learned to enjoy" sex, and said, "I don't know." But she continued to have intercourse because "the rest of the girls" enjoyed it.[86] Sandy's sexual choices were as much about her role in her social group of friends as in her actual romantic relationships. For migrant girls who may have been disconnected from their peers in the South due to their domestic work schedules and inability to socialize at school and public events, northern friendships were especially fulfilling and exciting. Girls developed camaraderie, as well as competition, with each other, and these new peer groups became nearly as important as families in helping them establish a sense of belonging.

The teenage mothers interviewed recognized that their unplanned pregnancies relegated them to the margins of their communities. They agreed with Frazier that their community and parents had failed them in many ways, but the girls believed that the failures were avoidable, and they expressed their dissatisfaction with not being taken seriously or properly educated on sex. Girls attributed their unplanned pregnancies to a lack of sexual knowledge, coercion, and pressure from peers. Knowing that community members—and perhaps the interviewers and social workers at their school—judged their parents because of their pregnancies, some girls defended their mothers against claims of bad parenting. One girl praised her mother for trying to supervise her daughters from what she saw as a predatory city. The girl said that she "always went to dances at home [in the South] but I would have to have a chaperone . . . I can hardly get out anywhere." Her mother vetted every acquaintance. "Mamma's got to know the people, you see, and if she hear anything about their parents, she won't let me around with those girls . . . So now I hardly have but two or three girl friends . . . My mother is very strict with me." The girl's mother also mistrusted their neighbors and required her to stay in her apartment. "Last night the people on the first floor were out in the sun parlor playing cards and Mamma thought it was awful. She thinks Chicago awful. All men will try to get fly with you, but I know what to say to them. Mama always wants me to hurry home before night.[87] Caroline Leakes assumed full responsibility for her pregnancy. "My mother's advice stayed long in remembrance with me. She told me everything a girl should know about boys and what I should know. It wasn't my mother's fault because I was taught . . . right." In Caroline's defense of her mother, she also revealed a common experience among the teenage mothers when she said that she had sex with a boyfriend because "I was some what afraid of him."[88]

Coercive sex and sexual abuse were common stories among girls, and in these cases they indicted families and communities for not warning them about sexual assault and manipulation. Belinda Matthews was fifteen years old when she met a boy at a local candy store. The boy promised Belinda a ring if she followed him into the basement of a building. She initially refused, but she admitted that her curiosity had led her to comply and she had sex with him. When the interviewer pressed her to talk more about her sexual experience, she hesitated. "Why don't you want to talk?" She replied simply, "Because I don't want to tell you . . . cause it ain't nice to tell what happened." When the interviewer asked if the boy had forced her to have sex she said no, but revealed she had not wanted to have intercourse and had not enjoyed it. Their sexual relationship continued, although she admitted that she never enjoyed sex with him. The boy claimed to love Belinda; but she only liked him. When she discovered she was pregnant, their families did not force them to marry; she admitted that she was relieved because after delivering her baby, the child died.[89]

Frazier concluded that pregnant girls "in the urban environment" did not choose marriage because the North held no "folkways" or community expectation of it. He acknowledged that girls were sometimes subject to "the formal control exercised by the courts and the social agencies" and then got married. Although some girls did not see the necessity in getting married, it did not mean that they did not value their relationships, did not grapple with being forced to marry men significantly older than them, or did not have reasons to believe that the institution did not guarantee happiness. Girls suffered abuse from their stepfathers, watched their parents' marriages disintegrate under the weight of Migration-induced stress, and realized that adults sometimes shirked their family responsibilities. One fourteen-year-old mother told Frazier of mixed feelings about a court-mandated marriage to the father of her child. "We were married the same day after school . . . Did I do right?"[90]

Negro Family's researchers collected disturbing accounts of girls sexually victimized by newly acquired stepfathers and teenagers exposed to prostitution in their neighborhoods. One of his informants, a fourteen-year-old mother, remarked on having "learned too much down there," referring to her cousin's neighborhood where solicitation was common. In the city, women could easily meet and socialize with young men at beer gardens, dance halls, even on the street, without scrutiny or permission from elders.[91] Frazier blamed the absence of small communities and their accompanying moral standards for courtship and marriage, as well as inadequate parental supervision, for the premarital sexual relationships among youth. Yet he did not discuss the abuse that originated in homes. Although the newspapers reported on rape and molestation cases regularly in terms of perpetrators within communities, it is apparent from the reports of the Court of Domestic Relations, black girls often suffered from sexual abuse within the home as well.

Seventeen-year-old Rhonda Martins's stepfather was incarcerated for raping her. This Georgia migrant and live-in domestic was the mother of two children; her stepfather fathered one child, and her sexual abuse was a source of shame and ostracism. Rhonda recounted that her stepfather had raped her in retaliation for exposing his stealing from her mother. "He would take things away from our house and give them to his sisters." She described the assault in graphic detail: "I was downstairs and so I went up stairs to dress for the afternoon. He was shaving and said, "Oh yes, you little devil, you told your mother on me didn't you? I said yes, because I had heard the plot in the kitchen and I was certainly going to tell mother. So that was the time he did it. Well, I hate to tell you, it was that bad. He almost broke my neck, got me between his two knees and pushed me up against the wall."

After the attack, he fled to his sisters' house, and the girl reported the crime to the police. Rhonda placed the baby for adoption in an Indianapolis orphanage after telling her mother she would "feel ashamed to take it around." A couple years later, Rhonda met Morris, a local boy, who promised that he wanted to marry her. They began a sexual relationship soon after meeting. Her mother had an "awful dream" that Rhonda was pregnant, and the girl shortly discovered that her mother's dream was indeed a premonition. The short-lived romance, which Rhonda estimated had led to only three or four instances of "relations," ended with Rhonda's regret over meeting Morris. Their baby was in the care of a neighborhood family, who threatened to place the boy in an orphanage if the couple failed to pay for its board. When asked what she dreamed about, Rhonda responded: "Not much." "I have nothing to dream about now only trouble and disgrace." Her feelings of disgrace led her to leave her "brick front" church. She focused her attention on her new goal of becoming a stage dancer, secure in the knowledge that performing was not a sin, because it was a "benefit" to her. Rhonda was shamed by the social services system that sought to reform and repair girls like her. "The probation officer, she never says anything but the worse about me. When she took me to the court, she said: This is Rhonda Martins and this is her baby and she has had intercourse with her stepfather and he is now in the penn. She kept on saying second baby."[92]

Sometimes courts responded favorably to girls, arresting abusers and removing children from homes. One case of a mixed-race girl revealed how racial identity shaped the way people perceived the problems within homes. Greta and Nella, two girls, appeared before the courts due to the abuse they had suffered at the hands of their Swedish father. The father was accused of raping his daughter and stepdaughter, but when the girls were questioned in court they said he "treated them all right." Convinced the girls misunderstood the questions presented by the prosecution, the courts remained vigilant, investigating the family as they moved frequently around the city in order "to lose their contact with the court." The girls' mother believed that the allegations against her husband were rooted in community members' jealousy over her interracial marriage. Eventually, the court used evidence from a medical examination to prosecute the man, whose first lawyer abandoned his client because he was "too obviously guilty."[93]

These and other stories in Frazier's reports provide counterarguments to his claims that families in the South were inherently more stable and less disorganized. Sexual abuse from fathers and stepfathers was a recurring issue for girls, and the North may have only added their exposure to more abusers in the form of male roomers. Families took in roomers to make ends meet, and the presence of more men around them did not reduce their vulnerability to abuse from a parent.

Frazier's suggestion that girls refused to marry because migrant communities did not demand that from their daughters also ignores girls' own reasons for resisting marrying their boyfriends. In some cases, like Rhonda's, boyfriends denied paternity, and their parents encouraged them to do so. When Rhonda sought Morris's parents to discuss her pregnancy, they accused the women of being after the family's wealth. Morris avoided the Martins women's request to meet with his mother, and Rhonda's mother appealed to the courts to try to adjudicate the issue. Morris and his mother claimed that he was "abnormal" and unable to complete school past the sixth grade. The court ruled in his favor."[94]

Having a child out of wedlock did not necessarily mean a girl had no marriage prospects. Nineteen-year-old Harriet Crane had been surprised that her husband, Harpo, had wanted to marry her. She had already had a child at sixteen, and she met him when he rented a room at her mother's house. She swore that she did not "have intercourse . . . in the house," with the boarder but said that they did have premarital sex. "I didn't think he would marry me, but he said his sister had one and that she wasn't married. So, we married."[95]

The girls in the study, perhaps the ones Frazier found most precocious, did not place great value on monogamy, and they understood dating as a crucial social activity in and of itself. One girl explained: "I have a beau. You know how it is . . . You have about two or three. But you have a main one to fall back on you know." The teenage girl could not openly spend time with her boyfriends or fellow girlfriends because her mother was highly distrustful of Chicago teens.[96] Charlene McCourt, who enjoyed the Savoy and Warwick Hall, balanced "four or five" beaus. Despite the relationships, she claimed that she had never been in love. "No there is no such thing as love. I have liked them real hard. Love ain't nothing, just a lot of worry. I once thought I was in love but I changed my mind." She claimed that she never enjoyed sex and considered abstaining from sex because of a diagnosis of "bad blood," most likely syphilis. "I don't think it [premarital sex] is right. It isn't right to have it until you get married. I realize now how bad it is."[97]

Charlene also held a negative opinion of black people in her community. "You know how your people are. That's the reason the white people don't want them in the rich neighborhoods, because they get drunk and lay out and around in the streets." Migrant girls were clearly not immune to the castigating opinions of racial uplifters, and in their criticisms they indicate that they were better or more adjusted than their neighbors and community. In seeing themselves as separate, or different from, those around them, these girls insulated themselves from the judgments and criticisms of others.

In Burgess's study of South Chicago teens, boys and girls described their communities in similar ways when discussing the sexual culture of their neighborhood. South Chicago girls and teenage women could depend on few community and recreational resources to engage their interests, but boys, dance parties, and alcohol were in regular supply for girls seeking excitement after school or while their parents were away at work. Girls sometimes exchanged sex for money with a regular partner, and one informant believed that these girls did not consider themselves involved in prostitution but merely enxjoying one of the benefits of a sexual relationship. A Mississippi migrant teen talked about the common practice of eschewing monogamy for multiple boyfriends. "Ain't none of the young girls start out hustlin' hardly, but they all 'jazz' with the boys, they is too green to get money for it, even when they has men."[98] The boy added: "All the kids I knows about out here drink whiskey and I don't know any girls out here that don't go around with boys, all those over fourteen do anyhow." He blamed parents for their girls' sexual activity and in his accusation he makes a tacit plea for black childhood; he told the researcher, "when you are fourteen or fifteen these people out here thinks their kids are half grown and so they can run around."[99]

The distinctions that teenagers in South Chicago made among their sexual practices reflected the overlapping and enmeshed systems that shaped the ways urban youth perceived their sexual and economic autonomy in the city. In her study on New York in the first half of the twentieth century, Elizabeth Ann Clement untangles the way young people understood "prostitution, treating, and courtship," which she categorized as "distinct practices," though the same individual may have engaged in all these categories of activity.[100]

"I JUST AIN'T HAD NO BODY TO RAISE ME"

Frazier castigated black families for not controlling their daughters as they would have in the South, and girls concurred that their parents changed when they arrived in Chicago. While Frazier's research, again, was a way for him to argue against migration, girls' revelations of their parents' shortcomings was their way of suggesting that they deserved more than the larger society was offering them. Teenage girls were especially sensitive about feelings of alienation when their pregnancies became public. May Ellen Brown articulated becoming isolated after she became pregnant, and despite feeling that she was competent and smart, community members regularly degraded her. May Ellen migrated to Chicago via Tennessee, and mourned her father, who was murdered when she was fourteen years old.

Her mother was indifferent to her children and sometimes threatened them:

> Papa raised seven children, you see, my mother left him when we was all real young and she came up here. She even left my sister who was only six months old. Well, a man cut my father with a four pound knife over some moonshine . . . They was at a party . . . and he cut my father's heart right in two. He died right away. My two youngest sisters stays over there with my mother but she says sometimes she feels like throwing them in the lake. My stepfather is nice sometimes and sly sometimes.

May Ellen missed her father, who used to praise her intelligence. Neighbors and family members made her feel badly about her pregnancy: "My father used to be on me cause I was so smart for my age. That's why I don't pay no attention to what people said. I just only got fooled once and that's all. I just ain't had no body to raise me. You see people said that I was so smart, but after this trouble . . . they have all turned me down." Rumors and gossip dominated her decision to leave the South, after boarding in a teacher's home. The woman accused her of sleeping with her husband, which the girl vehemently denied, and she named the father of her baby, a twenty-year-old classmate at her high school:

> Some others said that the baby was a white man's—that was before it was even born. But I didn't fool with no white man at all, cause those white folks don't care nothing bout no colored down there. Those people sho talk a heap. This schoolteacher's sister-in-law come over to my house last week and she said she didn't believe it. You know this teacher is trying to bring this up in court. I told her if she want to be out $25.00 she could take my baby and her husband down to the doctor and have a blood test, and then she could see for herself.

The stress of the lies affected her health. "And some days . . . I don't even put a piece of bread in my mouth or drink a glass of water. I go to eat and git so filled up thinking over things, I just can't eat."[101]

A South Chicago man reported that parents forced girls into perilous situations not because of changes in the North but because of a continuity in life choices: "Girls around seventeen and eighteen working in those houses [of prostitution], some of them work in houses run by their own mothers." Raising the possibility that South Chicago prostitutes from the

South had done sex work long before they migrated and merely continued their line of work in Chicago, he concluded: "They don't know better, they think that it is all there is for women to do."[102]

May Ellen's lament that she "had no body to raise me" was shared by a number of migrant youth, who questioned the authority and ability of their parents. Frazier believed that families could not provide adequate supervision to their girls, and some girls agreed. Yet they did not just critique their parents in their answers; they also intimated that they had a strong notion of what families are supposed to do. While Frazier saw parental failure as being internalized by girls and marked on their bodies, these young people actually agreed with Frazier, and they longed for better, stronger parents and communities. They also imagined themselves as capable of resisting their parents' negative models and being better citizens in the future. They criticized their parents' permissiveness and criminal activity and their community's inability to intercede. Some informants may have used the interviews to resist the sociologists' stereotypes of lower-class migrant communities, but others may have seen the exchanges as an opportunity to distance themselves from the worst conditions in the Black Belt and South Chicago.

"AND I AM SURE THAT I DON'T WANT TO GO THERE"

When parents could not or did not step in to protect them, girls asked for assistance from Chicago's various institutions, hoping that they could be of service to them. Girls received an array of responses to their problems—from indifference to sympathy. The girls in Frazier's study demonstrated their knowledge of Chicago's various institutions in the process of sharing their narratives. They used public schools, Urban League social programs, and health clinics. In using these community resources, they were also exercising their rights to the city's institutions. These girls did not navigate these spaces naively, and they made choices about the extent to which they wanted outsiders involved with their personal lives.

For teen girls afraid of being shunned for their pregnancies, the city's maternity homes offered a discreet place for them to hide from communities and families. While inside the homes, they endured reprisals for their pregnancies and disciplinary interventions to prevent them from another unwed pregnancy. One girl, who claimed to have become sexually active only ten weeks prior to being interviewed at the Urban League, expressed fear of such a home. "The only thing I am afraid of that is going to a home to stay until I am 21 years old. And I am sure that I don't want to go there. That is if I can keep from it. And I hope the good lord that I won't have to go." She revealed her sadness about being sent to a special school, and she feared surviving childbirth. "And I hope when I have my baby it won't kill me as the people said it will." Her fear of motherhood was compounded by a fear of greater alienation from her family. "Oh . . . I am sorry of my condition as I said before. Because, it has make all of my people forget that they are my people and they are the only people I have and know any . . . about."[103]

Teen wives sometimes reported to the Domestic Relations Court that their married life was filled with disappointments, including abandonment and infidelity. Thelma Marsh Bates, a seventeen-year-old from New Orleans, lamented that her husband, Grey, brought his mistress to their room in a boardinghouse when he thought his wife was away. Though the young woman was not happy to find his husband's other woman in her room, she reported being unable to confront the pair because "she had a knife."[104]

The delinquency case of fifteen-year-old Ellen Minter was an example of the way girls' victimization could turn into criminalization and how the Juvenile Court failed girls. City truancy officers investigated a claim of bastardy stemming from Minter's sexual relationship with a man ten years her senior.[105] Minter graduated from the local elementary school in 1934 but did not participate in commencement exercises because she was pregnant. Her social exclusion did not end when she eventually married the father of her child, per the order of a court.[106]

A South Chicago truant officer was equally frustrated with her colleagues on a local police force for not intervening in Minter's and the case of a twelve-year-old-girl who was sexually assaulted in her home. "The girl's mother was a prostitute, the police knew about her. The girl should have been taken away from her and put in a decent home." The truant officer was "simply furious" when the girl was arrested and put in a patrol car. He acknowledged that race was a factor in the police's decision. "They wouldn't have dared do that in any other type of neighborhood. They knew they could get away with that rough stuff over there. Someone should have reported the arresting officers."[107]

Frazier's research fueled debates about black families, urbanization, gender, and patriarchy for decades after the publication of *The Negro Family in Chicago*. His summary of the interviews with girls shaped the way social scientists, politicians, and historians viewed the Great Migration. By looking beyond the material Frazier included in his study and delving into the complex stories these girls told, we gain a multifaceted perspective on girls who were all too often deemed bad citizens. As teen mothers, recipients of public assistance, and girls open about their sexuality, they were rarely applauded or recognized for more than their choices. Black girls' articulation of their abuse and their clarity in identifying the failed systems around them called attention to the gender dynamics, social barriers, and inequalities in the city. Although Frazier's subjects did not exist in the same social or ideological spaces as the model girl citizens of the Minute Girls or the Oececa Camp Fire council, the interviewees still had an understanding that their expectations and experiences were valuable.

CONCLUSION

Camp Fire Girls, a creation of the Progressive Era, was a national girls' organization devoted to training girls for the modern era by connecting them to a mythical pioneer past when settler women and girls tended the communal campfire and used nature's resources to maintain their family's well-being. Although Camp Fire did not wholeheartedly embrace African American participation, black women in Chicago successfully brought Camp Fire to black girls. These Camp Fire leaders redefined the organization's mission and practices to conform to their vision of what black girls needed and to circumvent the reality of segregation in recreational facilities and programs. When civic-minded girls arrived at children's hospitals to distribute toys during the holidays, wore carefully stitched badges on their uniform sashes, or posed for pictures for the *Defender*, they symbolized the best of African American parents and communities.

Of all the issues facing black migrant girls, why did camping emerge as a high priority for black community leaders? Camping is not as essential as safe housing or as aspirational as college attendance and subsequent entry into professional life, yet access to recreational opportunities was not simply a matter of playing games or sharing a tent with a friend. African American girls' ability to participate equally in an ever-growing series of experiences that were deemed quintessentially part of American childhood was proof that racial equality and equal opportunity could perhaps be achieved and could bolster belief in and action on behalf of the fundamental innocence of black girls.

As the Migration entered its third decade, girls expressed their frustrations with the racism that kept their schools poor and with communities devoid of resources like safe parks and swimming pools. Research on Migration girls' experiences uncovered girls' criticism of their parents' inability to adapt to city life and their families' clinging to "back home" ways. These girls suffered from the aftershocks of the Great Depression, navigated generational tensions, and spoke of disappointment with a lack of substantive opportunities awaiting them after they completed school. Black leaders feared that these factors engendered a restlessness and rebelliousness among girls, and they hoped that Camp Fire Girls, camping trips, and youth clubs could suppress these emotions and channel girls away from sex and crime.

Black Camp Fire advocates gained community support and strengthened their movement by soothing anxieties about black girls and juvenile delinquency as Chicago's Black Belt widened geographically and its bleak housing and poverty conditions reduced girls' opportunities and personal safety. Camping advocates also believed that black girls deserved to experience, on equal grounds, the cherished youthful activities available to white girls. Outdoor culture, in the eyes of its proponents, could provide the discipline and opportunity that families, especially fathers, did not or could not provide their daughters. Black women also supported camping initiatives through black women's clubs. In addition, settlement houses and community trusts selected black girls to participate in camping programs with the explicit goal of forging interracial friendship and connections.

Meanwhile, scores of other girls, who did not fit the image of the ideal girl citizen, were also making claims to belonging in the city. Among the archived interviews with teenage girls about their Migration experiences are consistent themes that reveal how they constructed a sense of self in the face of family problems, betrayals, and disappointment. Frazier and Burgess uncovered disillusionment with Chicago's promises, conflicts with authority, and confusion about sex and love. The majority of the interviews include serious grievances against family and community, but the girls acknowledged the aspects of city life they cherished, from dancing at the Savoy Ballroom to friendships with other girls at school.

While representative race girls made a case for black equality, these girls at the margins undermined respectability politics and played no visible role in the politics of play. They made claims for their own belonging in Chicago, redefined what a citizen could be by acting on their desires and defenses, and contributed in significant ways to urban scholarship through their candor. Social scientists recorded their experiences and used them to devise theories about black families and urbanization; these studies were sometimes the basis of racialized social policy and could contribute to further stereotyping of black people. Yet the consequences of the ways these studies led these girls' experiences to be interpreted should not foreclose on recognizing the value of these studies' preservation of these girls' perspectives on the Migration. All of these confessions and contestations alert us to black girls' sense of their own rights to experience autonomy, to receive loving guidance, and to assume, ultimately, that their citizenship mattered.

· CONCLUSION ·

"SHE WAS FIGHTING FOR HER FATHER'S FREEDOM"

Black Girls after the Great Migration

In May 1960, Chicago's West Woodlawn Woman's Club and local AKA chapters presented a $1,300 gift to Daisy Bates, the civil rights activist who represented the first nine African American students who integrated Little Rock Central High School. Bates, a former Arkansas state president of the NAACP, recounted to five hundred Chicagoans the desegregation battle waged nearly three years earlier. Images of mobs of segregationists, frightened black children, and, eventually, National Guardsmen accompanying the students to school riveted the world.[1] At the close of that fateful 1957–1958 school year, the city's leaders had closed all public schools in an attempt to circumvent further school desegregation.[2] While some white students attended private schools and others enrolled at newly opened "segregation academies," many black students were left without access to public schools. Three black girls from Little Rock suddenly found themselves migrants to Chicago after their local high school closed. The girls enrolled in Wendell Phillips High School. Chicagoans raised money to pay for the girls' nonresident tuition of nearly $1,500.

Bates also shared an anecdote that illustrated the conditions of black girls' lives in the South as the First Great Migration moved into its final decade and school integration battles were propelling a new generation of southern black girls to ponder their futures. A teenaged girl approached Bates about enrolling at Central High, but her father stopped her because he "feared retaliation on his job." Bates argued that the father's decision was wrongheaded; the girl had already been active in local demonstrations, and she was simply trying to make a difference. The man failed to see that "she was fighting for her father's freedom." She continued: "Children are tired of the fear and slavery of their parents."[3]

Bates's story about the girl's frustration mirrors some of the feelings of the teenage girl from Louisiana mentioned in the introduction who wrote to the *Chicago Defender* for help more than forty years earlier. Both girls questioned their fathers' resignation to the ways of the Jim Crow South. Both girls longed to shape their own destiny. Both girls looked outside their families' confines to search for opportunities in an era of rapid changes for black people. Despite the similar conflicts these girls shared across time, African American girls' lives had changed dramatically from the days following Abbott's announcement of the Great Northern Migration Day in both the North and the South. Yet the lingering questions about black girls and girlhood as symbols of black progress would remain at the surface of the next, transformative period in African American life and culture: the civil rights movement.[4]

Bates's battle in Little Rock and her continued encouragement of girls to take part in the movement contributed to Glenda Gilmore's argument that the Supreme Court's 1954 *Brown* decision placed the "weight of Jim Crow's destruction" on the "backs of schoolchildren."[5] Yet when we take a wider view of how black girls interacted with the dynamic changes of Migration-era Chicago, we realize just how long girls had been carrying similar "weight" for black communities. From the early awakenings of the Great Migration, black girls, and the idea of black girlhood, were powerful forces of agitation for change. Before a family packed a cardboard suitcase with their prized possessions or packed a shoebox with southern fare for a train ride up North, black girls' working conditions and lack of educational opportunities in the South concerned black families. With few legal mechanisms in place to take their sexual victimization seriously, and with their crucial contributions to the financial welfare of their families, the Migration provided a hopeful avenue in which to protect them. When families arrived in Chicago, they could believe that it was possible for their daughter to escape domestic service, feel safe at work, and for the first time enjoy being a child.

The realities of Chicago did not come close to meeting the expectations. Chicago's most vulnerable girls—the destitute, dependent, and delinquent—realized that Jim Crow had also boarded the train and followed them everywhere. The segregation of children's facilities, the lack of trust in black leaders by white philanthropists, and an inability to find suitable homes for black girls who most needed them shaped early Migration social services. Black women who assumed leadership of the Amanda Smith Industrial School for Colored Girls, and similar institutions that followed, found themselves crafting precarious arguments about the value of girls to the larger community. Black women pled that black girls were innocent and worthy of protection and benevolence, while also grounding their value in their usefulness to adults. By centering race motherhood as the favorable outcome in investing in girls, leaders did not create a concrete vision of black girlhood. Rather, they tied black girls' care to the needs of the race. In doing so, black women leaders were expressing notions consistent with the era's maternalist politics. This rhetorical strategy of focusing on future mothers of the race was not exclusive to black communities. However black women envisioned black girlhood, it did not provide for a true child status, and it did not address the racialized, sexual stereotyping girls encountered in integrated spaces.

As the Migration era progressed, black intellectual, literary, and political figures also emerged to engage with how migrants understood their new, urban identities. Girls were no different. In examining how girls interacted with religions and popular culture, we are given a broader look into the ways consumer culture provided black girls with the experience of choice, pleasure, and rebellion. Black girls' uses of clothes, makeup, and social spaces illustrated how much Migration changed family dynamics and relationships. Although girls worked to help support their families, the Migration transformed them into shoppers and, more important, choosers. Girls could choose styles of dress and adornment, as well as social groups and leisure activities, in unprecedented ways. They knew their choices could disrupt family dynamics, but the goods and experiences found in Chicago's commercial districts were too exhilarating to ignore. Similarly, the array of religious communities that emerged from the Migration served to fracture some families, transforming once steady and devout people into occasional churchgoers, wanderers, or perpetual visitors to new churches. In hearing girls' experiences of mainline churches, New Negro–inspired religious movements, and storefront churches, we understand how gender and age formed these emerging movements.

The Moorish Science Temple's early history also provides a vehicle for understanding how girlhood as a symbolic state, rather than an actual lived experience, operated in Migration-era Chicago. In its joining of the ideologies of New Negro thinking and the beauty enterprises that captured the attention of so many Chicagoans, the Moorish Science Temple is an example of how rhetoric about girls and girlhood could serve the purposes of gaining legitimacy, validation, and power. New Negro cults, as they were called, were judged by their ability to seemingly resist the dominant culture through its control of girls and teenage women's expressive culture. In its position as different from other religious groups and impervious to the manifestations of the flapper culture, the Moorish Science Temple deployed language and regulations around black girlhood that exalted and controlled. Like its New Negro ancestor, the Garvey movement, the Moorish Science Temple engaged black women migrants directly and offered them new identities and opportunities to enjoy aspects of Migration culture. For actual girls in the Moorish Science Temple, their obedience to the doctrines and self-fashioning helped form the basis of one of the most influential black religious movements of the twentieth century: the Nation of Islam. The sex scandal that was revealed after Noble Drew Ali's death was not merely another lurid tale in the *Defender* that could discredit New Negro organizations. It represents an opportunity to consider how New Negro rhetoric coincided and collided with actual girls' lives.

The distance between rhetoric and reality is also clear in the Great Depression responses to how black girls would participate in the nation's massive economic recovery. The three varying perspectives on where girls fit after the crisis alert us to how black Chicagoans used ideas about black girls to promote political stances, situate early feminist work, and forge improved race relations. Alpha Kappa Alpha sorority women, many of whom were excluded from pursuing their own professional goals due to racism and sexism, found mutual benefit in bringing vocational guidance programs to girls. Work with girls in Chicago's public schools—which did not always fully embrace migrant girls—allowed black women to make a case for their own professional competence. It also redirected the form of racial uplift targeted to girls, urging them away from race motherhood and instead toward race leadership. AKA women's work with girls reflected the membership's exceptional status in black communities, and it projected onto girls the task to ignore racial and gender limitations in careers. AKA women were undoubtedly aware of the challenges that girls—even the most educated ones—faced in securing professional work. Their message was not just about girls, but a feminist critique of the limits they experienced themselves as professional black women.

The "Don't Buy Where You Can't Work" campaigns in Chicago's Black Belt were more realistic than the vocational guidance movement in the goals of securing clerk jobs for black teenage women. The movement wedded calls for economic justice to the concerns about girls' safety at work and their inability to escape domestic labor. Although the boycott movement's leaders admitted that work as a store clerk was not especially interesting to high school–educated teenagers, they were relying on girls to be the most acceptable race representatives in public work. The campaign organizers used girls' employment struggles to bolster their introduction of economic sanctions and commercial boycotting to Black Belt residents.

While black leaders were agitating for better jobs and professional work for black people, girls at Chicago's NYA Resident School for Girls were shaping the path that would lead to *Brown* and Little Rock Central High School. Prior to 1954, African Americans challenged school segregation and sent their children into integration fights across the country. The NYA school is an early example of an interracial program, and the black girls there highlighted the possibilities and limits of integration. Black NYA program graduates, like their peers at high schools and colleges across the country, found that their race kept them from securing jobs after graduation. Despite the good intentions and goodwill of the schoolteachers and white students, black girls soon realized that they faced public scrutiny from outside forces that did not tolerate the most modest integration. Stories of black girls engaging in interracial sex and assaults on black girls' character undermined the educational and social goals of the NYA. Black girls continued to hear narratives about their sexual impropriety and inability to be educated with whites. The decades after the NYA school closed would be no different.

Amid the difficulties black girls faced in shaping their futures as young women, a group of black leaders were committed to making a case for black childhood, and they used black participation in children's organizations to demonstrate their worthiness for play. In the Girl Scouts, the Camp Fire Girls, and the YWCA Girls Reserves, black girls could join a social group devoted to their personal growth and physical well-being. These groups were not designed with black girls in mind, but black women leaders adapted their instructions and ideas to make them relevant and accessible to black girls. One of the major challenges in providing the Camp Fire program to girls was that segregation made camping a difficult call to fulfill. Black women leaders organized to provide camping opportunities for girls in their own communities. In addition to providing a childhood experience, black girls in these organizations were also participating in a tacit appeal for black citizenship and equality. By teaching girls the importance of civic responsibility and community stewardship, black girls were playing a role in African Americans' calls for their rights as citizens. Understanding how girls participated as citizens reminds us of the multifaceted way citizenship is exercised and communicated.

Girls who were not among the fighters in the public acts of black citizenship are also significant in the ways they discussed Migration, race, and black life. Sociological studies of black girls deemed juvenile delinquents provide us with a broader frame in which to understand how black girls interpreted the various messages about change during the Migration. While black leaders and elites carefully displayed the activities of and images surrounding black girls who symbolized achievement and race progress, other girls were voicing their thoughts and realities. E. Franklin Frazier and Ernest W. Burgess's interviewees remind us that although citizens may not always be compliant, that does not mean that they do not contribute to the society they inhabit.

By the time a well-groomed fifteen-year-old named Elizabeth Eckford met a screaming crowd obstructing her legally protected path into Little Rock's Central High School, black girls had long been working on behalf of their race. The civil rights movement did not introduce black girls to the gravity of black struggle or the insults or abuse that sprang from racialized perceptions of their morality.[6] In looking at how girls lived Chicago's Great Migration, we realize the importance of black girls in shaping black activism, as well as ideas about stagnation and hope. We are also warned about ensuring that girls—not images—shape our historical inquiries, public policy, and racial discourses.

....

On January 29, 2013, fifteen-year-old Hadiya Pendleton was murdered on Chicago's South Side, a few blocks from the Hyde Park home where Michelle Obama had lived before her family's move to the White House. Chicago's South Side and West Side communities, where black migrants settled more than a century earlier, has come to represent the vitality of the Great Migration era and the viciousness of urban decline in the decades that followed its end. In 2012 Chicago logged hundreds of homicides; the majority of victims were people of color living across some of the city's most blighted South Side neighborhoods. Hadiya was an atypical victim—a teenage girl, with no criminal ties, simply enjoying a city park. Her death became national news after it was revealed that she had performed for the first family in the nation's capital a week earlier as part of the Inaugural Day parade. Hadiya's death brought Michelle Obama back to the South Side to attend the girl's funeral and deliver a speech to local business leaders. The First Lady's remarks connected Hadiya's life with her own upbringing on the South Side:

> She was 15 years old, an honor student. . . . And she came from a good family—two devoted parents, plenty of cousins, solid godparents and grandparents, and adoring little brother. The Pendletons are hardworking people. They're churchgoing folks. And Hadiya's mother did everything she could for her daughter. She enrolled her in every activity you could imagine . . . anything to keep her off the streets and keep her busy. As I visited with the Pendleton family . . . I realized . . . Hadiya's family was just like my family . . . Hadiya Pendleton was me.[7]

Obama's speech included pointed recommendations about providing youth with alternatives to violence, investing in education, and creating opportunities to gain job training. Chicago's mayor was poised to close dozens of city schools, and the city's homicide rate the previous year had ended at more than five hundred deaths, many of them a result of the type of gun violence that claimed Hadiya's life. As one South Side girl eulogized another, Michelle Obama was doing what black women before her had done—she was alerting Chicago's leadership to the need to protect black girls, and making a case for their value in a moment when their lives and their safety seemed unimportant to so many.

NOTES

INTRODUCTION. "I WILL THANK YOU ALL WITH ALL MY HEART"

1 Emmet J. Scott, "Additional Letters of Negro Migrants, 1916–18," *Journal of Negro History* 4, no. 4 (October 1919): 413.

2 Scott, "Additional Letters of Negro Migrants, 1916–18," 413.

3 Throughout this book, I use pseudonyms for girls whose stories appear in unpublished manuscripts and court records. Real names are used in the book when the name appeared in a newspaper or magazine. "What I Can Remember," E. Franklin Frazier Papers, MSRC.

4 For more on the Great Migration, see: James Grossman, *Land of Hope: Chicago, Black Southerners, and the Great Migration* (Chicago: University of Chicago Press, 1989); Nicholas Lemann, *The Promised Land: The Great Black Migration and How It Changed America* (New York: Vintage Books, 1992); Farrah Jasmine Griffin, *Who Set You Flowin'? The African-American Migration Narrative* (Oxford: Oxford University Press, 1996); Adam Green, *Selling the Race: Culture, Community, and Black Chicago, 1940–1955* (Chicago: University of Chicago Press, 2007), and Isabel Wilkerson, *The Warmth of Other Suns: The Epic Story of America's Great Migration* (New York: Random House, 2010). The majority of Great Migration scholarship focuses on northern and eastern cities, but the story of the migration to the West is also important. For more on the Migration's national implication, see Annelise Orleck, *Storming Caesar's Palace: How Black Mothers Staged Their Own War on Poverty* (Boston: Beacon Press, 2005), and Donna Jean Murch, *Living for the City: Migration, Education, and the Rise of the Black Panther Party in Oakland, California* (Chapel Hill: University of North Carolina Press, 2010).

5 Michele Mitchell captures black hopes and cautious optimism in her study of the "politics of racial destiny" after the decline of Reconstruction reforms. See Michele Mitchell, *Righteous Propagation: African Americans and the Politics*

of Racial Destiny after Reconstruction (Chapel Hill: University of North Carolina Press, 2004).

6 Joe William Trotter, "Blacks in the Urban North: The "Underclass Question in Historical Perspective," in *The Underclass Debate: Views from History*, ed. Michael B. Katz (Princeton, NJ: Princeton University Press, 1993), 68. By 1920, 1.5 million African Americans became official city dwellers, with large concentrations in the Black Belt in Chicago (182,274 people) and New York City (198,483). See Campbell Gibson and Kay Jung, *Historical Census Statistics on Population Totals by Race, 1790 to 1990, and by Hispanic Origin, 1970 to 1990, for the United States, Regions, Divisions, and States* (Washington, DC: US Census Bureau, 2006). By 1920, 83 percent of all African American Chicagoans were born outside Illinois, with 65 percent of that group hailing from southern states. See Allan H. Spear, *Black Chicago: The Making of a Negro Ghetto, 1890–1920* (Chicago: University of Chicago Press, 1967), 142–43.

7 For more on Chicago's Black Belt, see St. Clair Drake and Horace Cayton, *Black Metropolis: A Story of Negro Life in a Northern City* (Chicago: University of Chicago Press, 1962), Spear, *Black Chicago*, and Joe Allen, *People Wasn't Meant to Burn: A True Story of Housing, Race and Murder in Chicago* (Chicago: Haymarket Books, 2011).

8 James G. Gentry, a theatre reviewer for the black newspaper the *Chicago Bee*, coined the term "Bronzeville" to replace the demeaning references to the South Side, including Darkie Town or Black Belt. Bronzeville was the heart of the South Side's economic and cultural institutions during the Great Migration and the home of such institutions as Anthony Overton's Hygienic Building, the Wabash Avenue Colored YMCA, the *Chicago Defender*, and the Victory Monument. Originally bound by Thirty-First and Thirty-Ninth Streets, Bronzeville extended an additional eight blocks to Forty-Seventh Street. By the 1960s, it was the site of large-scale public housing. By the 1980s, Bronzeville suffered from mass unemployment due to the movement of factories and businesses out of the South Side to the suburbs. From the late 1990s, the area has been the target of a redevelopment effort that has included the expansion of the Illinois Institute of Technology, the rehabilitation of Bronzeville's grand mansions, and the opening of new businesses. Milwaukee's black business district was also called Bronzeville. See Michelle R. Boyd, *Jim Crow Nostalgia: Reconstructing Race in Bronzeville* (Minneapolis: University of Minnesota Press, 2008), Derek S. Hyra, *The New Urban Renewal: The Economic Transformation of Harlem and Bronzeville* (Chicago: University of Chicago Press, 2008), Robert Bone, Richard A. Courage, and Amritjit Singh, *The Muse in Bronzeville: African American Creative Expression in Chicago, 1932–1950* (New Brunswick, NJ: Rutgers University Press, 2011). Bronzeville is also the center of the landmark study of Chicago, Cayton and Drake's *Black Metropolis*.

9 The research on African Americans in suburban Chicago is sparse, but a few

historians have examined black communities in the surrounding cities of Evanston and Chicago's North Shore and Chicago's south suburbs before mass black suburbanization in the 1980s. See James Dorsey, *Up South: Blacks in Chicago's Suburbs 1719–1983* (Bristol, IN: Wyndham Hall Press, 1986), and Andrew Wiese, *Places of Their Own: African American Suburbanization in the Twentieth Century* (Chicago: University of Chicago Press, 2005).

10 Scholars from a variety of disciplines have debated the migration patterns of southern women to the North, yet there are no definitive answers to questions of whether women mostly traveled as members of families or independently. Darlene Clark Hine's Migration research suggests that in midwestern cities, "throughout the First World War era, the number of black males far exceeded female migrants." Compared to eastern and southern migration cities, the Midwest provided the most and the best jobs for men. Hine highlights that women tended to migrate directly to one location, as opposed to men, who often moved to several cities in the South and North before settling on one location. See Darlene Clark Hine, *Hine Sight: Black Women and the Re-construction of America* (Bloomington: Indiana University Press), 89.

11 Wilma King has explored African American childhoods during the Migration era. She has examined the experience of Hattie Lee Cochran, a black teenage girl in Depression-era Cleveland. See "What a Life This Is: African American Girl Comes of Age during the Great Depression in Urban America," in Wilma King, *African-American Childhoods: Historical Perspectives from Slavery to Civil Rights* (New York: Palgrave-McMillan, 2005).

12 The literature on the study of childhood and youth has engaged questions of whether childhood is a biological stage or cultural production. The history of children and childhood has been greatly influenced by Philippe Aries, *Centuries of Childhood: A Social Study of Family Life* (New York: Vintage Books, 1962). See also Steven Mintz, *Huck's Raft: A History of American Childhood* (Cambridge, MA: Harvard University Press, 2004). Mintz argues that childhood is indeed a great American myth, and he argues that class has determined which children participated in the sentimentalities of childhood. He also argues that few children were truly protected from the social, political, and economic circumstances of their parents. Karen Sanchez-Eppler, *Dependent States: The Child's Part in Nineteenth-Century American Culture* (Chicago: University of Chicago Press, 2005) uses children's literature to examine how texts impressed on children and families the notion of childhood.

13 Darlene Clark Hine, "Rape and the Inner Lives of Black Women in the Middle West," *Signs* 14, no. 4 (Summer 1989): 912.

14 Valerie Grim, "From the Yazoo Mississippi Delta to the Urban Communities of the Midwest: Conversations with Rural African-American Women," *Frontiers: A Journal of Women Studies* 22, no. 1 (2001): 133.

15 "Child Nurse Poisons Baby, Negro Girl in Alabama Kills Charge Because She Was Forbidden to Go to Excursion," *Chicago Defender*, May 16, 1910.

16 R. R. Wright, "Causes of the Migration from the Viewpoint of a Northern Negro," *Chicago Defender*, November 9, 1916.

17 Chicago Commission on Race Relations, *The Negro in Chicago: A Study of Race Relations and a Race Riot* (Chicago: University of Chicago Press, 1922), 265.

18 "Night Schools," *Chicago Defender,* October 25, 1913.

19 "Night Schools."

20 Grossman, *Land of Hope*, 36.

21 Grim, "From the Yazoo Mississippi Delta to the Urban Communities of the Midwest," 137.

22 Emmet J. Scott, "Letters of Negro Migrants of 1916–1918," *Journal of Negro History* 4, no. 3 (July 1919): 316.

23 Scott, "Letters of Negro Migrants of 1916–1918."

24 Annelise Orleck, *Storming Caesar's Palace: How Black Mothers Staged Their Own War on Poverty* (Boston: Beacon Press, 2005), discusses black women's early entry into the workplace in the South. Orleck traces the Migration experiences of women who settled in Las Vegas and African American history in the West. Rebecca Sharpless, *Cooking in Other Women's Kitchens: Domestic Workers in the South, 1865–1960* (Chapel Hill: University of North Carolina Press, 2011), and Anne Valk and Leslie Brown, *Living with Jim Crow: African-American Women and Memories of the Segregated South* (New York: Palgrave McMillan, 2010), also discuss black women's memories of their girlhood labors.

25 Racial uplift encompasses both the ideological and applied notions of middle-class, Victorian values as essential to shaping poor and uneducated blacks into morally upright citizens. For more on the dynamics of racial uplift, see Kevin K. Gaines, *Uplifting the Race: Black Leadership, Politics, and Culture in the Twentieth Century* (Chapel Hill: University of North Carolina Press, 1996), Stephanie Shaw, "Black Club Women and the Creation of the National Association of Colored Women," in *We Specialize in the Wholly Impossible: A Reader in Black Women's History*, ed. Darlene Clark Hine, Wilma King, and Linda Reed (Brooklyn: Carlson, 1995), 433–42; and Jacqueline Moore, *Booker T. Washington, W. E. B. Du Bois and the Struggle for Racial Uplift* (Wilmington, DE: Scholarly Resources, 2003).

26 Susan K. Cahn, *Sexual Reckonings: Southern Girls in a Troubling Age* (Cambridge, MA: Harvard University Press, 2007), 4. Cahn's study of girls and sexuality in the New South examines how discourses on juvenile delinquency, youth sexuality, school integration, and southern urbanization shifted along racial lines.

27 African American girls and young women were often ignored in efforts to establish and enforce age-of-consent laws in the postbellum South. The language surrounding these initiatives reveals debates about whether African American girls could truly be victims of sexual assault. Leslie K. Dunlap, "The Reform of Rape Law and the Problem of White Men: Age of Consent Campaigns in

the South, 1885–1910," in *Sex, Love, Race: Crossing Boundaries in North American History*, ed. Martha Hodes (New York: New York University Press, 1999), 352–72.

28 The Phillis Wheatley Home was established in 1896, under the leadership of Elizabeth Davis Lindsay, who led the Phillis Wheatley Club of Chicago for twenty-eight years and published a history of the National Association of Colored Women (NACW). The home was seen as a refuge for young, southern women who came to Chicago searching for work or, in rare cases, education. The organization's mission was "to maintain a home and to safeguard and protect the young woman who is a stranger without friends or relatives in Chicago. Surround them with Christian influences; to aid in securing employment." See Anne Meis Knupfer, *Toward a Tenderer Humanity and Nobler Womanhood: African-American Women's Clubs in Turn-of-the-Century Chicago* (New York: New York University Press, 1996). Young, single, wage-earning women were sometimes restricted as to how they spent their money when they resided in working girls' homes. A number of women's historians have explored the relationship between young women laborers and the public amusements in early twentieth-century cities, yet we still have much to learn about how young African American women indulged in these leisure practices and spent their discretionary income. For more on white women laborers in the early twentieth century, see Kathy Peiss, *Cheap Amusements: Working Women and Leisure in Turn of the Century New York* (Philadelphia: Temple University Press, 1987), Nan Enstad, *Ladies of Labor, Girls of Adventure: Working Women, Popular Culture, and Labor Politics at the Turn of the Century* (New York: Columbia University Press, 1999), and Laura Rabinovitz, *For the Love of Pleasure: Women, Movies and Culture in Turn of the Century Chicago* (New Brunswick, NJ: Rutgers University Press, 1998). For African American women and public amusements, see Tera W. Hunter, *To 'Joy My Freedom: Southern Black Women's Lives after the Civil War* (Cambridge, MA: Harvard University Press, 1998).

29 For more on women's reform culture in Chicago, see Maureen A. Flanagan, *Seeing with Their Hearts: Chicago Women and the Vision of the Good City, 1871–1933* (Princeton, NJ: Princeton University Press, 2002).

30 "Social Control," *Crisis*, January 1911, 22. Jane Addams was representative of white women Progressives' uneasy relationship to black civil rights in the early twentieth century. The founder of the Hull House Settlement and supporter of black community and civil rights groups, Addams still held on to the racialized notions of her day in her perceptions of black Chicagoans. See Elisabeth Lasch-Quinn, *Black Neighbors: Race and the Limits of Reform in the Settlement House Movement, 1890–1945* (Chapel Hill: University of North Carolina Press, 1993). Lasch-Quinn chronicles the involvement of black Chicagoans in the famed Hull House. The formation of a black mothers' club in 1927 was little more than the group using the Hull House space. The black mothers were

never included in community meetings or official Hull House rosters. In 1930, there was only one black settlement house in Chicago. Other programs, such as the summer camps and boarding program for working girls, were segregated well into the 1940s. Black participation in other projects was minimal and sporadic at best. Lasch-Quinn notes that the enlistment of black participation in Hull House began in 1938, when it employed its first black staff member, Dewey Jones of the Works Progress Administration. Jones died shortly after his appointment, in 1939, putting an end to formal integration attempts.

31 "Old Settlers Social Club Membership Application," Hope Ives Dunmore/ Old Settlers Social Club Collection, box 2, folder 6, DMAAH. Old settlers were particularly concerned about how migrants would disrupt the implicit racial agreement of pre-Migration Chicago, in which black citizens could enjoy limited rights and economic opportunities. For an engaging discussion of how the Great Chicago Fire helped to segregate the city along various lines and bring class, race, and ethnic tensions to the surface, see Karen Sawislak, *Smoldering Cities: Chicago and the Great Fire 1871–1874* (Chicago: University of Chicago Press, 1996).

32 See Knupfer, *Toward a Tenderer Humanity and a Nobler Womanhood*. African American women's clubs in the North made important contributions to a wide range of social, economic, and political movements in their communities, yet it is important to remember that the South was also home to a vibrant network of women's clubs. The *Chicago Whip* reported in the fall of 1919 that there were 1,553 women's clubs and 1,962 girls' clubs in the South in 1918. These clubs represented a total of 103,377 women and girls, with the majority of that figure representing girls. "Reports Show Southern Colored People Waking Up," *Chicago Whip*, September 20, 1919.

33 Irene McCoy Gaines, "Views on Many Topics by Readers of the Daily News: Plea for the Colored Girl," *Daily News,* May 27, 1920, clipping, Irene McCoy Gaines Collection, box 1, folder 6, CHM. Irene McCoy Gaines was born in Ocala, Florida, in 1892. From 1930 to 1945 she worked for the Cook County Welfare Department, and she also led the Chicago Council of Negro Organizations from 1939 to 1953. A Republican Party activist, Gaines made Illinois history by becoming the first African American woman to run for the state legislature and county commissioner. She died in 1964 after a long career in public service. For more on Irene McCoy Gaines, see Sandra M. O'Donnell, "The Right to Work Is the Right to Live": The Social Work and Political and Civic Activism of Irene McCoy Gaines," *Social Science Review* 75 (2001): 456–78, and Darlene Clark Hine, ed., *Black Women in America: An Historical Encyclopedia*, vols. 1 and 2 (Brooklyn, NY: Carlson), 1993. For analysis of black women's work in Illinois politics, see Lisa G. Masterson, *For the Freedom of Her Race: Black Women and Electoral Politics in Illinois, 1877–1932* (Chapel Hill: University of North Carolina Press, 2010).

34 Grossman details the tensions engendered by Migration and the reactions

of the "old settler" community to migrants, whom they referred to as "home people," in *Land of Hope*, 123–60.

35 The literature on antivice and prostitution crusades charts Progressive Era campaigns to rehabilitate young women in the sex trade. These reformers created professional opportunities by "mothering" the society around them. For an excellent discussion of black women and Chicago's sex trade, see Cynthia Blair, *I've Got to Make My Living: Black Women's Sex Work in Turn-of-the-Century Chicago* (Chicago: University of Chicago Press, 2010).

36 For more on the construction of "the girl problem" among white, black, and immigrant girls in the late nineteenth and early twentieth centuries, see Ruth Alexander, *The Girl Problem: Female Sexual Delinquency in New York, 1900–1930* (Ithaca, NY: Cornell University Press, 1995), Regina Kunzel, *Fallen Women, Problem Girls: Unmarried Mothers and the Professionalization of Social Work, 1890–1945* (New Haven, CT: Yale University Press, 1995), Mary E. Odem, *Delinquent Daughters: Protecting and Policing Adolescent Female Sexuality in the United States, 1885–1920* (Chapel Hill: University of North Carolina Press, 1995), and Cheryl Hicks, *Talk with You Like a Woman: African American Women, Justice, and Reform in New York, 1890–1935* (Chapel Hill: University of North Carolina Press, 2011). Cheryl Hicks's study of black, working-class women in New York prisons and Cynthia Blair's examination of Chicago's black women sex workers and antivice campaigns have brought much needed nuance to the conversations about moral panic, race, authority and female agency in women's and gender history and urban studies. Kali Gross's work on black women and criminality in Philadelphia also engages issues of race and crime. See Kali Gross, *Colored Amazons: Crime, Violence, and Black Women in the City of Brotherly Love, 1880–1910* (Durham, NC: Duke University Press, 2006).

37 For more on girls and the construction of girlhood in the United States, see Cahn, *Southern Reckonings*, Rachel Devlin, *Relative Intimacy* (Chapel Hill: University of North Carolina Press, 2007), and Miriam Brunell-Forman, *Babysitter: An American History* (New York: New York University Press, 2010). While social scientists and social psychologists have long studied girls, the history of girls and girlhood is an emerging offshoot of women's and gender studies and the history of childhood and youth.

38 William Lester Bodine, *Bodine's Reference Book on Juvenile Welfare: A Review of the Chicago Social Service System* (Chicago: Bodine, 1913), 120.

39 Bodine, *Bodine's Reference Book on Juvenile Welfare*, 34.

40 Stephen Robertson, "Age of Consent Laws," in Children and Youth in History website, Center for History and New Media, item #230, Children and Youth in History, http://chnm.gmu.edu/cyh/teaching-modules/230 (accessed June 30, 2014). Also see Leslie K. Dunlap, "The Reform of Rape Law and the Problem of White Men: Age-of-Consent Campaigns in the South, 1885–1910," in Hodes, *Sex, Love, and Race*, 352–72. The issue of consent shifted

along racial lines in early twentieth-century America, with white middle-class girls the focus of campaigns to raise the age of consent for sexual relationships.

41 E. Franklin Frazier, *The Negro Family in Chicago* (Chicago: University of Chicago Press, 1932), 106. Sociologist E. Franklin Frazier (1864–1962) was one of the most influential scholars of black life in Chicago. He earned his PhD in sociology from the University of Chicago in 1931, while also teaching at Fisk University. A harsh critic of the black middle class, Frazier argued against theories of black racial inferiority and connection to African cultures and cited the disruptive effects of the slave trade, slavery, Emancipation, and migration on the collective character of black people and families.

42 White House, "First Lady Michelle Obama," website of the White House, www.whitehouse.gov/administration/first-lady-michelle-obama (accessed June 30, 2014).

CHAPTER 1. "DO YOU SEE THAT GIRL?"

1 Amanda Smith News, "Do You See That Girl?" box 4, folder 49, Ellen M. Henrotin Papers (EMHP), AESL.

2 As quoted in David C. Bartlett and Larry A. McClellan, "The Final Ministry of Amanda Berry Smith," *Illinois Heritage* 1, no. 2 (Winter 1998): 22–31.

3 Amanda Smith's autobiography captures an array of experiences from slavery into the Progressive Era. Smith was internationally known for her orations and deep, heartfelt passion at meetings; her testimonies of faith and performances of praise songs attracted audiences across the country. Methodist bishop James Mills Thoburn recalled hearing her speak and determined that she possessed a "rare degree of spiritual power." Smith, *Autobiography of Mrs. Amanda Smith*, vi. The national AME press also praised her. In an 1895 edition of the *Christian Recorder*, Bishop Wyman Parker described Smith as "that great female evangelist," and he believed that the orphanage would flourish because its leader was "a woman so well known." Smith, *An Autobiography: The Story of the Lord's Dealings with Mrs. Amanda Smith the Colored Evangelist; Containing an Account of Her Life Work of Faith, and Her Travels in America, England, Ireland, Scotland, India, and Africa, as an Independent Missionary* (Chapel Hill: University of North Carolina Press, 1999), 505.

4 Bartlett and McClellan, "Final Ministry of Amanda Berry Smith," 22–31.

5 Smith, *Autobiography*, 255–60.

6 For more on black women missionaries see Bettye Collier-Thomas, *Daughters of Thunder: Black Women Preachers and Their Sermons, 1850–1979* (San Francisco: Jossey Bass, 1998), Elizabeth Brooks Higginbotham, *Righteous Discontent: The Women's Movement in the Black Baptist Church 1880–1920* (Cambridge, MA: Harvard University Press, 1994), and Anthea Butler, *Women in the Church of God in Christ: Making a Sanctified World* (Chapel Hill: University of North Carolina Press, 2007).

7 The initial colonization of Liberia commenced in 1820 after the American Colonization Society moved to create a free, black nation in which to repatriate black freed people. On arrival, the American colonists contended with an unfamiliar terrain, violent clashes with the native population, and a struggle to articulate their vision in Africa. They established the modern-day nation of Liberia in 1847. See Claude Clegg III, *The Price of Liberty: African American girlhoods and the Making of Liberia* (Chapel Hill: University of North Carolina Press, 2003), Bronwen Everil, *Abolition and Empire in Sierra Leone and Liberia* (New York: Palgrave McMillan, 2012), and James Climent, *Another America: The Story of Liberia and the Former Slaves Who Ruled It* (New York: Hill and Wang, 2013).

8 Smith, 57, 218–19.

9 Smith, 58, 496.

10 Smith, 390, 342, 421.

11 Amanda Smith, "Africa," *Christian Standard and Home Journal*, February 20, 1886.

12 In 1890, Frances Willard gave an interview to *Voice* in which she defended the southern practice of lynching, suggesting that southern white men were merely protecting the "safety of woman, of childhood, of the home" when "menaced in a thousand localities at this moment." Speaking against full suffrage for blacks, Willard linked her opposition to universal voting rights to her concerns about black sobriety and intellect. See Frances E. Willard, "The Race Problem: Miss Willard on the Political Puzzle of the South," *Voice*, October 23, 1890, 8. These comments incensed Ida B. Wells-Barnett, who had chronicled the lynching problem and posited that white women perpetuated rape myths to hide consensual, sexual relationships with black men. She responded, referring to the schism between white women and black people in the fight for universal suffrage by mentioning Frederick Douglass's split from Willard and her faction of suffragists who only supported the vote for white women. "Here we have Miss Willard's words in full, condoning fraud, violence, murder, at the ballot box; rapine, shooting, hanging, and burning; for all these things are done and being done now by the Southern white people. She does not stop there, but goes a step further to aid them in blackening the good name of an entire race, as shown by the lines in italics. These utterances, for which the coloured people have never forgiven Miss Willard, and which Frederic Douglass has denounced as false." See "About Southern Lynchings," *Baltimore Herald*, October 20, 1895. Temperance and Prohibition Papers microfilm (1977), sec. 3, reel 42, scrapbook 70, frame 153, Women and American Social Movements. Willard wrote back, situating her rebuttal in the issue of temperance: "Furthermore, I said that the nameless outrages perpetrated upon white women and little girls were a cause of constant anxiety, and this I still believe to be true; but I wish I had said then, as I do now, that the immoralities of white men in their relations with colored women are the source of intolerable race prejudice

and hatred, and that there is not a more withering curse upon the manhood of any nation than that which the eternal laws of nature visited upon those men and those homes in which the helpless bondwoman was made the victim of her master's base desire. . . . An average colored man when sober is loyal to the purity of white women; but when under the influence of intoxicating liquors the tendency in all men is toward a loss of self-control, and the ignorant and vicious, whether white or black, are most dangerous characters." See doc. 32, Frances E. Willard, "The Colored People," *National WCTU Annual Meeting Minutes of 1894* (Chicago: Woman's Temperance Publication Association, 1894), 129–31 (Temperance and Prohibition Papers microfilm (1977), sec. I, reel 4). For more on Amanda Smith and interracial networks in the Methodist Church community, see Priscilla Pope-Levison, "Methodist Interracial Cooperation in the Progressive Era: Amanda Berry Smith and Emma Ray," *Methodist History* 49, no. 2 (January 2011): 68–85. For the heart of Wells-Barnett's antilynching perspectives, see Jacqueline Jones Royster, ed., *Southern Horrors and Other Writings* (New York: Bedford Press, 1997).

13 Kenneth Cmiel, *Home of Another Kind: One Chicago Orphanage and the Tangle of Child Welfare* (Chicago: University of Chicago Press, 1995). An analysis of the decline of orphanages and the expansion of welfare-state approaches to child poverty is found in Matthew A. Crenson, *Building the Invisible Orphanage: A Prehistory of the American Welfare System* (Cambridge, MA: Harvard University Press, 2001). Linda Gordon examines the history of illegal orphan placement practices in the Southwest in *The Great Arizona Abduction* (Cambridge, MA: Harvard University Press, 2001). For more on the history of orphanages and race, see William Seraile, *Angels of Mercy: White Women and the History of New York's Colored Orphans* (New York: Fordham University Press, 2011). Jessie B. Ramey, *Child Care in Black and White: Working Parents and the History of Orphanages* (Urbana: University of Illinois Press, 2012) compares two Pittsburgh orphanages, one all-white and the other all-black, to understand how the child-care system perpetuated racial inequality among poor children and families. Also John E. Murray, *The Charleston Orphan House: Children's Lives in the First Public Orphanage in America* (Chicago: University of Chicago Press, 2013).

14 "Death at Girls Home," *Geneva (IL) Republican*, August 28, 1897.

15 Illinois Children's Home and Aid Society, to the ICHAS in Regard to Facilities for the Care of Dependent Colored Children, 1913, box 1, folder 1, Illinois Children's Home and Aid Society Papers ICHASP), RJDL.

16 Illinois Children's Home and Aid Society, Memorandum to the ICHAS in Regard to Facilities for the Care of Dependent Colored Children.

17 Charlotte Ashby Crawley, "Dependent Negro Children in Chicago in 1926," master's thesis, University of Chicago, 1927, 97.

18 Crawley, "Dependent Negro Children in Chicago in 1926," 93–95.

19 Celia Parker Woolley (1848–1918) was born in Toledo, Ohio, and graduated

from the Coldwater Female Seminary. She served as the pastor of the Geneva (Illinois) Unitarian Church and the Independent Liberal Church of Chicago. A prolific novelist and essayist, she eventually moved to the city's South Side to provide social work services to migrants. For more on Woolley, see Maureen A. Flanagan, *Seeing with their Hearts: Chicago Women and the Vision of the Good City, 1871–1933* (Princeton, NJ: Princeton University Press, 2002).

20 "Mrs. Celia Parker Woolley Speaks, The Douglass Center President Takes a Deeper Interest in the Welfare of Colored Girls Than All the Negro Societies and Churches—This Was the Only Letter Sent Out to Park Ridge to Find Out What Is Being Done for the Colored Girl. Will the Northern Negro Ever Wake Up?," *Chicago Defender*, September 23, 1911.

21 "The Park Ridge Home," *Chicago Defender*, October 11, 1911.

22 "Charges at Mrs. Covington's," *Chicago Defender*, November 4, 1911.

23 Anna Meis Knupfer, *Toward a Tenderer Humanity and a Nobler Womanhood: African American Women's Clubs in Turn-of-the-Century Chicago* (New York: New York University Press, 1996), 78–79.

24 Suellen Hoy, *Good Hearts: Catholic Sisters and Chicago's Past* (Urbana: University of Illinois Press, 2006), 72. The Sisters of the Good Shepherd remained committed to the cause of black girls' education into the civil rights era. For more on the work of Catholic nuns and child care, see Judith Estrine and Edward Rohs, *Raised by the Church: Growing Up in New York City's Catholic Orphanages* (New York: Fordham University Press, 2011), and Margaret M. McGuiness, *Called to Serve: A History of Nuns in America* (New York: New York University Press, 2013).

25 Hoy, *Good Hearts*, 98.

26 Sophonisba Breckenridge (SB) to (WSR), April 4, 1918, box 1, folder 3, ICHASP, RJDL.

27 Crawley, "Dependent Negro Children in Chicago in 1926," 134–35.

28 "Amanda Smith School for Girls Formed in Court Room," *Chicago Defender*, August 16, 1913.

29 C. Spencer, "Negro Children Sold into Slavery," *Chicago Inter-Ocean*, May 1913, clipping, folder 39–13, Illinois Writers Project (IWP), Vivian C. Harsh Collection (VCHC), CGWRL. See Arthur Alden Guild, *Baby Farms in Chicago: An Investigation Made for the Juvenile Protective Association* pamphlet, (Chicago: Juvenile Protective Association, 1917).

30 Guild, "Baby Farms in Chicago."

31 Anne Meis Knupfer, 26.

32 "Home visited by Jesse Binga and Mrs. Booker T. Washington," *Broad Ax*, August 7, 1909, and "Chicago Bureau," *Indianapolis Freeman*, August 7, 1909. Jesse Binga (1865–1950), a Detroit native, founded one of the first black-owned banks in Chicago, serving African Americans barred from using other banking outlets. After rising to phenomenal success during the Great Migration, Binga lost his wealth after the Great Depression and his subsequent im-

prisonment for running an illegal bank. See Carl R. Osthaus, "The Rise and Fall of Jesse Binga, Black Financier," *Journal of Negro History* 58, no. 1 (January 1973), 36–60. For more on blacks in banking, see Nicholas A. Lash, "Black-Owned Banks: A Survey of the Issues," *Journal of Developmental Entrepreneurship* 10, 2 (2005), 187–202.

33 Nannie Burroughs, "Miss Burroughs Appeals to Parents to Save Their Girls—Now," boxes 46–47, Nannie Helen Burroughs Papers (NHBP), LOC.

34 For more on an analysis of black self-help organizations, see Emmett Devon Carson, *A Hand Up: A Black Philanthropy and Self-Help America* (Ann Arbor: University of Michigan Press, 1993), and John Sibley Butler, *Entrepreneurship and Self-Help Among Black Americans: A Reconsideration of Race and Economics* (Albany: State University Press of New York, 2005).

35 Adrienne Israel, *Amanda Berry Smith: From Washerwoman to Evangelist* (Lanham, Md.: Scarecrow Press, 1998), 131–34.

36 Israel, *Amanda Berry Smith*, 134.

37 Charles Virden (CV) to Julius Rosenwald (JR), box 37, file 3, Julius Rosenwald Papers (JRP), JRLSC.

38 State of Illinois Board of Public Charities, *Report of the Illinois Board of Public Charities, 19: 1904-1906* (Springfield, IL: State Journal Company State Printers, 1907), 337.

39 US Census Bureau, "1910 Census, Amanda Smith Industrial Home for Destitute and Dependent Colored Children" (Washington, DC: 1910).

40 "Amanda Smith's Birthday," *Broad Ax*, January 7, 1911.

41 Israel, 141.

42 For more on the Smith and Manual homes, see Sandra M. O'Donnell, "The Care of Dependent African-American Children in Chicago: The Struggle between Black Self-Help and Professionalism," *Journal of Social History* 27, no. 4 (Summer 1994): 763–76.

43 "Training School for Colored Girls," *Chicago Defender*, August 9, 1913.

44 Juvenile delinquency in America has been a topic of inquiry in a number of disciplines, from sociology to criminology and social psychology. Scholars of race and gender have brought nuance to the history of the category of the delinquent youth offender. See David B. Wolcott, *Cops and Kids: Policing Juvenile Delinquency in Urban America, 1890–1945* (Columbus: Ohio State University Press, 2005), and Miroslava Chavez-Garcia, *States of Delinquency: Race and Science in the Making of California's Juvenile Justice System* (Berkeley: University of California Press, 2012).

45 Crawley, "Dependent Negro Children in Chicago in 1926," 65, 135, 137.

46 Crawley, "Dependent Negro Children in Chicago in 1926," 132.

47 Crawley, "Dependent Negro Children in Chicago in 1926," 133.

48 Crawley, "Dependent Negro Children in Chicago in 1926," 145.

49 Adah M. Waters (AMW), *The Amanda Smith Industrial School for Colored Girls*, pamphlet, box 37, folder 3, JRP, JRSCL.

50 "Condensed Report of the Amanda Smith Industrial School for Girls," June 18, 1915, CV to JR, box 37, folder 3, JRP, JRSCL.

51 "Amanda Smith," pamphlet, box 4, folder 49, EMHP, AESL.

52 Israel, *Amanda Berry Smith*, 143–44.

53 "Negro Education: A Study of the Private and Higher Schools for Colored People in the United States, Prepared in Cooperation with the Phelps-Stokes Fund Under the Direction of Thomas Jesse Jones, Specialist in the Education of Racial Groups" (Washington, DC: Bureau of Education, 1916).

54 AMW to WSR, dated March 27, 1918, box 75–18, folder 75–107, ICHASP, RJDL.

55 Julius S. Rosenwald (1862–1932) was born in Springfield, Illinois, into a working-class Jewish family. His early career was in the clothing business, and he established a successful business in Chicago with his brother, Morris Rosenwald. In 1895, he purchased an interest in the mail-order company Sears and Roebuck. In 1912 he became a board member of Booker T. Washington's Tuskegee Institute, a training school for black students in Alabama. Over the course of twenty years, he devoted a significant portion of his personal wealth to black education. Peter Ascoli, *Julius Rosenwald: The Man Who Built Sears, Roebuck and Advanced The Cause of Black Education in the American South* (Bloomington: Indiana University Press, 2006). See also Stephanie Deutsch, *You Need a Schoolhouse: Booker T. Washington, Julius Rosenwald and the Building of Schools for the Segregated South* (Evanston, IL: Northwestern University Press, 2011), and Mary S. Hoffschwelle, *The Rosenwald Schools of the American South* (Gainesville: University Press of Florida, 2006).

56 Israel, *Amanda Berry Smith*, 146.

57 Although the name of the institution from 1912 onward was the Amanda Smith Industrial School for Colored Girls, the *Chicago Defender*, *Broad Ax*, and organizations continued to refer to it for years afterward as the "Amanda Smith Home," "Amanda Smith Home School," and "Amanda Smith's Industrial Home." "Take Positions with Amanda Smith Home," *Chicago Defender*, March 9, 1918, and "Amanda Smith Home Gets Field Sec.," *Chicago Defender*, March 2, 1918.

58 AMW to WSR, March 27, 1918. For more on racial uplift, see Kevin Kelly Gaines, *Uplifting the Race: Black Leadership, Politics, and Culture in the Twentieth Century* (Chapel Hill: University of North Carolina, 1996), and Willard B. Gatewood, *Aristocrats of Color: The Black Elite, 1880–1920* (Bloomington: Indiana University Press, 1990).

59 AMW to WSR, March 27, 1918.

60 For more on the politics of maternalism, see Peggy Pascoe, *Relations of Rescue: The Search for Female Moral Authority in the American West, 1874–1939* (Oxford: Oxford University Press, 1993), Robin Muncy, *Creating a Female Dominion in American Reform, 1890–1935* (Oxford: Oxford University Press, 1994), Molly Ladd-Taylor, *Mother-Work: Women, Child Welfare, and the State, 1890–

1930 (Urbana: University of Illinois Press, 1995), Linda Gordon, *Pitied but Not Entitled: Single Mothers and the History of Welfare, 1890–1935* (Cambridge, MA: Harvard University Press, 1998). For maternalism as it relates to black women specifically, see Cynthia Edmonds-Cady, "Mobilizing Motherhood: Race, Class, and the Uses of Maternalism in the Welfare Rights Movement," *WSQ: Women's Studies Quarterly* 37, nos. 3/4 (Fall/Winter 2009): 206–22. For work on Chicago specifically, see Joanne L. Goodwin, *Gender and the Politics of Welfare Reform: Mothers' Pensions in Chicago, 1911–1929* (Chicago: University of Chicago Press, 1997).

61 "Grace Lyceum Sunday," *Chicago Defender*, March 16, 1918.

62 CV to JR, June 18, 1915, box 37, folder 3, JRP, JRSCL.

63 Ferdinand Lee Barnett (c. 1864–1932) was a Tennessee-born attorney, who founded the *Chicago Conservator*, the city's first black newspaper in 1878. He married activist Ida B. Wells in 1895, and the couple were active in a number of initiatives on behalf of black Chicagoans. See Alfreda Duster, ed., *A Crusade for Justice: The Autobiography of Ida B. Wells* (Chicago: University of Chicago Press, 1970), 376.

64 "Amanda Smith, Race Martyr Sleeps Near Her Monument," *Chicago Defender*, March 6, 1915.

65 Edith Abbott (EA) to the ICHAS, January 10, 1913, box 30, folder 6, ICHASP, RJDL.

66 Sophonisba Breckinridge (SB) to JR, June 1, 1912, box 11, folder 21, JRP, JRSCL.

67 For more on Chicago's Provident Hospital (1891–1987, reopened 1993–) and its founder, Dr. Daniel Hale Williams (c. 1856–1931), see Helen Buckler, *Daniel Hale Williams, Negro Surgeon* (New York: Pittman, 1968). For more on black women's experiences learning and working at Provident's nurse training program, see Susan L. Smith, *Sick and Tired of Being Sick and Tired: Black Women's Health Activism, 1890–1950* (Philadelphia: University of Pennsylvania Press, 2005). For more on the Wabash Avenue YMCA, see Nina Mjagkij, *Light in the Darkness: African Americans and the YMCA, 1852–1946* (Lexington: University of Kentucky Press, 2003). For more on the Frederick Douglass Center Settlement and black settlement houses, see Elisabeth Lasch-Quinn, *Black Neighbors: Race and the Limits of Reform in the American Settlement House Movement, 1890–1945* (Chapel Hill: University of North Carolina Press, 1993).

68 Esther W. Brophy (EWB) to CV, June 22, 1915, box 49, folder 15, JRP, JRSCL.

69 EWB to JR, December 7, 1915, box 49, folder 15, JRP, JRSCL. Rosenwald suggested a similar idea to the Phillis Wheatley Club of Cleveland after they requested funding for a home. Rosenwald suggested that they merge with an already established YWCA. That idea was met with opposition from the YWCA. See JR to Phillis Wheatley Club, Cleveland, box 49, folder 7, JRP, JRSCL.

70 SB to WSR, April 4, 1918, box 1, folder 7, ICHASP, RJDL.

71 For more on sex and girls' institutions, see Agnes Bennett Murphy, "The Girls'

Industrial School of the State of Ohio" (PhD diss., School of Social Service Administration, University of Chicago, 1935), and Philip Morris Hauser, "Motion Pictures in Penal and Correctional Institutions: A Study of the Reactions of Prisoners to Movies" (master's thesis, University of Chicago, 1933), 75, and Anne Meis Knupfer, " 'To Become Good, Self-Supporting Women': The State Industrial School for Delinquent Girls at Geneva, Illinois, 1900–1935," *Journal of the History of Sexuality* 9, no. 4 (October 2000): 420–46.

72 EWB to JR, nd, folder 37, box 1, JRP, JRSCL.

73 Anne Meis Knupfer, *Reform and Resistance: Gender, Delinquency, and America's First Juvenile Court* (New York: Routledge, 2001), 145. For more on race and women's penal institutions, see Cheryl D. Hicks, *Talk with You Like a Woman: African American Women, Justice and Reform in New York, 1890–1935* (Chapel Hill: University of North Carolina Press, 2010), and Ruth Rosen, *The Girl Problem: Female Sexual Delinquency in New York, 1900–1930* (Ithaca, NY: Cornell University Press, 1999).

74 Knupfer, *Reform and Resistance*, 145.

75 Michael Rembis, *Defining Deviance: Sex, Science and Delinquent Girls, 1890–1960* (Urbana: University of Illinois Press, 2011), 103–5.

76 See Knupfer, "To be Good, Self-Supporting Women," 420–46.

77 As the black population of Geneva increased, school matrons and officials monitored interracial mixing and punished black girls for resisting the institutional culture. In 1941, seven black Geneva students were "sentenced to terms of one year each at the state reformatory for women at Dwight" by the local sheriff for shouting "encouragement to three white girls who were trying to escape." The girls fled to the living room of their segregated Hope Cottage "and were only quieted after Sherriff Damisch and his deputies had removed them to cells in the county Jail." The girls finally left the cottage "on the threat of tear gas but put up a bit of resistance when the officers tried to handcuff them." The state's attorney who prosecuted the girls announced that "local authorities are through tolerating disturbances at the schools in Kane County and that any that are brought to trial here will be sent on to the state prisons." He warned: We are going to treat them all alike in the future." "State School Girls Sentenced to Prison after Riot Sunday," *Geneva Republican*, August 1, 1941.

78 Deborah Gray White frames black women's activism in the late nineteenth century club movement as black women "in defense of themselves." See *Too Heavy a Load: Black Women in Defense of Themselves* (New York: Norton, 1999).

79 "Amanda Smith's Industrial Home," *Broad Ax*, February 13, 1909.

80 Untitled Article, *Broad Ax*, April 27, 1907.

81 "Amanda Smith News," folder 4, box 49, EMHP, AESL.

82 "Girls Perish in Fire at Amanda Smith School," *Chicago Defender*, November 30, 1918.

83 AMW, "The Amanda Smith Industrial School for Colored Girls," folder 37, box 3, JRP, JRSCL.

84 "Girls Perish in Fire at Amanda Smith School."

85 "Girls Perish in Fire at Amanda Smith School."

86 "Minutes of the Special Meeting Called to Consider Plans for the Amanda Smith Home for Girls," December 6, 1918, box 75–18, folder 75–107, ICHASP, RJDL.

87 Crawley, "Dependent Negro Children in Chicago in 1926," 61.

88 Crawley, 60.

89 Duster, 373. Amelia Sears is credited with writing one of the first guides on social work: *The Charity Visitor, a Handbook for Beginners*. An active member of Chicago's Urban League, she worked at the city's United Charities and Bureau of Public Welfare. Amelia Sears, *The Charity Visitor* (Chicago: Chicago School of Civics and Philanthropy, 1917).

90 Duster, 394.

91 William Lester Bodine, *Bodine's Reference Book on Juvenile Welfare: A Review of the Chicago Social Service System* (Chicago: Bodine, 1913), 24.

92 Bodine, *Bodine's Reference Book on Juvenile Welfare*, 114.

93 Illinois State Charities Commission, *Second Annual Report of the State Charities Commission to the Honorable Charles S. Deneen, Gov. of Illinois, December 31, 1911* (Springfield, IL: State Journal Company State Printers, 1912).

94 Crawley, 120.

95 "Take Positions with Amanda Smith Home," *Chicago Defender*, March 9, 1918, and "Amanda Smith Home Gets Field Sec.," *Chicago Defender*, March 2, 1918.

96 "Notes of the ICHAS," 1918, ICHASP, RJDL.

97 I. E. Putnam to WSR, dated January 2, 1919, box 30, folder 6, ICHASP, RJDL.

98 Mrs. S. E. Cooper to ICHAS, dated December 28, 1918 (box 75–18, folder 75–107), ICHASP, RJDL.

99 Roberta Church, Report to the ICHAS, September 22, 1944, folder 7, box 30, ICHASP, RJDL.

100 WSR to Mary F. Waring, May 14, 1917 (box 30, folder 9), ICHASP, RJD.

101 Katherine Briggs to Illinois Children's Home and Aid Society, January 11, 1913, box 30, folder 6, ICHASP, RJDL.

102 Maude Mary Firth, "The Use of the Foster Home for the Care of the Delinquent Girls of the Cook County Juvenile Court," master's thesis, University of Chicago, 1924), 53.

103 Firth, "The Use of the Foster Home," 56.

104 *Chicago Defender*, September 27, 1919.

105 "Wants Home for Girls."

106 For more on Mary Bartelme, see "America's Only Woman Judge," *Law Student's Helper* 21, no. 7 (July 1913): 7.

107 "Big Sisters Benefit," *Pittsburgh Courier*, December 3, 1927.

108 "Dependent Negro Children in Chicago in 1926," 147–48.

109 Crawley, 141.

110 "Amanda Smith Home Entered by Burglars," *Chicago Defender*, July 9, 1921.

111 "Amanda Smith Musicale," *Chicago Defender*, September 17, 1921; "Will Aid Amanda Smith Home Building Fund," *Chicago Defender*, October 8, 1921.

112 Crawley, 83.

113 "Amanda Smith Home," *Broad Ax*, June 16, 1923.

114 "Students Hear Prince at Both Universities," *Chicago Defender*, November 8, 1924.

115 Regina Kunzel, *Fallen Women, Problem Girls: Unmarried Mothers and the Professionalization of Social Work, 1890–1945* (New Haven, CT: Yale University Press, 1995).

116 "Open School for Negro Girls," *Broad Ax,* September 2, 1913.

117 "Two Girls Perish in Fire," *Chicago Defender*, and Duster, *Crusade for Justice,* 373–74.

118 "Amanda Smith School for Girls Formed in Court Room," *Chicago Defender*, August 16, 1913.

119 Carolyn A. Stroman, "The *Chicago Defender* and the Mass Migration of Blacks, 1916–1918," *Journal of Popular Culture* 15, no. 2 (Fall 1981): 62–67.

120 See Knupfer, *Toward a Tenderer Humanity and a Nobler Womanhood.*

CHAPTER 2. "MODESTY ON HER CHEEK"

1 "Address of the Council of Bishops, A.M.E. Church," *Christian Recorder*, August 16, 1917, in *African-American Religious History: A Documentary Witness*, ed. Milton C. Sernett, 2nd ed. (Durham, NC: Duke University Press, 1999), 361, 362. Prominent African Americans Carter G. Woodson and Booker T. Washington were skeptical of the movement. Woodson's prediction was blunt and arguably accurate: "The maltreatment of the Negroes will be nationalized by this exodus." Washington departed from Woodson's concern and instead wanted African Americans to remain loyal to the South, and he encouraged them to acquire the economic skills necessary to make themselves invaluable to the rising New South manufacturing centers. See Carter G. Woodson, *A Century of Negro Migration* (Washington, DC: Association for the Study of Negro Life and History, 1919), 7.

2 Benjamin E. Mays and Joseph William Nicholson, *The Negro's Church* (New York: Arno Press, 1933), 108.

3 Milton C. Sernett, *Bound for the Promised Land: African-American Religion and the Great Migration* (Durham, NC: Duke University Press, 1997), 157.

4 Mays and Nicholson, *Negro's Church,* 179.

5 S. Mattie Fisher and Mrs. Jessie Mapp, "Social Work at Olivet Baptist Church," in Sernett, *African-American Religious History*, 368–70.

6 Fisher and Mapp, "Social Work at Olivet Baptist Church," 368–69.

7 Fisher and Mapp, "Social Work at Olivet Baptist Church," 368.

8 Fisher and Mapp, "Social Work at Olivet Baptist Church," 369–70.

9 Nannie H. Burroughs, "Report of the Work of Baptist Women, Twentieth Annual Report," *Journal of the Twentieth Annual Session of the Woman's Convention Auxiliary to the National Baptist Convention, Held with Second Baptist Church, Indianapolis, Indiana*, September 8–13, 1920, in Sernett, *African-American Religious History*, 387.

10 Burroughs, "Report of the Work of Baptist Women," 391.

11 Burroughs, "Report of the Work of Baptist Women," 388.

12 Burroughs, "Report of the Work of Baptist Women," 38.

13 Ruth Evans Pardee, "A Study of the Functions of Associations in a Small Negro Community in Chicago" (master's thesis, University of Chicago, 1937), 35.

14 Elizabeth Clark-Lewis, *Living in, Living Out: African American Domestics in Washington, DC, 1910–1940* (Washington, DC: Smithsonian Institution Press, 1994), 33.

15 Clark-Lewis, *Living in, Living Out*, 36.

16 Interview (names withheld to respect privacy of subjects), June 19, 1929 "Research Projects, The Negro Family in the United States, Illegitimacy Documents—Chicago (RPTNFUSID-C), folder 2, box 131-82, E. Franklin Frazier Papers (EFFP), Moorland-Spingarn Research Center (MSRC).

17 Case 16: Southern Family with Daughter Finishing High School, nd, "Research Projects, The Negro Family in the US, Documents of Families Coming to the Urban League" (RPTNFUSDFCUL), folder 12, box 131-81, EFFP, MSRC.

18 Case 18: Woman Shot by Husband, nd, RPTNFUSDFCUL, folder 12, box 131-81, EFFP, MSRC.

19 Interview, May 8, 1929, RPTNFUSID-C, folder 2, box 131-82 EFFP, MSRC.

20 Clark-Lewis, *Living in, Living Out*, 44.

21 Tera W. Hunter's examination of black working-class women's lives in Atlanta highlights the importance of popular culture. See Hunter, *To 'Joy My Freedom: Southern Black Women's Lives and Labors after the Civil War* (Cambridge, MA: Harvard University Press, 1997).

22 *Crisis*, the official magazine of the NAACP, featured the dolls and the book in a special issue devoted to children filled with pictures of African American girls of various phenotypes. It is interesting that the doll and the illustration for the book *Hazel* feature a girl that appears white. See *The Crisis Advertiser, The Crisis Magazine* (New York: Crisis, 1913). Critics noted Hazel's picture and remarked that the child on the book cover looked European. One reviewer noted: "Unfortunately, the frontispiece drawing of Hazel does not portray a typical Negro child." See "Book Reviews," *Southern Workman* 43 (January–December 1914): 59–60. For more on African American girls and dolls in popular culture, see Robin Bernstein, *Racial Innocence: Performing American Childhood* (New York: New York University Press, 2011).

23 Oliver Cromwell Cox, "The Negroes' Use of Their Buying Power in Chicago as a Means of Securing Employment, a New Application of an Old Method," 8, nd, unpublished manuscript, Everett Cherrington Hughes Papers, JRSCL.

24 Case 16, RPTNFUSDFCUL, EFFP, MSRC.

25 Annie Malone (1869–1957) was a pioneer in the manufacturing and sales of black women's hair products. The child of slaves, Malone created a beauty empire with the Poro Company, originally headquartered in St. Louis and then in Chicago's Bronzeville. A committed philanthropist, she trained sales agent turned entrepreneur Sarah Breedlove (1867–1919), who later became known as Madam C. J. Walker. For more on Malone and Poro, see Graham White and Shane White, *Stylin': African American Expressive Culture, from Its Beginnings to the Zoot Suit* (Ithaca, NY: Cornell University Press, 1999). For more on Sarah Breedlove and the epic rise of the Madam C. J. Walker Manufacturing Company and her impact on black women's lives in the Migration era, see A'Leila Bundles, *On Her Own Ground: The Life and Times of Madam C. J. Walker* (New York: Scribner, 2002). Anthony Overton (1865–1946) was founder of the Hygienic Manufacturing Company, the first black-owned cosmetics business in America. Overton also founded the Bronzeville-based Douglass National Bank. For more on Overton, see "Anthony Overton," *Journal of Negro History* 32, no. 32 (July 1947): 394–96. For more on black women's beauty culture and Chicago's Migration, see Davarian Baldwin, *Chicago's New Negroes: Modernity, the Great Migration, and Black Urban Life* (Chapel Hill: University of North Carolina Press, 2007), and Tiffany Gill, *Beauty Shop Politics: African American Women's Activism in the Beauty Industry* (Urbana: University of Illinois Press, 2010).

26 Chicago Commission on Race Relations, *The Negro in Chicago: A Study of Race Relations and a Riot* (Chicago: University of Chicago Press, 1922), 443.

27 Interview, May 8, 1929, RPTNFUSID-C, folder 2, box 131-82 EFFP, MSRC.

28 Charlotte Ashby Crawley, "Dependent Negro Children in Chicago in 1926" (master's thesis, University of Chicago, 1927), 120.

29 Case 18, RPTNFUSDFCUL, EFFP, MSRC.

30 The most noted Chicago women to take up the challenge of establishing their own congregations were Lucy Smith and Mary Evans. The most famous woman-led group was the All Nations Pentecostal Church, organized by Lucy Smith, a prominent faith healer. In the 1930s, Mary Evans left the AME Church and became the leader of the debt-ridden Cosmopolitan Community Church, which she turned into a "singing, praying, and tithing" church to which 98 percent of the members regularly gave 10 percent of their income. See Wallace Best, *Passionately Human, No Less Divine: Religion and Culture in Black Chicago, 1915–1952* (Princeton, NJ: Princeton University Press, 2005), 147–80.

31 *Chicago Defender Junior*, September 10, 1921.

32 "The True Brownies," *Crisis*, October 1919, 285–86.

33 Interview, November 22, 1929, RPTNFUSID-C, folder 2, box 131-82, EFFP, MSRC.

34 Case 16, RPTNFUSDFCUL, EFFP, MSRC.

35 For more on the New Negro movement in Chicago, see Robert Bone and

Richard A. Courage, *The Muse in Bronzeville: African American Creative Expression in Chicago, 1932–1950* (New Brunswick, NJ: Rutgers University Press, 2011), and Darlene Clark Hine and John McCluskey, Jr., *The Black Chicago Renaissance* (Chicago: University of Illinois Press, 2012).

36 For more on the Garvey movement, see E. David Cronon, *Black Moses: The Story of Marcus Garvey and the Universal Negro Improvement Association* (Madison: University of Wisconsin Press, 1960), Marcus Garvey, *Marcus Garvey Life and Lessons: A Centennial Companion to the Marcus Garvey and the University Negro Improvement Association Papers,* edited by Barbara Bair and Robert Hill (Berkeley: University of California Press, 1988), and Colin Grant, *Negro with a Hat: The Rise and Fall of Marcus Garvey* (New York: Oxford University Press, 2010).

37 Allan Spear, *Black Chicago: The Making of a Negro Ghetto, 1890–1920* (Chicago: University of Chicago Press, 1967), 196.

38 Abbott was also one of many cosigners of a letter requesting the US attorney general to investigate the UNIA. The letter accused the movement of stimulating "the violent temper of the dangerous element" and called Garvey "an unscrupulous demagogue." The letter appears in Amy Jacques Garvey, ed., *Philosophy and Opinions of Marcus Garvey, or Africa for the Africans* (New York: Athenaeum, 1969). For more on the dispute between Abbott and Garvey, see Shawn Leigh Alexander, "Marcus Garvey and the *Chicago Defender*, 1917–1923" (PhD diss., University of Iowa, 1995).

39 Spear, *Black Chicago*, 194–96.

40 Spear, *Black Chicago*, 196.

41 "Black Nationalist by Lionel Yard, Oral Historian of the Garvey Movement, Organizer of UNIA Branches, 1975," box 1, folder 1919–1975, Moorish Science Temple of America Collection (MSTAC), SCRBC.

42 Illinois Workers Project, "Early Studies in Black Nationalism, Cults, and Churches in Chicago by the WPA, circa 1941," notes, Negro in Illinois Project (NIP), Vivian Harsh Collection (VHC), CGWRL.

43 Illinois Workers Project, "The WPA Study of the Moorish Science Temple, 1940," NIP, VHC, CGWRL.

44 Illinois Workers Project, "The WPA Study of the Moorish Science Temple, 1940." For more on the Chicago Race Riots, see William M. Tuttle, *Race Riot: Chicago in the Red Summer of 1919* (Urbana: University of Illinois Press, 1996), and Janet L. Abu-Lughod, *Race, Space and Riots in Chicago, New York and Los Angeles* (New York: Oxford University Press, 2006).

45 Noble Drew Ali (NDA), "Koran Questions for Moorish Children," box 1, folder 1, MSTAC, SCRBC.

46 NDA, "Circle Seven Koran," box 1, folder 1, MSTAC, SCRBC.

47 Arthur Huff Fauset, *Black Gods of the Metropolis: Negro Religious Cults of the Urban North* (Philadelphia: University Press of Pennsylvania, 1944), 41.

48 Fauset, *Black Gods of the Metropolis*, 42.

49 E. Franklin Frazier, *The Negro Church in America* (Liverpool: University of Liverpool Press, 1963), 70–71.

50 Frazier, *Negro Church in America*.

51 Kevin Kelly Gaines, *Uplifting the Race: Black Leadership, Politics, and Culture in the Twentieth Century* (Chapel Hill: University of North Carolina Press, 1996), 127.

52 Rollin Hartt, "When the Negro Comes North," *World's Work Magazine*, report, "Wilbur Owens Woods" file, box 1, folder 8, Marcy Newberry Association Records, RJDL.

53 Arna Bontemps and Jack Conroy, "Registered with Allah," in *Anyplace but Here* (Columbia: University of Missouri Press, 1997), 219.

54 NDA, *Moorish Voice*, box 1, folder 5, MSTAC, SCRBC.

55 NDA, "Circle Seven Koran."

56 Barbara Bair, "Comparing the Role of Women in the Garvey Movement," 2000 American Experience: Marcus Garvey, website of Public Broadcasting Service, http://www.pbs.org/wgbh/amex/garvey/sfeature/sf_forum_14.html (accessed July 1, 2014).

57 Miles Mark Fisher, "Organized Religion and the Cults," *Crisis*, January 1937, 8–10.

58 Fisher, "Organized Religion and the Cults."

59 "List of Moorish Temples," in *Moorish Guide*, 1928, box 1, folder 5, MSTAC, SCRBC.

60 Richard Brent Turner, *Islam in the African-American Experience* (Bloomington: Indiana University Press, 2003), 101.

61 NDA, *Moorish Guide*, 1928, "Economics," box 1, folder 5, MSTAC, SCRBC.

62 "Mrs. Drew Ali Organizes Young Moorish People," *Chicago Defender*, December 1, 1928.

63 "Daily Topics," *Moorish Guide*, April 1935.

64 "Daily Topics."

65 Debra Washington Mubashshir, "Forgotten Fruit of the City: Chicago and the Moorish Science Temple of America," *Cross Currents*, March 22, 2001.

66 Martin Summers, *Manliness and Its Discontents: The Black Middle Class and the Transformation of Masculinity, 1900-1930* (Chapel Hill: University of North Carolina Press, 2004), 89.

67 "The Moorish Science Temple of America's First Annual Convention," 1928, unspecified Moorish publication, box 1, folder 5, MSTAC, SCRBC.

68 "Moorish Science Temple of America's First Annual Convention."

69 "Moorish Head Makes Plans for Conclave," *Chicago Defender*, July 21, 1928.

70 Advertisement in *Moorish Voice*, "Moorish Science Temple History," www.moorishsciencetempleofamerica.com (accessed July 16, 2014).

71 [Untitled], folder 4, box 1, MSTAC, SCRBC.

72 Yvonne Yazbeck Haddad and Jane Idleman Smith, *Mission to America: Five Islamic Sectarian Communities in North America* (Gainesville: University Press of Florida, 1993), 88.

73 For more on this form of activism, called "Don't Buy Where You Can't Work," see Cheryl Greenberg, "Don't Buy Where You Can't Work," in *Or Does It Explode? Black Harlem in the Great Depression* (New York: Oxford University Press, 1991). See also "Marshall Field & Co. Again Refuses to Sell to Colored Girl," *Chicago Whip*, August 1919.

74 Noble Drew Ali, "Moorish Leader's Historic Message to America," website of Moorish Science Temple of America, www.moorishsciencetempleofamerica .com (accessed July 16, 2014).

75 Turner, *Islam in the African-American Experience*, 100.

76 Bundles, *On Her Own Ground*, 288–89.

77 Pamphlets, box 1, folder 5, MSTAC, SCRBC.

78 Rosemary Skinner Keller, Rosemary Radford Ruether, and Marie Cantlon, "The Moorish Science Temple," in *The Encyclopedia of Women and Religion in North America* (Bloomington: Indiana University Press, 2006), 611.

79 For more on flappers in the 1920s and African American women, see Deborah Gray White, *Too Heavy a Load: Black Women in Defense of Themselves, 1894–1994* (New York: Norton, 1999), 128–30, and Margaret A. Lowe, *Looking Good: College Women and Body Image, 1875–1930* (Baltimore: Johns Hopkins University Press, 1993), 103–33. For an insightful look into how African American women mediated what she calls the "whirlpools of representation" in the "sex-race marketplace," see Erin Chapman, *Prove It on Me: New Negroes, Sex and Popular Culture in the 1920s* (New York: Oxford University Press, 2012).

80 "Physician Has Fears for the Young Flappers," *Chicago Defender*, June 17, 1922.

81 "The Flapper Age," *Chicago Defender*, July 29, 1922.

82 "Noble Drew Ali Returns after Long Visit South," *Chicago Defender*, November 19, 1927. Incidentally, Ali visited Marcus Garvey in Atlanta during his trip to the South. Garvey was serving his term in a federal prison.

83 "Birthday of Moorish Leader Is Celebrated," *Chicago Defender*, January 12, 1929.

84 Oscar Stanton De Priest (1871–1951) was born in Alabama and moved to Kansas as a child. He moved to Chicago in 1899 and became a successful realtor. He served as the Second Ward's alderman, the first African American on the Chicago City Council, between 1915 and 1917. He served as a Republican congressman from Illinois from 1929 to 1935. For more on De Priest's rise and eventual political defeat in the 1930s, see S. Davis Day, "Herbert Hoover and Racial Politics: The De Priest Incident," *Journal of Negro History* 65 (Winter 1980): 6–17, and Wanda Hendricks, "Vote for the Advantage of Ourselves and Our Race": The Election of the First Black Alderman in Chicago," *Illinois Historical Journal* 87, no. 3 (Autumn 1994): 171–84.

85 "Cult Leader Being Held in Murder Case," *Chicago Defender*, May 18, 1929, "'Prophet' of Moorish Cult Dies Suddenly," *Chicago Defender*, July 27, 1929, and "Five Moors Indicted in Murder Case," *Chicago Defender*, October 12, 1929.

86 "Murder Exposes Murdered Leaders Amours, Three Women Named in Case," *Pittsburgh Courier*, March 23, 1929.

87 See Earnest Allen, Jr., "Religious Heterodoxy and Nationalist Tradition: The Continuing Evolution of the Nation of Islam," *Black Scholar* 26, nos. 3–4 (Fall 1996/Winter 1997): 2–34, 3; Vibert L. White, Jr., *Inside the Nation of Islam: A Historical and Personal Testimony by a Black Muslim* (Gainesville: University Press of Florida, 2001), 5, and Juan Williams and Quinton Dixie, "Black Gods of the City," in *This Far by Faith: Stories from the African-American Religious Experience* (New York: HarperCollins Morrow 2003), 177. For a contemporary look at the Moorish Science Temple see "The Aging of the Moors," *Chicago Reader*, November 15, 2007.

88 "Cult Leader Lured Girls to Harem," *Chicago Defender*, March 23, 1929. "Murder Exposes Murdered Leaders Amours, Three Women Named in Case."

89 "Murder Exposes Murdered Leaders Amours, Three Women Named in Case."

90 "Murder Exposes Murdered Leaders Amours, Three Women Named in Case."

91 Turner, *Islam in the African-American Experience*, 100.

92 "'Prophet' of Moorish Cult Dies Suddenly."

93 Turner, *Islam in the African-American Experience*, 100.

94 Susan Nance, "Respectability and Representation: The Moorish Science Temple, Morocco, and Black Public Culture in 1920s Chicago," *American Quarterly* 54, no. 4 (December 2002): 623–57.

95 Spear, *Black Chicago*, 193.

96 "Religious Cult Raided: Rescue Girls in Harem," *Chicago Defender*, February 27, 1926.

97 John Givens-El stated that after Ali's death, he fainted. While being examined, an observer noted that "the sign of the star and the crescent were in his eyes," indicating the reincarnation of Drew Ali. See Aminah Beverly McCloud, *African-American Islam* (New York: Routledge, 1995), 55.

98 For more on the history of the Nation of Islam, see Steven Tsoukalas, *The Nation of Islam: Understanding the Black Muslims* (New York: P and R, 2001).

99 See Louis E. Lomax, *When the Word Is Given: A Report on Muhammad, Malcolm X and the Black Muslim World* (New York: World, 1963).

100 Clifton Hugo Marsh, *The Lost Found Nation of Islam in America* (New York: Scarecrow Press, 2000), 44.

101 Marsh, 44.

102 Andrew Claude Clegg III, "Rebuilding the Nation: The Life and Work of Elijah Muhammad, 1946–1954," *Black Scholar* 26, nos. 3–4 (Fall 1996/Winter 1997): 51.

103 Clegg, "Rebuilding the Nation," 55.

104 Davarian Baldwin, *Chicago's New Negroes: Modernity, the Great Migration and Black Urban Life* (Chapel Hill: University of North Carolina Press, 2007). Baldwin notes: "Many migrants endured social programs on hygiene and domestic arts and sermons on public behavior in order to have access to childcare and obtain referral networks while also acquiring social status through church attendance," 159.

105 Evelyn Brooks Higginbotham, *Righteous Discontent: The Woman's Movement in the Black Baptist Church* (Cambridge, MA: Harvard University Press, 1993), 15–16.

106 Historians of African American churches in the Great Migration era have examined the response of mainline Christian churches to migrants, the rise of storefront churches and gospel music, and groups deemed cults. See Benjamin E. Mays and Joseph William Nicholson, *The Negro's Church* (New York: Arno Press, 1933), C. Eric Lincoln, *Black Muslims in America* (Grand Rapids, Mich.: Eerdmans, 1961), Robert Gregg, *Sparks from the Anvil of Oppression: Philadelphia's African Methodists and Southern Migrants, 1890–1940* (Philadelphia: Temple University Press, 1993), Jill Watts, *God, Harlem, USA: The Father Divine Story* (Berkeley: University of California Press, 1995), Timothy E. Fulop and Albert J. Raboteau, *African-American Religion: Interpretive Essays in History and Culture* (New York: Routledge, 1996), Wallace D. Best, *Passionately Human, No Less Divine: Religion and Culture in Black Chicago, 1915–1952* (Princeton, NJ: Princeton University Press, 2007), and Jacob S. Dorman, *Chosen People: The Rise of American Black Israelite Religions* (New York: Oxford University Press, 2013).

107 Ula Taylor, *The Veiled Garvey: The Life and Times of Amy Jacques Garvey* (Chapel Hill: University of North Carolina Press, August, 2002), 2.

CHAPTER 3. "THE POSSIBILITIES OF THE NEGRO GIRL"

1 See Philip T. K. Daniel, "A History of Discrimination against Black Students in Chicago Secondary Schools," *History of Education Quarterly* 20, no. 2 (Summer 1980), 147–62.

2 Daniel, "History of Discrimination against Black Students in Chicago Secondary Schools," 147–48, 149.

3 Daniel, "History of Discrimination against Black Students in Chicago Secondary Schools," 150.

4 Note on Chicago School Census, May 2, 1912, Illinois Children's Home Aid Society Papers, box 30, folder 6, RJDL. For more on African American education during the Migration era, see Michael W. Homel, "The Politics of Public Education in Black Chicago, 1910–1941," *Journal of Negro Education* 45, no. 2 (Spring 1976), 179–91.

5 Homel, "Politics of Public Education in Black Chicago," 149.

6 Valerie Grim, "From the Yazoo Mississippi Delta to the Urban Communi-

ties of the Midwest: Conversations with Rural African-American Women," *Frontiers: A Journal of Women Studies* 22, no. 1 (2001): 133.

7 For more on African American women's work with issues of truancy and juvenile justice, see Ann Meis Knupfer, *Toward a Tenderer Humanity and a Nobler Womanhood: African American Women's Clubs in Turn-of-the-Century Chicago* (New York: New York University Press, 1996), and Sandra M. O'Donnell, " 'The Right to Work Is the Right to Live': The Social Work and Political and Civic Activism of Irene McCoy Gaines," *Social Science Review* 75 (2001): 456–78.

8 James R. Grossman, *Land of Hope: Chicago, Black Southerners, and the Great Migration* (Chicago: University of Chicago Press, 1989), 246.

9 Dionne Danns, "Thriving in the Midst of Adversity: Educator Maudelle Brown Bousfield's Struggles in Chicago, 1920–1950," *Journal of Negro Education* 78, no. 1 (Winter 2009): 3–16.

10 Grossman, *Land of Hope*, 246.

11 Allan H. Spear, *Black Chicago: The Making of a Negro Ghetto, 1890–1920* (Chicago: University of Chicago Press, 1967), 203–4. Often, adults unexpectedly benefited from Chicago's educational system more than their children. For instance, the Phillips High School established night schools that allowed adults to enroll in remedial courses for elementary grades for $1 and attend high school for $2. By 1921, four thousand African Americans enrolled in these courses. See Grossman, *Land of Hope*, 246.

12 Chicago Commission on Race Relations, *The Negro in Chicago: A Study of Race Relations and a Race Riot* (Chicago: University of Chicago Press, 1922), 267.

13 Chicago Commission on Race Relations, *Negro in Chicago*.

14 Ione Margaret Mack, "The Factor of Race in the Religious Education of the Negro High School Girl" (master's thesis, University of Chicago, 1927), 33.

15 Mack, "Factor of Race in the Religious Education of the Negro High School Girl," 38, 41.

16 Robert Cohen, ed. *Dear Mrs. Roosevelt: Letters from Children of the Great Depression* (Chapel Hill: University of North Carolina Press, 2002), 202.

17 "Report on the Meeting of the Secret Knights Social Club," February 22, 1934, box 89, folder 5, Ernest Watson Burgess Papers (EWBP), JRSCL.

18 Mack, "Factor of Race in the Religious Education of the Negro High School Girl," 1.

19 For more on W. E. B. Du Bois and the concept of the Talented Tenth, see W. E. B. Du Bois, *The Negro Problem* (New York: James Pott, 1903).

20 Mack, "Factor of Race in the Religious Education of the Negro High School Girl," 66, 67.

21 Mack, "Factor of Race in the Religious Education of the Negro High School Girl," 104–5, 109.

22 Interview, November 22, 1929, Notes on the Negro Family in Chicago, E. Franklin Frazier Papers, MSRC.

23 Howard University, one of the nation's preeminent black colleges, was founded in 1867 as part of the expansive Reconstruction plan that established institutions for the black elite to train and teach newly emancipated African Americans. Women were integral to this mission, and that legacy continued into the 1900s, with the majority of women students enrolled in the Teacher's College. Paula Giddings, in her study of the sorority Delta Sigma Theta, claimed that Howard in its early years was "tolerant of ideas when it came to race" but "behind" when dealing with women students, faculty, and staff. See Giddings, *In Search of Sisterhood: Delta Sigma Theta and the Challenge of the Black Sorority Movement* (New York: Morrow, 2007), 43.

24 For more on the University of Chicago's pioneering position in the education of women scholars in the social sciences, see Ellen Fitzpatrick, *Endless Crusade: Women Social Scientists and Progressive Reform* (New York: Oxford University Press, 1994). Henry Yu examines the work of Robert Park and what became known as the Chicago School of Sociology in the formation on ideas about Asians in America in Henry Yu, *Thinking Orientals: Migration, Contact, and Exoticism in Modern America* (New York: Oxford University Press, 2002). For analysis of the Chicago School of Sociology and claims about its perceptions of black family life and about the sociologist E. Franklin Frazier, see Daryl Michael Scott, *Contempt and Pity: Social Policy and the Image of the Damaged Black Psyche, 1880–1996* (Chapel Hill: University of North Carolina Press, 1997).

25 University of Chicago Special Collections Research Center, *How U. Chicago Became a Hub for Black Intellectuals,* online exhibit, and Amy Braverman Puma, "Colorlines," *University of Chicago Magazine*, January–February 2009. For more on black women's experiences at colleges during the Reconstruction and Great Migration eras, see Giddings, *In Search of Sisterhood,* and Linda M. Perkins, "Lucy Diggs Slowe: Champion of the Self-Determination of African-American Women in Higher Education," *Journal of Negro History* 81, nos. 1–4 (Autumn/Winter 1996): 89–104. Linda Perkins characterized Howard University's policies on women students as "infringements upon their independence and freedom" that "prevented them from maturing and taking advantage of all that college life had to offer," 95.

26 "University of Chicago," *Chicago Defender*, March 13, 1915.

27 Prominent AKA member Georgiana Simpson battled the University of Chicago for the right to live in campus housing in 1907. Sociologist Sophonisba Breckinridge was the university's assistant dean of women at the time, and she allowed Simpson to move into a women's residence hall. When university president Pratt Judson demanded Breckinridge remove Simpson from the hall, she reflected: "I pointed out that the announcements distributed by the University with reference to the Houses said nothing of this, but he was immovable and Miss Simpson moved out." See Fitzpatrick, *Endless Crusade*, 182.

28 Ella Mae Johnson and Marjorie W. Turner, eds., "Here's Zelma: The Dr. Zelma Watson George Appreciation Dinner Program," October 24, 1971, 11–13.

29 "Theta Omega Chapter," *The Ivy Leaf*, 1921.

30 "Mrs. E. Frank Turner Jr. to Direct Girls' Y Camp," *Chicago Defender*, August 10, 1929.

31 "A Scrap Book for Women in Public Life, Mrs. Prescott Is Most Youthful of Deans," *Chicago Defender*, August 24, 1929.

32 "2500 Alphas Launch 3rd Annual Education Drive," *Chicago Defender*, April 7, 1923.

33 "2500 Alphas Launch 3rd Annual Education Drive," and "Go to High School and College Meeting," *Chicago Defender*, May 29, 1920.

34 "Sorority to Have Vocational Week," *Chicago Defender*, May 24, 1924.

35 Richard W. Stephens, "Birth of the National Vocational Guidance Association," *Career Development Quarterly* 36, no. 4 (June 1988): 293–306.

36 "Wins Scholarship," *Chicago Defender*, October 6, 1923.

37 "Sorority Plans to Give Big Scholarship Dance," *Chicago Defender*, October 31, 1925.

38 "Sorority Helps Girls Pick Work, AKA Observes National Vocational Guidance Celebration," *Chicago Defender*, May 15, 1926.

39 Photograph, *Chicago Defender*, May 26, 1928.

40 "Prize Winner," *Chicago Defender*, June 15, 1929.

41 "A Scrap Book for Women in Public Life, Girl Receives Degree from Chicago U.," *Chicago Defender*, April 5, 1930.

42 "Vocational Guidance," *The Ivy Leaf* 13, no. 4 (1935): 10, 28. Also see "Alpha Kappa Alphas Sponsoring Youth Week," *Chicago Defender*, May 4, 1935.

43 "Soror to Arms," *The Ivy Leaf*, 1927, 35–36. .

44 "Soror to Arms," 26.

45 "Soror to Arms," 26.

46 "Address Delivered in University Hall, Ohio State University: On Occasion of Public Meeting Boulé, Alpha Kappa Alpha Society, December 28, 1926," *The Ivy Leaf*, 1927, no. 7.

47 "Our National Program," *The Ivy Leaf*, 1927, 26.

48 "AKA's National Basileus Talks Guidance in Drive," *Chicago Defender*, May 15, 1937.

49 Dionne Danns, "Thriving in the Midst of Adversity: Educator Maudelle Brown Bousfield's Struggles in Chicago, 1920–1950," *Journal of Negro Education* 78, no. 1 (Winter 2009): 3–16.

50 See Adele Hast and Rima Lunin Schultz, "Maudelle Bousfield," in *Women Building Chicago 1790–1990: A Biographical Dictionary* (Bloomington: Indiana University Press, 2001), and Dionne Danns, *Something Better for Our Children: Black Organizing in Chicago Public Schools, 1963–1971* (New York: Taylor and Francis, 2002).

51 Phillips High School Yearbook, 1924, Arthur Logan Papers (ALP), Vivian G. Harsh Collection (VGHC), CGWRL.

52 Phillips High School Yearbook, 1927, ALP, VGHC, CGWRL.

53 Phillips High School Yearbook, 1927. The Chicago Normal School, formerly the Cook County Normal School founded in 1867, was led by some of the city's leading educators, including Francis Parker, Arnold Tomkins, and Ella Flagg Young. Renamed the Normal School in 1913, the institution innovated outreach to immigrants, the laboratory school system, and curriculum reforms in the city's public school. In 1938 it was renamed again the Chicago Teachers College. It is currently Chicago State University, a predominately African American college, reflecting the changing demographics of the city's South Side. For more on Ella Flagg Young, see Joan K. Smith, "Progressive School Administration: Ella Flagg Young and the Chicago Schools, 1905–1915," *Journal of the Illinois State Historical Society* 73, no. 1 (Spring 1980): 27–44, and for an analysis of her generation of women educators and sexuality, see Jackie Blount, *Fit to Teach: Same-Sex Desire, Gender, and School Work in the Twentieth Century* (Albany: State University Press of New York, 2006); also Anne Durst, *Women Educators in the Progressive Era: The Women Behind Dewey's Laboratory School* (New York: Palgrave Macmillan, 2010). The University of Illinois at Urbana-Champaign (established 1867) first admitted black students in 1887. Yet it did not enroll a critical mass of black students until the 1960s. For more on the history of black students there, see Joy Ann Williamson, *Black Power on Campus: The University of Illinois, 1965–1975* (Urbana: University of Illinois Press, 2003).

54 "Alpha Kappa Alpha in Vocational Guidance," *Chicago Defender*, May 5, 1928.

55 Kelly Schrum, *Some Wore Bobbysox: The Emergence of Teenage Girls' Culture, 1920–1945* (New York: Palgrave Macmillan, 2006), 12.

56 Millie E. Hale, "Possibilities of the Negro Girl," *Alpha Kappa Alpha Ivy Leaf*, 1927, no. 45.

57 Horace Cayton and St. Clair Drake, *Black Metropolis: A Story of Negro Life in a Northern City* (Chicago: University of Chicago Press, 1962), 258.

58 Fannie Barrier Williams, "The Problem of Employment for Negro Women," in *The New Woman of Color: The Collected Writings of Fannie Barrier Williams*, ed. Mary Jo Deegan (DeKalb: Northern Illinois University Press, 2005), 56. The *Voice of the Negro* was established in Atlanta in 1904 as a moderate publication to bridge the opinions of radical and accommodationist African Americans. Eventually the magazine embraced a more radical identity, alienating Booker T. Washington and other African American conservatives. After the Atlanta Race Riots, the magazine moved to Chicago in 1906 and folded a year later. For more about the *Voice of the Negro* and its political writing, see Louis R. Harlan, "Booker T. Washington and the *Voice of the Negro*, 1904–1907," *Journal of Southern History* 45 (February 1979): 45–62.

59 Katherine Davis Chapman Tillman, "Paying Professions for Colored Girls," *Voice of the Negro* (January–February 1907): 54–56.

60 Sophia Boza, A.P. Drucker, A.L. Harris, Miriam Schaffner, Louise deKoven

Bowen, *The Colored People of Chicago: An Investigation Made for the Juvenile Protective Association* (Chicago: Juvenile Protective Association, 1913), 19.

61 Grossman, *Land of Hope*, 246.

62 Grossman, *Land of Hope*, 246.

63 For more on sexual violence and black domestic workers, see Isabel Wilkerson, *The Warmth of Other Suns: The Epic Story of America's Great Migration* (New York: Vintage, 2011), David W. Jackson, Charletta Sudduth, and Katherine Van Wormer, *The Maid Narratives: Black Domestics and White Families in the Jim Crow South* (Baton Rouge: Louisiana State University Press, 2012).

64 E. Franklin Frazier, *The Negro Family in Chicago* (Chicago: University of Chicago Press, 1932), 269.

65 Chicago Commission on Race Relations, *Negro in Chicago*, 96.

66 Cayton and Drake, *Black Metropolis*, 246.

67 Chicago Commission on Race Relations, *Negro in Chicago*, 626.

68 Richard Wright, *Twelve Million Black Voices: A Folk History of the Negro in the United States* (New York: Basic Books, 2012), 135.

69 "A Message from Our Basileus," *The Ivy Leaf*, March 1932, no. 2.

70 Christopher Robert Reed, *The Chicago NAACP and the Rise of the Black Professional Leadership, 1910–1966* (Bloomington: Indiana University Press, 1997), 74.

71 Jacqueline Jones, *Labor of Love, Labor of Sorrow: Black Women, Work, and the Family, from Slavery to the Present* (New York: Basic Books, 2009), 164. Also Cheryl Greenberg, *To Ask for an Equal Chance: African Americans in the Great Depression* (Lanham, MD: Rowan and Littlefield, 2009).

72 For more on Oliver Cromwell Cox, see Christopher A. McAuley, *The Mind of Oliver C. Cox* (South Bend, IN: University of Notre Dame Press, 2004).

73 Oliver Cromwell Cox, "The Negroes' Use of Their Buying Power in Chicago as a Means of Securing Employment, a New Application of an Old Method," unpublished manuscript, Everett Cherrington Hughes Papers, JRSCL.

74 Cohen, *Dear Mrs. Roosevelt*, 238.

75 "Labor Survey," June 11, 1937, box 14, folder 12, Illinois Writers Project (IWP), VGHC, CGWRL.

76 For more on the politics of these types of initiatives see Greenberg, "Don't Buy Where You Can't Work," in *Or Does it Explode? Black Harlem in the Great Depression* (New York: Oxford University Press, 1991), 114–39. Prior to the Great Depression, access to simply buying at Chicago stores was a hot-button issue among African American activists. The *Chicago Whip* reported that a Miss Viola Penn was refused service at the famed Marshall Field and Company department store. The newspaper took the matter up with the management of the stores, to find out "why our people cannot spend the coin of the realm in their establishment." Penn planned on bringing suit against the retailer. "Marshall Field & Co. Again Refuses to Sell to Colored Girl," *Chicago Whip*, 1919.

Gareth Canaan argues that though the Depression was economically devastating for black Chicagoans, in the decades preceding it they were chronically underpaid and underemployed. See Gareth Canaan, "Part of the Loaf: Economic Conditions of Chicago's African-American Working Class during the 1920s," *Journal of Social History* 35 (Fall 2001): 147–74.

77 "Girls Quit Downtown Firm When Color Line Is Drawn," *Chicago Defender*, July 13, 1918.

78 Cox, "Negroes' Use of Their Buying Power in Chicago," 6.

79 Cox, "Negroes' Use of Their Buying Power in Chicago," 38.

80 [Untitled], *Provident Phalanx*, July 1946, box 1, folder 2, Joseph Bibb Papers (JBP), CHM. Joseph D. Bibb (1895–1966) was a well-known lawyer and civil rights activist in Chicago. He was the first black Chicagoan to be appointed to a state cabinet; Governor William Stratton named him the Illinois director of public safety in 1953. He was editor of the *Chicago Whip* between 1919 and 1932. See "Joseph Dandridge Bibb," in Henry Louis Gates and Evelyn Brooks Higginbotham, ed. *Harlem Renaissance Lives from African American National Biography* (New York: Oxford University Press), 51–52.

81 Cayton and Drake, *Black Metropolis*, 84.

82 Cox, "Negroes' Use of Their Buying Power in Chicago," 39.

83 Albion L. Holsey to Joseph Bibb, October 27, 1930, box 1, folder 2, JBP, CHM.

84 Arvarh E. Strickland, *History of the Chicago Urban League* (Columbia: University of Missouri Press, 2001), 50.

85 Cayton and Drake, *Black Metropolis*, 246.

86 Cox, "Negroes' Use of Their Buying Power in Chicago," 110–11.

87 Cayton and Drake, *Black Metropolis*, 257.

88 For more on the NYA, see Betty Grimes Lindley and Ernest K. Lindley, *A New Deal for Youth: The Story of the National Youth Administration* (New York: Viking Press, 1938).

89 "NYA Circular 7," April 1938, box 68, folder 3, EWBP, JRSCL.

90 "NYA Circular 7." The coverage of the opening of the NYA School for girls was headlined in the *Chicago Daily Tribune*: "Boondoggling Seminary Holds Open House: 100 Girls Enter," *Chicago Daily Tribune*, January 12, 1936.

91 Hilda W. Smith (HWS) to Wilfred S. Reynolds, November 6, 1935, National Youth Administration (NYA), Records of the National Advisory Committee on Educational Camps for Unemployed Young Women (RNACECUEYW), Correspondence of the Chairman of the Deputy Executive Directory of the NYA with State Youth And Camp Directors on Camp Policies and Problems, 1935–36, Arkansas-New Mexico, E 321, box no. 1, folder "Correspondence Camps, 1935, Illinois," Record Group (RG) 119.55, NARA.

92 Marguerite Gilmore (MG), Memo to Federal Emergency Relief Administration, November 9, 1935, NYA, RNACECUEYW, RN 119.55, NARA.

93 "State of Illinois National Youth Administration Resident School for Girls Request for Staff Appointment," NYA, RNACECUEYW, RN 119.55, NARA.

94 William J. Campbell to HWS, January 15, 1936, NYA, RNACECUEYW, RN 119.55, NARA.

95 MG, Letter dated January 10, 1936, NYA, RNACECUEYW, RN 119.55, NARA.

96 "20 Race Girls Are Studying at NYA School," *Chicago Defender*, January 25, 1936. The NYA created a similar program focusing on training boys in trades in Chicago. See "Champaign-Urbana," *Chicago Defender*, February 18, 1939.

97 "Class Schedule from January 10, 1936," NYA, RNACECUEYW, RN 119.55, NARA.

98 "Class Schedule from January 10, 1936."

99 "NYA School Here Offers Fine Opportunity for Girls," *Chicago Defender*, February 1, 1936.

100 "NYA Turns Loose Class of Girl Leaders Today," *Chicago Daily Tribune*, April 2, 1936.

101 "NYA School Here Offers Fine Opportunity for Girls."

102 "NYA School Here Offers Fine Opportunity for Girls."

103 "Asst. NYA Agent Makes State Tour," *Chicago Defender*, May 30, 1936.

104 "NYA Report on the Field Visit in the State of Illinois, by Leah K. Dickinson, Regional Supervisor of Service Projects, Region II, dated November 7, 1941," NYA, Records of the Service Projects Section Field Inspection Reports and related correspondence of the section chief concerning administration of Girls' Projects, Alabama-Michigan, E304, box no. 1, folder "Illinois," RN119.55, NARA.

105 "Letter from Ora B. Stokes, Field Investigator, to Mrs. Marie Dresden Lane regarding Illinois Report—Chicago, IL, dated July 9, 1941," NYA, Records of the Service Projects Section Field inspection Reports and related correspondence of the section chief concerning administration of Girls' Projects, Alabama-Michigan, E304, box no. 1, folder "Illinois," RN119.55, NARA.

106 See Lindley and Lindley, *New Deal for Youth,* and Richard A. Reiman, *The New Deal and American Youth: Ideas and Ideals in a Depression Decade* (Athens: University of Georgia Press, 1992).

107 NYA Is Dead—Killed by Race-Baiting of GOP and Southern Demo Clique," *Chicago Defender*, July 19, 1943.

108 See Susan L. Smith, *Sick and Tired of Being Sick and Tired: Black Women's Health Activism in America, 1890–1950* (Philadelphia: University of Pennsylvania Press), 153–67.

109 "Preface by Consuelo Young-Megahy," *Chicago Defender*, May 28, 1938.

110 Susan Ware, ed., "Dorothy Boulding Ferebee," in *Notable American Women: A Biographical Dictionary Completing the Twentieth Century* (Cambridge, MA: Harvard University Press, 2004), 203–5.

111 See Smith, *Sick and Tired.*

1 For more on the concept of black women's self-defense through organizing, see Deborah Gray White, *Too Heavy a Load: Black Women in Defense of Themselves* (New York: Norton, 1999).

2 Leslie Paris, *Children's Nature: The Rise of the American Summer Camp* (New York: New York University Press), 2. For more on the history of summer camps and gender, see Sue Miller, *Growing Girls: The Natural Origins of Girls' Organization in America* (New Brunswick, NJ: Rutgers University Press, 2007).

3 Miller, *Growing Girls.*

4 Elizabeth Clark-Lewis, *Living In, Living Out: African American Domestics in Washington, D.C., 1910–1940*, 47.

5 Clark-Lewis, *Living In, Living Out*, 47.

6 "White House Conference on Child Health and Protection survey, box 79, folder 3, Ernest Watson Burgess Papers (EWBP), JRLSC. Ernest Watson Burgess (1886–1966) was a University of Chicago–trained sociologist who worked with fellow sociologist Robert Park in developing the tenets of the Chicago's Sociology department, known as the Chicago School of Sociology, the center of critical research during the Great Migration. His research hypothesized a concentric circle mapping of urban areas. He contributed to the White House Conference on Child Health, an event that began in 1909 under the name White House Conference on Dependent Children. Burgess's most notable work includes Ernest W. Burgess and Robert Ezra Park, *An Introduction to the Science of Sociology* (Chicago: University of Chicago Press, 1921).

7 Camp Fire Girls of America, *The Book of the Camp Fire Girls* (New York: Camp Fire Girls of America, 1913), 5. Camp Fire Girls is now Camp Fire USA, a coeducational group. The process of integrating boys into Camp Fire began in 1969, when the Boy Scouts of America opened up their Explorers program to Camp Fire Girls. In 1975, the national Camp Fire organization welcomed boys in all its programs and renamed the organization Camp Fire Boys and Girls. In 2001, the organization became Camp Fire USA.

8 The Gulick children and grandchildren kept the campsite at Lake Sebago within their family for nearly a century. Louise Gulick and her husband, Davis Van Winkle, ran the camp, called WoHeLo, for more than thirty years. The camp is still in existence. For a comprehensive history of Camp Fire and gender in twentieth-century America, see Jennifer Hillman Helgren, *Inventing American Girlhood: Gender and Citizenship in the Twentieth-Century Camp Fire Girls* (PhD diss., Claremont Graduate University, 2005).

9 "Program," in Camp Fire Girls of America, *The Camp Fire Guide* (New York: Camp Fire Girls of America, 1940), 19.

10 Camp Fire Girls of America, *Wo-He-Lo: The Camp Fire History* (New York: Camp Fire, Inc., 1980), 6.

11 See Gail Bederman, *Manliness and Civilization: A Cultural History of Gen-*

der and Race in the United States, 1880–1917 (Chicago: University of Chicago Press, 1996).

12 For more on racial panics and children's organizations see Shari Huhndorf, *Going Native: American Indians in the American Cultural Imagination* (Ithaca, NY: Cornell University Press, 2001), and Phil Deloria, *Playing Indian* (New Haven, CT: Yale University Press, 1999). For a specific conversation on Camp Fire and American Indian identity, see Jennifer Helgren, "Native American and White Camp Fire Girls Enact Modern Girlhood, 1910–39," *American Quarterly* 66, no. 2 (2014), 333–60.

13 A. E. Hamilton, "Putting Over Eugenics: Making It a Living Force Depends on Sound Application of Psychology and Sociology—Camp Fire Girls an Organization Which Will Create Eugenic Ideals in Women in an Indirect but Effective Way," *Journal of Heredity* 6, no. 6 (1915): 281–88.

14 Hamilton, "Putting Over Eugenics."

15 For the role of girls' organizations in assimilation, see Laureen Tedesco, "Progressive Era Girl Scouts and the Immigrant: *Scouting for Girls* (1920) as a Handbook for American Girlhood," *Children's Literature Association Quarterly* 31, no. 4 (Winter 2006): 346–68.

16 June 6, 1912, Ruth S. Baldwin (RSB) to L. H. Wood (LHW), L. Hollingsworth Wood Papers (LHWP), box 53, folder 1, Quaker Collection, HC.

17 Helgren, *Inventing American Girlhood*, 275. For more on the Blue Triangle League, 1919–1974, see the website of the Tennessee State University's digital library, http://ww2.tnstate.edu/library/digital/Blue.htm, (accessed July 9, 2014). For more on Nashville in the Migration era, see Louis M. Kyriakoudes, *The Social Origins of the Urban South: Race, Gender and Migration in Nashville and Middle Tennessee* (Chapel Hill: University of North Carolina Press, 2003). Girls in the Blue Triangle League and the Girls Reserves worked together to overcome the racial segregation in the organization throughout the 1940s. For a rich institutional history of how YWCA members understood their Christian mission in the fight against racial segregation, see Nancy Marie Robertson, *Christian Sisterhood, Race Relations, and the YWCA, 1906–1946* (Urbana: University of Illinois Press, 2007). For more on the YWCA movement among African Americans see Judith Weisenfeld, *African American Women and Christian Activism: New York's Black YWCA, 1905–1945* (Cambridge, MA: Harvard University Press, 1997).

18 Helgren, *Inventing American Girlhood*, 275.

19 For more on the racial politics of Girls Scouts, especially their exclusion of African American girls in spite of their openness to girls of other races and ethnicities and disabled girls, see Stacy A. Cordery, *Juliette Gordon Low: The Remarkable Founder of the Girl Scouts* (New York: Viking Press, 2012), 248–50.

20 Tedesco, "Progressive Era Girl Scouts and the Immigrant," 346–68.

21 "The Clotee Scott Settlement," *Chicago Defender*, January 23, 1915, and "The Clotee Scott Settlement," *Chicago Defender*, August 7, 1915.

22 "Clubs and Societies," *Chicago Defender*, July 22, 1916.

23 Benjamin E. Mays and Joseph Nicholson, *The Negro's Church* (New York: Arno Press, 1933), 155.

24 Luther Gulick, "Girls Work, #10," *Annals of the American Academy of Political and Social Science* 79, September 1918, 190.

25 Gulick, "Girls Work, #10."

26 Memo from Abbie Condit, regarding Minute Girls Program, June 3, 1918, Irene McCoy Gaines Papers, box 1, folder 2, Chicago History Museum.

27 For more on black military service and patriotism claims see Adrienne Lentz-Smith, *Freedom Struggles: African Americans and World War I* (Cambridge, MA: Harvard University Press, 2011).

28 Irene McCoy Gaines, "Views on Many Topics by Readers of the Daily News: Plea for the Colored Girl," *Chicago Daily News*, May 27, 1920.

29 "Clubs and Fraternal," *Chicago Defender*, March 2, 1918. Irene Goins (1876 or 1877–1929) was a prominent clubwoman and activist. She was a member of Chicago's City Federation of Colored Women's Clubs, the Illinois Federation of Colored Women's Clubs, the Frederick Douglass League of Women Voters, and the Women's Trade Union League. See Elizabeth Davis Lindsay, *The Story of Illinois Federation of Colored Women's Clubs* (Chicago: S.N., 1922) and Lisa G. Materson, *For the Freedom of Her Race: Black Women and Electoral Politics in Illinois, 1877–1932* (Chapel Hill: University of North Carolina Press).

30 "Loma Camp Fire Girls Give Beautiful Pageant," *Chicago Defender*, June 10, 1918.

31 Untitled advertisement, *Chicago Defender*, May 18, 1918.

32 Wilma, "Social Calendar: Items of Special Interest," *Chicago Defender*, March 13, 1943.

33 "Seen and Heard along the North Shore," *Chicago Defender*, September 30, 1916.

34 Luther H. Gulick, "Recreation and Youth," *Proceedings of the Academy of Political Science in the City of New York* 2, no. 4 (July 1912): 592.

35 "Seen and Heard Along the North Shore."

36 "In Concert," *Chicago Defender*, March 14, 1931. Pilgrim Baptist Church is often referred to as the birthplace of gospel music, under the leadership of their music minister, Thomas A. Dorsey.

37 The literature on juvenile delinquency is incredibly vast, with studies from disciplines and perspectives as varied as sociology, social psychology, criminology, gender studies, economics, and critical race theory contributing to the analysis of the causes, and potential remedies, of juvenile delinquency. Anthony M. Platt's groundbreaking work *The Child Savers: The Invention of Delinquency* (Chicago: University of Chicago Press, 1969) interrogates the idea that work with youth was merely benevolent by looking at the punitive nature of juvenile institutions and the ideological work of the movement's leaders. For a

historical account of delinquency and race, particularly racial segregation in juvenile facilities, see Barry C. Feld, *Bad Kids: Race and the Transformation of the Juvenile Court* (New York: Oxford University Press, 1999), and Geoff K. Ward, *The Black Child Savers: Racial Democracy and Juvenile Justice* (Chicago: University of Chicago Press, 2012). For more about the historical roots of current problems in gendering juvenile delinquency, see Meda Chesney-Lind, *The Female Offender: Girls, Women and Crime* (Thousand Oaks, CA: Sage, 1997), and Ruth Alexander, *The Girl Problem: Female Sexual Delinquency in New York, 1900–1930* (Ithaca, NY: Cornell University Press, 1995); "Progressive," *Chicago Defender*, January 7, 1933.

38 "Oececa Camp Fire Officers Plan Affair; Florence I. Williams to Be Guest Speaker," *Chicago Defender*, July 7, 1940.

39 "Girl Given Scholarship by Rep. William E. King," *Chicago Defender*, October 3, 1931.

40 "A.K.A. Sorors Give Original 3-Act Comedy," *Chicago Defender*, May 14, 1932, and "Softball Tournament Starts September 5," *Chicago Defender*, September 4, 1932. At the urging of South Side Chicago community groups, the Chicago Park District acquired land from the South Park Commission to establish a park in 1934. In the 1940s, the federal government purchased more land in the area around the park to create the Ida B. Wells Home, one of the first housing projects open to African-American families exclusively.

41 "Hawaiian Goddess," *Chicago Defender*, July 25, 1942.

42 "Camp Fire Sponsors in Outing and Program," *Chicago Defender*, August 31, 1940.

43 See Adam Green, *Selling the Race: Culture, Community, and Black Chicago, 1940–1955* (Chicago: University of Chicago Press, 2007).

44 Sophonisba Breckinridge and Edith Abbott, *The Delinquent Child and the Home* (1912; reprint, New York: Arno Press, 1970), 57.

45 Regina Kunzel, *Fallen Women, Problem Girls: Unmarried Mothers and the Professionalization of Social Work, 1890–1945* (New Haven, CT: Yale University Press, 1995); E. Franklin Frazier, *The Negro Family in Chicago* (Chicago: University of Chicago Press, 1932), 273.

46 Frazier, *Negro Family in Chicago*, 348.

47 Frazier, *Negro Family in Chicago*, 206.

48 Horace Cayton and St. Clair Drake, *Black Metropolis: A Study of Negro Life in a Northern City*, 3rd ed. (Chicago: University of Chicago Press, 1993), 589.

49 Frazier, *Negro Family in Chicago*, 204.

50 "Bud's Easter Celebration Boon to Youth of Race," *Chicago Defender*, April 11, 1936.

51 Cayton and Drake, *Black Metropolis*, 3rd ed., 589.

52 "What the People Say," *Chicago Defender*, March 6, 1940.

53 "Advantages of Camping Are Cited," *Chicago Defender*, July 6, 1935.

54 "Colored Girl Reserves," *Southern Workman* 50 (August 1921): 353–56.

55 "Summer Camp Program Set," *Chicago Defender*, July 1, 1944.

56 "Illinois State News," *Chicago Defender*, December 10, 1930.

57 Belle Fountain, "Race Women in Club Work," *Chicago Defender*, May 4, 1935.

58 "Illinois," *Chicago Defender*, August 22, 1936.

59 "Coleman's Camp to Hold Benefit Party April 18th; Camp Shows Progress since 1935 Opening," *Chicago Defender*, April 15, 1939.

60 "Summer Day Camp, 1944," box 2, folder: Chicago Commons, Clubs and Groups, 1943–1947, Chicago Commons Association Records (CCAR), CHM. The Chicago Commons Settlement House (established 1894) was founded by Graham Taylor and modeled after Jane Addams's Hull House. The Chicago Commons settlement began serving black and Mexican neighborhood residents in the 1930s and 1940s, promoting integration. His daughter Lea Demarest Taylor (1883–1975) assumed leadership of the Settlement in 1922. Lea Taylor was especially interested in race relations and oversaw the integrated children's activity at the settlement. See Mina Carson, *Settlement Folk: Social Thought and the American Settlement Movement, 1885–1930* (Chicago: University of Chicago Press, 1990).

61 "Fall Report on Evening Work, 1945–1946," box 2, folder: Chicago Commons, 1943–1947, CCAR, CHM.

62 "January Report, 1946," box 2, folder: Chicago Commons, 1943–1947, CCAR, CHM.

63 "Additional Information Obtained from Interviews," box 2, folder: Chicago Commons, 1945–1946, CCAR, CHM.

64 "Additional Information Obtained from Interviews."

65 "Interview, 1950," box 2, folder: Chicago Commons, 1948–1952, CCAR, CHM.

66 "Chicago Commons Association Individual Summary, Joann Lyles," box 2, folder: Chicago Commons-Summer Camps, CCAR, CHM.

67 "V. Davis," box 2, folder: Chicago Commons, 1943–1947, CCAR, CHM.

68 Founded in Chicago in 1919, the National Association of Negro Musicians worked to educate black students in music and support black performers and composers.

69 Lewis Walker and Benjamin C. Wilson, *Black Eden: The Idlewild Community* (East Lansing: Michigan State University Press, 2007). For an analysis of the social class dynamics of Idlewild and other black elite vacation spots, like Martha's Vineyard, see Lawrence Otis, *Our Kind of People: Inside America's Black Upper Class* (New York: Harper Perennial, 2009).

70 "Our Town," *Chicago Daily Tribune*, October 5, 1947.

71 "Woman's Club Celebrates 46th Year," *Chicago Defender*, January 28, 1939.

72 "Carefree Hours of Enjoyment are Anticipated by Supporters of Second Annual Women's Amateur Minstrel," *Chicago Defender*, November 5, 1938.

73 "Camp Fire Girls Will Honor Bud Billiken at Autumn Soiree," *Chicago Defender*, November 1, 1947.

74 Photograph, *Chicago Defender*, May 8, 1954.

75 "National Hails Campfire Girls and Girl Scouts," *Chicago Defender*, March 10, 1956.

76 "On Good Friday," *Chicago Daily Defender*, May 10, 1958.

77 Frazier, *Negro Family in Chicago*, 49.

78 Frazier, *Negro Family in Chicago*, 49.

79 E. Franklin Frazier, "Problems and Needs of Negro Children and Youth Resulting from Family Disorganization," *Journal of Negro Education* (Summer 1960), 276–77.

80 For more on critiques of black matriarchy beyond Frazier's *Negro Family*, see E. Franklin Frazier, "Certain Aspects of Conflict in the Negro Family," *Social Forces* 10, no. 1 (October 1932): 76–84.

81 For more on readings of E. Franklin Frazier and blacks, see Daryl Michael Scott, *Contempt and Pity: The Black Psyche: Social Policy and the Image of the Damaged Black Psyche, 1880–1996* (Chapel Hill: University of North Carolina Press, 1997), 41–56.

82 For more on South Chicago and Chicago's Mexican community, as well as other Latino populations, see Lilia Fernandez, *Brown in the Windy City: Mexicans and Puerto Ricans in Postwar Chicago* (Chicago: University of Chicago Press, 2012), and Michael Innis-Jimenez, *Steel Barrio: The Great Mexican Migration to South Chicago, 1915–1940* (New York: New York University Press, 2013).

83 Frazier, *Negro Family in Chicago*, 19.

84 Frazier, *Negro Family in Chicago*, 19.

85 Interview with Woman who worked in Men's Hotel on South Side Hotel, Court of Domestic Relations Interviews (CDRI), box 131–81, folder 11, Research Projects, The Negro Family in the US Case Studies (RPNFUSCS), E. Franklin Frazier Papers (EFFP), MSRC.

86 Interview dated November 22, 1929, box 131–82, folder 2, Research Projects, The Negro Family in the US (RPNFUS), Cases of Illegitimacy (CI), EFFP, MRSC.

87 CI Notes, RPNFUS, EFFP, MSRC.

88 "I Remember" essay, RPNFUS, EFFP, MSRC.

89 CI Notes dated July 1929, RPNFUS, EFFP, MSRC.

90 CI Notes, RPNFUS, EFFP, MSRC.

91 CI Notes, RPNFUS, EFFP, MSRC.

92 Interview, RPNFUS EFFP, MRSC.

93 Ashley Crawley, "Dependent Negro Children in Chicago in 1926" (PhD diss., University of Chicago, 1928), 142–43.

94 Interview, RPFNUSCS EFFP, MRSC.

95 CI Note #15, RPNFUS, EFFP, MSRC.

96 CI Note #16, RPNFUS, EFFP, MSRC.

97 Interview dated July 23, 1915, RPNFUS, EFFP, MSRC.

98 Interview dated July 23, 1915, RPNFUS.

99 "Personal Interview with a South Chicago Boy," February 14, 1934, box 89, folder 5, EWBP, JRSCL.

100 Elizabeth Ann Clement, *Love for Sale: Courting, Treating, and Prostitution in New York City, 1900–1945* (Chapel Hill: University of North Carolina Press, 2006).

101 Interview dated May 8, 1929, RPNFUS, EFFP, MSRC.

102 "Interview with Rev. E. N. Wainwright," box 89, folder 5, EWBP, JRSCL.

103 "When I Was Small," May 4, 1929, RPNFUS, EFFP, MSRC.

104 CI Note #20, RPNFUS, EFFP, MSRC.

105 "Interview with Mr. Frejeau, Truant Officer," January 20, 1934, box 89, folder 5, EWBP, JRSCL.

106 "Interview with Rev. E. N. Wainwright, Pilgrim Baptist Church," 1934, EWBP, JRSCL.

107 "Interview with Rev. E. N. Wainwright, Pilgrim Baptist Church," 1934, EWBP.

CONCLUSION. "SHE WAS FIGHTING FOR HER FATHER'S FREEDOM"

1 For more on television and civil rights, see Sasha Torres, *Black, White, and in Color: Television and Black Civil Rights* (Princeton, NJ: Princeton University Press, 2003), Kay Mills, *Changing Channels: The Civil Rights Case that Transformed Television* (Oxford: University of Mississippi Press, 2004), and Aniko Bodroghkozy, *Equal Time: Television and the Civil Rights Movement* (Urbana: University of Illinois Press, 2012).

2 For more on the Little Rock High School integration crisis, see Elizabeth Jacoway, *Turn Away Thy Son: Little Rock, The Crisis That Shocked the Nation* (New York: Simon and Schuster, 2007) and Karen Anderson, *Little Rock: Race and Resistance at Central High School* (Princeton, NJ: Princeton University Press, 2009). For more on Daisy Gatson Bates, see Daisy Bates, *The Long Shadow of Little Rock: A Memoir* (Fayetteville: University of Arkansas Press, 2007), and Grif Stockley, *Daisy Bates: Civil Rights Crusader from Arkansas* (Oxford: University Press of Mississippi, 2012).

3 "Banquet Brings Tears to Daisy Bates' Eyes," *Chicago Defender*, May 23, 1960.

4 For personal accounts of the Little Rock integration crisis, see Melba Pattillo-Beals, *Warriors Don't Cry: A Searing Memoir of the Battle to Integrate Little Rock's Central High School* (New York: Washington Square Press, 1995); Terrence Roberts, *Lessons from Little Rock* (Little Rock: Butler Center for Arkansas Studies, 2009); Carlotta Walls LaNier and Lisa Frazier Page, *A Mighty Long Way: My Journey to Justice at Little Rock Central High School* (New York: Ballantine, 2010); and David Margolick, *Elizabeth and Hazel: Two Women of Little Rock* (New Haven, CT: Yale University Press, 2011). For more on the relationship between Cold War politics and civil rights, see Mary

Dudziak, *Cold War Civil Rights: Race and the Image of American Democracy* (Princeton, NJ: Princeton University Press, 2011).

5 Glenda Gilmore, *Defying Dixie: The Radical Roots of Civil Rights, 1919–1950* (New York: Norton, 2008), 10.

6 In an episode that was quickly overshadowed by the desegregation standoff in Little Rock, fifteen-year-old Dorothy Counts briefly integrated a Charlotte, North Carolina, high school in 1957. See Susan Cahn, *Sexual Reckonings: Southern Girls in a Troubling Age* (Cambridge, MA: Harvard University Press, 2007), 269–301, and Frye Gaillard, *The Dream Long Deferred* (Chapel Hill: University of North Carolina Press, 1988), 3–17. Ruby Bridge integrated a primary school in New Orleans in 1960. See Liva Baker, *The Second Battle of New Orleans: The Hundred-Year Struggle to Integrate the Schools* (New York: HarperCollins, 1996).

7 Michelle Obama, "Remarks by the First Lady at the Joint Luncheon Meeting: Working Together to Address Youth Violence in Chicago," April 10, 2013, website of the White House, www.whitehouse.gov (accessed July 17, 2014).

BIBLIOGRAPHY

LIBRARIES AND ARCHIVES

AESL   Arthur and Elizabeth Schlesinger Library, Radcliffe Institute for Advanced Studies, Harvard University, Cambridge, MA

CGWRL   Carter G. Woodson Regional Library, Chicago Public Library, Chicago.

CHM   Chicago History Museum, Chicago.

DMAAH   Du Sable Museum of African-American History, Chicago.

HC   Haverford College Library, Haverford, PA

JRSCL   Joseph Regenstein Special Collections Library, University of Chicago, Chicago.

LOC   Library of Congress, Manuscripts Division, Washington, DC

MSRC   Moorland-Spingarn Research Center, Howard University, Washington, DC

NARA   National Archives and Records Administration, College Park, MD

RJDL   Richard J. Daley Library, University of Illinois-Chicago, Chicago.

SCRBC   Schomburg Center for Research in Black Culture, New York Public Library, New York.

MANUSCRIPT COLLECTIONS

Chicago History Museum
Harris Gaines Collection
Irene McCoy Gaines Collection
Joseph Bibb Papers
Lea Demarest Taylor Papers

Richard J. Daley Library, University of Illinois-Chicago
Illinois Children's Home and Aid Society Records
Juvenile Protective Association Papers

Lloyd O. Lewis Papers
Mary Bartelme Papers
Marcy Newberry Association papers
Phyllis Wheatley Association Papers
Urban League Annual Reports
Young Men's Christian Association-Wabash Avenue Records

DuSable Museum of African-American History
Hope Ives Dunmore/Old Settlers Social Club Collection

Haverford College Library
L. Hollingsworth Wood Papers, Quaker Collection

Library of Congress
Mary Church Terrell Papers
Nannie Helen Burroughs Papers

Moorland-Spingarn Research Center, Howard University
E. Franklin Frazier Papers

National Archives and Records Administration, College Park, MD
Records of the National Youth Administration

Joseph Regenstein Special Collections Library, University of Chicago
Ernest Watson Burgess Papers
Everett Cherrington Hughes Papers
Ida B. Wells-Barnett Papers
Julius Rosenwald Papers

Arthur and Elizabeth Schlesinger Library, Radcliffe Institute for Advanced Studies, Harvard University
Ellen M. Hernotin Papers

Schomburg Center for Research in Black Culture
Moorish Science Temple of American Collection
Melva Price Papers

Carter G. Woodson Regional Library, Vivian G. Harsh Collection
Arthur Logan Papers
Illinois Writers Project Papers

NEWSPAPERS, MAGAZINES AND JOURNALS

Alpha Kappa Alpha Ivy Leaf
Broad Ax
Chicago Daily News
Chicago Daily Tribune
Chicago Defender
Chicago Whip
The Crisis
Fellowship Herald
Moorish Guide
Moorish Voice
National Association Notes
New York Amsterdam News
Pittsburgh Courier
Second Ward News
Southern Workman
The Brownies' Book
University of Chicago Magazine
Voice of the Negro

INSTITUTIONAL HISTORIES

Chicago Northern District Association. *The Story of Seventy-Five Years of the Chicago and Northern District of Club Women, Inc., 1906–1981.* Chicago: Chicago Northern District Association, 1981.

Davis, Elizabeth Lindsay, ed. *Lifting as They Climb: An Historical Record of the National Association of Colored Women.* Washington, DC: NACW, Inc., 1933.

National Association of Colored Women. *A History of the Club Movement.* Washington, DC: NACW, Inc., 1902.

SECONDARY SOURCES

Adero, Malaika, ed. *Up South: Stories and Letters of this Century's African-American Migrations.* New York: New Press, 1993.

Alexander, Ruth. *The Girl Problem: Female Sexual Delinquency in New York, 1900–1930.* Ithaca, NY: Cornell University Press, 1995.

Allen, Jr., Earnest. "Religious Heterodoxy and Nationalist Tradition: The Continuing Evolution of the Nation of Islam." *Black Scholar* 26, nos. 3–4 (Fall 1996/Winter 1997): 2–34.

Allen, Joe. *People Wasn't Meant to Burn: A True Story of Housing, Race and Murder in Chicago.* Chicago: Haymarket Books, 2011.

Anderson, Alan B., and George W. Pickering. *Confronting the Color Line: The Broken Promise of the Civil Rights Movement in Chicago*. Athens: University of Georgia Press, 1986.

Anderson, Karen. *Little Rock: Race and Resistance at Central High School*. Princeton, NJ: Princeton University Press, 2009.

Aptheker, Bettina. *Woman's Legacy: Essays on Race, Sex, and Class in American History*. Amherst: University of Massachusetts Press, 1982.

Aptheker, Herbert, ed. *A Documentary History of the Negro People in the United States, Volume 2*. New York: Citadel Press, 1968.

Aries, Philippe. *Centuries of Childhood: A Social Study of Family Life*. New York: Vintage Books, 1962.

Ascoli, Peter. *Julius Rosenwald: The Man Who Built Sears, Roebuck and Advanced the Cause of Black Education in the American South*. Bloomington: Indiana University Press, 2006.

Baker, Liva. *The Second Battle of New Orleans: The Hundred-Year Struggle to Integrate the Schools*. New York: HarperCollins, 1996.

Baldwin, Davarian. *Chicago's New Negroes: Modernity, the Great Migration, and Black Urban Life*. Chapel Hill: University of North Carolina Press, 2007.

Bartlett, David C., and Larry A. McClellan. "The Final Ministry of Amanda Berry Smith." *Illinois Heritage* 1, no. 2 (Winter 1998): 22–31.

Bates, Daisy. *The Long Shadow of Little Rock: A Memoir*. Fayetteville: University of Arkansas Press, 2007.

Batterham, E. Rose. "Negro Girls and the Y.M.C.A." *Southern Workman* 48 (1919): 511–18.

Bederman, Gail. *Manliness and Civilization: A Cultural History of Gender and Race in the United States, 1880–1917*. Chicago: University of Chicago Press, 1995.

Bernstein, Robin. *Racial Innocence: Performing American Childhood from Slavery to Civil Rights*. New York: New York University Press, 2011.

Best, Wallace. *Passionately Human, No Less Divine: Religion and Culture in Black Chicago, 1915–1952*. Princeton, NJ: Princeton University Press, 2005.

Blair, Cynthia. *I've Got to Make My Living: Black Women Sex Workers in Turn-of-the-Century Chicago*. Chicago: University of Chicago Press, 2010.

Blauvelt, Mary Taylor. "The Race Problem as Discussed by Negro Women." *American Journal of Sociology* 6 (1900–1901): 662–72.

Blount, Jackie. *Fit to Teach: Same-Sex Desire, Gender, and School Work in the Twentieth Century*. Albany: State University Press of New York, 2006.

Bodine, William Lester. *Bodine's Reference Book on Juvenile Welfare: A Review of the Chicago Social Service System*. Chicago: Bodine, 1913.

Bodroghkozy, Aniko. *Equal Time: Television and the Civil Rights Movement*. Urbana: University of Illinois Press, 2012.

Bone, Robert and Richard A. Courage. *The Muse in Bronzeville: African American Creative Expression in Chicago, 1932–1950*. New Brunswick, NJ: Rutgers University Press, 2011.

Bontemps, Arna, and Jack Conroy. *Anyplace but Here*. Columbia: University of Missouri Press, 1997.

Boyd, Michelle R. *Jim Crow Nostalgia: Reconstructing Race in Bronzeville*. Minneapolis: University of Minnesota Press, 2008.

Boza, Sophia, A. P. Drucker, A. L. Harris, Miriam Schaffner, and Louise deKoven Bowen. *The Colored People of Chicago: An Investigation Made for the Juvenile Protective Association*. Chicago: Juvenile Protective Association, 1913.

Branham, Charles. "Black Chicago: Accommodationist Politics before the Great Migration." In *The Ethnic Frontier: Group Survival in Chicago and the Midwest*, eds. Melvin Holli and Peter Jones, 212–62. Grand Rapids, Mich.: Eerdmans, 1977.

Brawley, Benjamin. *Women of Achievement*. Chicago: Women's Baptist Home Mission Society, 1919.

Breckinridge, Sophonisba, and Edith Abbott. *The Delinquent Child and the Home*. New York: Charities Publication Committee, 1912.

Brown, Tamara L., Gregory S. Parks, and Clarenda M. Phillips, eds. *African-American Fraternities and Sororities: The Legacy and Vision*. Lexington: University Press of Kentucky, 2005.

Brunell-Forman, Miriam. *Babysitter: An American History*. New York: New York University Press, 2010.

Buckler, Helen. *Daniel Hale Williams, Negro Surgeon*. New York: Pittman, 1968.

Bundles, A'Leila. *On Her Own Ground: The Life and Times of Madam C. J. Walker*. New York: Scribner, 2002.

Burgess, Ernest W. and Robert Ezra Park. *An Introduction to the Science of Sociology*. Chicago: University of Chicago Press, 1921.

Butler, Anthea. *Women in the Church of God in Christ: Making a Sanctified World*. Chapel Hill: University of North Carolina Press, 2007.

Butler, John Sibley. *Entrepreneurship and Self-Help Among Black Americans: A Reconsideration of Race and Economics*. Albany: State University Press of New York, 2005.

Cahn, Susan. *Sexual Reckonings: Southern Girls in a Troubling Age*. Cambridge, MA: Harvard University Press, 2007.

Canaan, Gareth. "Part of the Loaf: Economic Conditions of Chicago's African-American Working Class during the 1920's." *Journal of Social History* 35.1 (Fall 2001): 147–74.

Carby, Hazel. "Policing the Black Woman's Body in an Urban Context." *Critical Inquiry* 18, no. 4 (Summer 1992): 738–55.

Carby, Hazel. *Reconstructing Womanhood: The Emergence of the Afro-American Woman Novelist*. New York: Oxford University Press, 1987.

Carlson, Shirley J. "Black Ideals of Womanhood in the Late Victorian Era." *Journal of Negro History* 77 (Spring 1992): 61–73.

Carson, Emmett Devon. *A Hand Up: A Black Philanthropy and Self-Help America*. Ann Arbor: University of Michigan Press, 1993.

Carson, Mina. *Settlement Folk: Social Thought and the American Settlement Movement, 1885–1930*. Chicago: University of Chicago Press, 1990.

Cayton, Horace, and St. Clair Drake. *Black Metropolis: A Story of Negro Life in a Northern City*. Chicago: University of Chicago Press, 1962.

Chapman, Erin D. *Prove It on Me: New Negroes, Sex and Popular Culture in the 1920s*. New York: Oxford University Press, 2012.

Chavez-Garcia, Miroslava. *States of Delinquency: Race and Science in the Making of California's Juvenile Justice System*. Berkeley: University of California Press, 2012.

Chesney-Lind, Meda. *The Female Offender: Girls, Women and Crime*. Thousand Oaks, CA: Sage, 1997.

Chicago Commission on Race Relations. *The Negro in Chicago: A Study of Race Relations and a Race Riot*. Chicago: University of Chicago Press, 1922.

Clark-Lewis, Elizabeth. *Living In, Living Out: African American Domestics in Washington, D.C., 1910–1940*. Washington, DC: Smithsonian Institution Press, 1994.

Clegg, Claude Andrew, III. *The Price of Liberty: African-Americans and the Making of Liberia*. Chapel Hill: University of North Carolina Press, 2003.

Clegg, Claude Andrew, III. "Rebuilding the Nation: The Life and Work of Elijah Muhammad, 1946–1954." *Black Scholar* 26, nos. 3–4 (Fall 1996/Winter 1 997): 51.

Clement, Elizabeth Ann. *Love for Sale: Courting, Treating, and Prostitution in New York City, 1900–1945*. Chapel Hill: University of North Carolina Press, 2006.

Climent, James. *Another America: The Story of Liberia and the Former Slaves Who Ruled It*. New York: Hill and Wang, 2013.

Cmiel, Kenneth. *Home of Another Kind: One Chicago Orphanage and the Tangle of Child Welfare*. Chicago: University of Chicago Press, 1995.

Cohen, Robert, ed. *Dear Mrs. Roosevelt: Letters from Children of the Great Depression*. Chapel Hill: University of North Carolina Press, 2002.

Collier-Thomas, Bettye. *Daughters of Thunder: Black Women Preachers and Their Sermons, 1850–1979*. San Francisco: Jossey-Bass, 1998.

Collins, Patricia Hill. *Black Feminist Thought: Knowledge, Consciousness and Politics of Empowerment*. Boston: Routledge, 1981.

Cordery, Stacy A. *Juliette Gordon Low: The Remarkable Founder of the Girl Scouts*. New York: Viking Press, 2012.

Crenson, Matthew. *Building the Invisible Orphanage: A Prehistory of the American Welfare System*. Cambridge, MA: Harvard University Press, 2001.

Cronon, E. David. *Black Moses: The Story of Marcus Garvey and the Universal Negro Improvement Association*. Madison: University of Wisconsin Press, 1960.

Curwood, Anastasia. *Stormy Weather: New Negro Marriage in the Interwar Years*. Chapel Hill: University of North Carolina Press, 2007.

Daniel, Phillip T. K. "A History of Discrimination against Black Students in Chicago Secondary Schools." *History of Education Quarterly* 2, no. 2 (Summer 1988): 147–62.

Danns, Dionne. *Something Better for Our Children: Black Organizing in Chicago Public Schools, 1963–1971*. New York: Taylor and Francis, 2002.

Danns, Dionne. "Thriving in the Midst of Adversity: Educator Maudelle Brown Bousfield's Struggles in Chicago, 1920–1950." *Journal of Negro Education* 78, no. 1 (Winter 2009) 3–16.

Davis, Angela. *Women, Race, and Class*. New York: Random House, 1981.

Day, S. Davis. "Herbert Hoover and Racial Politics: The De Priest Incident." *Journal of Negro History* 65 (Winter 1980): 6–17.

De Costa-Willis, Miriam, ed. *The Memphis Diary of Ida B. Wells*. New York: Beacon Press, 1995.

Deegan, Mary Jo, ed. *The New Woman of Color: The Collected Writings of Fannie Barrier Williams*. DeKalb: Northern Illinois University Press, 2005.

Deloria, Phil. *Playing Indian*. New Haven, CT: Yale University Press, 1999.

Dempsey, Travis. *An Autobiography of Black Chicago*. Chicago: Urban Research Institute, 1981.

Deutsch, Stephanie. *You Need a Schoolhouse: Booker T. Washington, Julius Rosenwald and the Building of Schools for the Segregated South*. Evanston, IL: Northwestern University Press, 2011.

Devlin, Rachel. *Relative Intimacy: Father and Daughters in Post–World War II America*. Chapel Hill: University of North Carolina Press, 2007.

Dill, Bonnie Thornton. "The Dialectics of Black Womanhood." *Signs* 4, no. 3 (1979): 543–55.

Diner, Steven J. "Chicago Social Workers and Blacks in the Progressive Era." *Social Science Review* 44 (December 1970): 393–410.

Dorman, Jacob S. *Chosen People: The Rise of American Black Israelite Religions*. New York: Oxford University Press, 2013.

Dorsey, James. *Up South: Blacks in Chicago's Suburbs 1719–1983*. Bristol, IN: Wyndham Hall Press, 1986.

Drake, St. Clair, and Horace R. Clayton. *Black Metropolis: A Study in the Negro Life in the Northern City*. New York: Harcourt, Brace, 1945.

Du Bois, W. E. B. *Some Efforts for Social Betterment among Negro Americans*. Atlanta: Atlanta University Press, 1909.

Du Bois, W. E. B. *The College Bred Negro: Report of a Social Study*. Atlanta: Atlanta University Press, 1900.

Dudziak, Mary. *Cold War Civil Rights: Race and the Image of American Democracy*. Princeton, NJ: Princeton University Press, 2011.

Durst, Anne. *Women Educators in the Progressive Era: The Women Behind Dewey's Laboratory School*. New York: Palgrave Macmillan, 2010.

Duster, Alfreda M., ed. *A Crusade for Justice: The Autobiography of Ida B. Wells*. Chicago: University of Chicago Press, 1970.

Edmonds-Cady, Cynthia. "Mobilizing Motherhood: Race, Class, and the Uses of

Maternalism in the Welfare Rights Movement," *WSQ: Women's Studies Quarterly* 37, nos. 3/4 (Fall/Winter 2009): 206–22.

Enstad, Nan. *Ladies of Labor, Girls of Adventure: Working Women, Popular Culture, and Labor Politics at the Turn of the Century*. New York: Columbia University Press, 1999.

Estrine, Judith and Edward Rohs. *Raised by the Church: Growing Up in New York City's Catholic Orphanages*. New York: Fordham University Press, 2011.

Everil, Bronwen. *Abolition and Empire in Sierra Leone and Liberia*. New York: Palgrave McMillan, 2012.

Fauset, Arthur Huff. *Black Gods of the Metropolis: Negro Religious Cults of the Urban North*. Philadelphia: University of Pennsylvania Press, 1944.

Feld, Barry C. *Bad Kids: Race and the Transformation of the Juvenile Court*. New York: Oxford University Press, 1999.

Feldstein, Ruth. *Motherhood in Black and White: Race and Sex in American Liberalism, 1930–1965*. Ithaca, NY: Cornell University Press, 2000.

Fernandez, Lillia. *Brown in the Windy City: Mexicans and Puerto Ricans in Postwar Chicago*. Chicago: University of Chicago Press, 2012.

Firth, Maude Mary. "The Use of the Foster Home for the Care of the Delinquent Girls of the Cook County Juvenile Court." Master's thesis, University of Chicago, 1924.

Fitzpatrick, Ellen. *Endless Crusade: Women Social Scientists and Progressive Reform*. New York: Oxford University Press, 1994.

Flanagan, Maureen. *Seeing with Their Hearts: Chicago Women and the Vision of the Good City, 1871–1933*. Princeton, NJ: Princeton University Press, 2002.

Frazier, E. Franklin. "Certain Aspects of Conflict in the Negro Family." *Social Forces* 10, no. 1 (October 1932): 76–84.

Frazier, E. Franklin. *The Negro Church in America*. New York: Schocken Books, 1963.

Frazier, E. Franklin. *The Negro Family in Chicago*. Chicago: University of Chicago Press, 1932.

Fulop, Timothy E. and Albert J. Raboteau. *African-American Religion: Interpretive Essays in History and Culture*. New York: Routledge, 1996.

Gaillard, Frye. *The Dream Long Deferred*. Chapel Hill: University of North Carolina Press, 1988.

Gaines, Kevin Kelly. *Uplifting the Race: Black Leadership, Politics, and Culture in the Twentieth Century*. Chapel Hill: University of North Carolina Press, 1996.

Garvey, Amy Jacques, ed. *Philosophy and Opinions of Marcus Garvey, Or Africa for the Africans*. New York: Athenaeum Press, 1969.

Garvey, Marcus. *Marcus Garvey Life and Lessons: A Centennial Companion to the Marcus Garvey and the University Negro Improvement Association Papers*, edited by Barbara Bair and Robert Hill. Berkeley: University of California Press, 1988.

Gatewood, Willard B. *Aristocrats of Color: The Black Elite, 1880–1920*. Bloomington: Indiana University Press, 1990.

Gibson, Campbell and Kay Jung. *Historical Census Statistics on Population Totals by Race, 1790 to 1990, and by Hispanic Origin, 1970 to 1990, for the United States, Regions, Divisions, and States*. Washington, DC: US Census Bureau, 2006.

Giddings, Paula. *In Search of Sisterhood: Delta Sigma Theta and the Challenge of the Black Sorority Movement*. New York: Morrow, 2007.

Giddings, Paula. *When and Where I Enter: The Impact of Black Women on Race and Sex in America*. New York: Morrow, 1984.

Gill, Tiffany. *Beauty Shop Politics: African American Women's Activism in the Beauty Industry*. Urbana: University of Illinois Press, 2011.

Gilmore, Glenda Elizabeth. *Defying Dixie: The Radical Roots of Civil Rights, 1919–1950*. New York: Norton, 2008.

Gilmore, Glenda Elizabeth. *Gender and Jim Crow: Women and the Politics of White Supremacy in North Carolina, 1896–1920*. Chapel Hill: University of North Carolina Press, 1996.

Gittens, Joan. *Poor Relations: The Children of the State of Illinois, 1818–1990*. Urbana: University of Illinois Press, 1994.

Gomez, Michael A. *Black Crescent: The Experience and Legacy of Black Muslims in the Americas*. Cambridge: Cambridge University Press, 2005.

Goodwin, Joanne L. *Gender and the Politics of Welfare Reform: Mothers' Pensions in Chicago, 1911–1929*. Chicago: University of Chicago Press, 1997.

Gordon, Linda. *Pitied but Not Entitled: Single Mothers and the History of Welfare, 1890–1936*. New York: Free Press, 1994.

Grant, Colin. *Negro with a Hat: The Rise and Fall of Marcus Garvey*. New York: Oxford University Press, 2010.

Green, Adam. *Selling the Race: Culture, Community, and Black Chicago, 1940–1955*. Chicago: University of Chicago Press, 2006.

Greenberg, Cheryl. *Or Does It Explode? Black Harlem in the Great Depression*. New York: Oxford University Press, 1991.

Greenberg, Cheryl. *To Ask for an Equal Chance: African Americans in the Great Depression*. Lanham, MD: Rowan and Littlefield, 2009.

Gregg, Robert. *Sparks from the Anvil of Oppression: Philadelphia's African Methodists and Southern Migrants, 1890–1940*. Philadelphia: Temple University Press, 1993.

Griffin, Farrah Jasmine. *Who Set You Flowin'? The African-American Migration Narrative*. New York: Oxford University Press, 1996.

Grim, Valerie. "From the Yazoo Mississippi Delta to the Urban Communities of the Midwest: Conversations with Rural African-American Women." *Frontiers: A Journal of Women Studies* 22, no. 1 (2001): 126–44.

Gross, Kali. *Colored Amazons: Crime, Violence, and Black Women in the City of Brotherly Love, 1880–1910*. Durham, NC: Duke University Press, 2006.

Grossman, James R. *Land of Hope: Chicago, Black Southerners, and the Great Migration*. Chicago: University of Chicago Press, 1989.

Gulick, Luther. "Recreation and Youth." *Proceedings of the Academy of Political Science in the City of New York* 2, no. 4 (July 1912): 592–96.

Haddad, Yvonne Yazbeck, and Jane Idleman Smith. *Mission to America: Five Islamic Sectarian Communities in North America*. Gainesville: University Press of Florida, 1993.

Hamilton, A. E. "Putting Over Eugenics: Making It a Living Force Depends on Sound Application of Psychology and Sociology—Camp Fire Girls an Organization Which Will Create Eugenic Ideals in Women in an Indirect but Effective Way." *Journal of Heredity* 6, no. 6 (1915): 281–88.

Harlan, Louis R. "Booker T. Washington and the *Voice of the Negro*, 1904–1907." *Journal of Southern History* 45 (February 1979): 45–62.

Helly, Dorothy O., and Susan M. Reverby, eds. *Gendered Domains: Rethinking Public and Private in Women's History*. Ithaca, NY: Cornell University Press, 1992.

Hendricks, Wanda. "Vote for the Advantage of Ourselves and Our Race": The Election of the First Black Alderman in Chicago." *Illinois Historical Journal* 87, no. 3 (Autumn 1994): 171–84.

Hicks, Cheryl. *Talk with You Like a Woman: African American Women, Justice and Reform in New York, 1890–1935*. Chapel Hill: University of North Carolina Press, 2010.

Higginbotham, Evelyn Brooks. *Righteous Discontent: The Women's Movement in the Black Baptist Church*. Cambridge, MA: Harvard University Press, 1993.

Hine, Darlene Clark. *Black Women in America: An Historical Encyclopedia*, vols. 1 and 2. Brooklyn, NY: Carlson, 1993.

Hine, Darlene Clark. *Hine Sight: Black Women and the Re-construction of American History*. Bloomington: Indiana University Press, 1997.

Hine, Darlene Clark. "Rape and the Inner Lives of Black Women in the Middle West." *Signs* 14, no. 4 (Summer 1989): 912–20.

Hine, Darlene Clark and John McCluskey, Jr., *The Black Chicago Renaissance*. Chicago: University of Illinois Press, 2012.

Hine, Darlene Clark, Wilma King, and Linda Reed, eds. *We Specialize in the Wholly Impossible: A Reader in Black Women's History*. Brooklyn, NY: Carlson Press, 1995.

Hodes, Martha, ed. *Sex, Love, Race: Crossing Boundaries in North American History*. New York: New York University Press, 1999.

Hoffschwelle, Mary S. *The Rosenwald Schools of the American South*. Gainesville: University Press of Florida, 2006.

Homel, Michael W. "The Politics of Public Education in Black Chicago, 1910–1941." *Journal of Negro Education* 45, no. 2 (Spring 1976): 179–91.

Hoy, Suellen. *Good Hearts: Catholic Sisters and Chicago's Past*. Urbana: University of Illinois Press, 2006.

Huhndorf, Shari. *Going Native: American Indians in the American Cultural Imagination*. Ithaca, NY: Cornell University Press, 2001.

Hunter, Tara W. *To 'Joy My Freedom: Southern Black Women's Lives and Labors after the Civil War*. Cambridge, MA: Harvard University Press, 1997.

Hyra, Derek S. *The New Urban Renewal: The Economic Transformation of Harlem and Bronzeville*. Chicago: University of Chicago Press, 2008.

Illinois State Charities Commission. *Second Annual Report of the State Charities Commission to the Honorable Charles S. Deneen, Gov. of Illinois, December 31, 1911*. Springfield, IL: State Journal Company State Printers, 1912.

Innis-Jimenez, Michael. *Steel Barrio: The Great Mexican Migration to South Chicago*. New York: New York University Press, 2013.

Israel, Adrienne. *Amanda Berry Smith: From Washerwoman to Evangelist*. Lanham, MD: Scarecrow Press, 1998.

Jackson, David W., Charletta Sudduth, and Katherine Van Wormer, *The Maid Narratives: Black Domestics and White Families in the Jim Crow South*. Baton Rouge: Louisiana State University Press, 2012.

Jacoway, Elizabeth. *Turn Away Thy Son: Little Rock, the Crisis That Shocked the Nation*. New York: Free Press, 2007.

Jones, Beverly W. "Mary Church Terrell and the National Association of Colored Women, 1896–1901." *Journal of Negro History* 67, no. 1 (1982): 20–33.

Jones, Jacqueline. *Labor of Love, Labor of Sorrow: Black Women, Work, and the Family, from Slavery to Present*. New York: Basic Books, 1985.

Katz, Michael B. *The Underclass Debate: Views from History*. Princeton, NJ: Princeton University Press, 1993.

King, Wilma. *African-American Childhoods: Historical Perspectives from Slavery to Civil Rights*. New York: Palgrave Macmillan, 2005.

Knupfer, Anne Meis. *Reform and Resistance: Gender, Delinquency, and America's First Juvenile Court*. New York: Routledge, 2001.

Knupfer, Anne Meis. "To Become Good, Self-Supporting Women: The State Industrial School for Delinquent Girls at Geneva, Illinois, 1900–1935." *Journal of the History of Sexuality* 9, no. 4 (October 2000): 420–46.

Knupfer, Anne Meis. *Toward a Tenderer Humanity and a Nobler Womanhood: African American Women's Clubs in Turn-of-the-Century Chicago*. New York: New York University Press, 1996.

Kunzel, Regina. *Fallen Women, Problem Girls: Unmarried Mothers and the Professionalization of Social Work, 1890–1945*. New Haven, CT: Yale University Press, 1993.

Kyriakoudes, Louis M. *The Social Origins of the Urban South: Race, Gender and Migration in Nashville and Middle Tennessee*. Chapel Hill: University of North Carolina Press, 2003.

LaNier, Carlotta Walls and Lisa Frazier Page. *A Mighty Long Way: My Journey to Justice at Little Rock Central High School*. New York: Ballantine, 2010.

Lasch-Quinn, Elisabeth. *Black Neighbors: Race and the Limits of Reform in the*

Settlement House Movement, 1890–1945. Chapel Hill: University of North Carolina Press, 1993.

Lemann, Nicholas. *The Promised Land: The Great Black Migration and How It Changed America*. New York: Vintage Books, 1992.

Lentz-Smith, Adrienne. *Freedom Struggles: African-Americans and World War I*. Cambridge, MA: Harvard University Press, 2009.

Lerner, Gerda. "Early Community Work of Black Club Women." *Journal of Negro History* 59 (April 1974): 158–67.

Lincoln, C. Eric. *Black Muslims in America*. Grand Rapids, Mich.: Eerdmans, 1961.

Lindley, Betty Grimes and Ernest K. Lindley. *A New Deal for Youth: The Story of the National Youth Administration*. New York: Viking Press, 1938.

Lomax, Louis. *When the Word Is Given: A Report on Muhammad, Malcolm X and the Black Muslim World*. New York: World, 1963.

Lowe, Margaret A. *Looking Good: College Women and Body Image, 1875–1930*. Baltimore: Johns Hopkins University Press, 1993.

Margolick, David. *Elizabeth and Hazel: Two Women of Little Rock*. New Haven, CT: Yale University Press, 2011.

Marsh, Clifton Hugo. *The Lost-Found Nation of Islam in America*. New York: Scarecrow Press, 2000.

Martin, Summers. *Manliness and Its Discontents: The Black Middle Class and the Transformation of Masculinity, 1900–1930*. Chapel Hill: University of North Carolina Press, 2004.

Materson, Lisa G. *For the Freedom of Her Race: Black Women and Electoral Politics in Illinois, 1877–1932*. Chapel Hill: University of North Carolina Press, 2010.

Mays, Benjamin E., and Joseph William Nicholson. *The Negro's Church*. New York: Arno Press, 1933.

McCloud, Aminah Beverly. *African-American Islam*. New York: Routledge, 1995.

McGuiness, Margaret. *Called to Serve: A History of Nuns in America*. New York: New York University Press, 2013.

Miller, Susan. *Growing Girls: The Natural Origins of Girls' Organizations in America*. New Brunswick, NJ: Rutgers University Press, 2007.

Mills, Kay. *Changing Channels: The Civil Rights Case that Transformed Television*. Oxford: University of Mississippi Press, 2004.

Mintz, Steven. *Huck's Raft: A History of American Childhood*. Cambridge, MA: Harvard University Press, 2004.

Mitchell, Michele. *Righteous Propagation: African Americans and the Politics of Racial Destiny After Reconstruction*. Chapel Hill: University of North Carolina Press, 2004.

Mjagkij, Nina. *Light in the Darkness: African Americans and the YMCA, 1852–1946*. Lexington: University of Kentucky Press, 2003.

Moore, Jacqueline. *Booker T. Washington, W. E. B. Du Bois and the Struggle for Racial Uplift*. Wilmington, Del.: Scholarly Resources, 2003.

Mumford, Kevin. *Interzones: Black/White Sex Districts in Chicago and New*

York in the Early Twentieth Century. New York: Columbia University Press, 1997.

Muncy, Robin. *Creating a Female Dominion in American Reform, 1890–1935*. Oxford: Oxford University Press, 1994.

Murch, Donna Jean. *Living for the City: Migration, Education, and the Rise of the Black Panther Party in Oakland, California*. Chapel Hill: University of North Carolina Press, 2010.

Murray, John. *The Charleston Orphan House: Children's Lives in the First Public Orphanage in America*. Chicago: University of Chicago Press, 2013.

Odem, Mary. *Delinquent Daughters: Protecting and Policing Adolescent Female Sexuality in the United States, 1885–1920*. Chapel Hill: University of North Carolina Press, 1995.

O'Donnell, Sandra. "The Care of Dependent African-American Children in Chicago: The Struggle between Self-Help and Professionalism." *Journal of Social History* 27 (Summer 1994): 763–76.

Orleck, Annelise. *Storming Caesar's Palace: How Black Mothers Staged Their Own War on Poverty*. Boston: Beacon Press, 2005.

Paris, Leslie. *Children's Nature: The Rise of the American Summer Camp*. New York: New York University Press, 2008.

Pascoe, Peggy. *Relations of Rescue: The Search for Female Moral Authority in the American West, 1874–1939*. Oxford: Oxford University Press, 1993.

Pattillo-Beals, Melba. *Warriors Don't Cry: A Searing Memoir of the Battle to Integrate Little Rock's Central High School*. New York: Washington Square Press, 1995.

Peiss, Kathy. *Cheap Amusements: Working Women and Leisure in Turn of the Century New York*. Philadelphia: Temple University Press, 1987.

Perkins, Linda M. "The Impact of the 'Cult of True Womanhood' on the Education of Black Women." *Journal of Social Issues* 39 (March 1983): 17–28.

Perkins, Linda M. "Lucy Diggs Slowe: Champion of the Self-Determination of African-American Women in Higher Education." *Journal of Negro History* 81, nos. 1–4 (Winter-Autumn 1996): 89–104.

Philpott, Thomas. *The Slum and the Ghetto: Immigrants, Blacks and Reformers in Chicago, 1880–1930*. Belmont, CA: Wadsworth, 1991.

Platt, Anthony M. *The Child Savers: The Invention of Delinquency*. Chicago: University of Chicago Press, 1969.

Powers, Jane Bernard. *The "Girl Question" in Education: Vocational Education for Young Women in the Progressive Era*. London: Falmer Press, 1992.

Rabinovitz, Lauren. *For the Love of Pleasure: Women, Movies, and Culture in Turn-of-the-Century Chicago*. New Brunswick, NJ: Rutgers University Press, 1998.

Ramey, Jessie B. *Child Care in Black and White: Working Parents and the History of Orphanages*. Urbana: University of Illinois Press, 2012.

Reed, Christopher Robert. *The Chicago NAACP and the Rise of the Black Professional Leadership, 1910–1966*. Bloomington: Indiana University Press, 1997.

Reiman, Richard A. *The New Deal and American Youth: Ideas and Ideals in a Depression Decade*. Athens: University of Georgia Press, 1992.

Rembis, Michael. *Defining Deviance: Sex, Science and Delinquent Girls, 1890–1960*. Urbana: University of Illinois Press, 2011.

Richings, G. F. *Evidence of Progress among Colored People*. Chicago: Afro-American Press, 1969.

Ritterhouse, Jennifer. *Growing Up Jim Crow: How Black and White Southern Children Learned Race*. Chapel Hill: University of North Carolina Press, 2006.

Roberts, Terrence. *Lessons from Little Rock*. Little Rock: Butler Center for Arkansas Studies, 2009.

Robertson, Nancy Marie. *Christian Sisterhood, Race Relations, and the YWCA, 1906–1946*. Urbana: University of Illinois Press, 2007.

Rolinson, Mary G. *Grassroots Garveyism: The University Negro Improvement Association in the Rural South, 1920–1927*. Chapel Hill: University of North Carolina Press, 2007.

Rosen, Ruth. *The Girl Problem: Female Sexual Delinquency in New York, 1900–1930*. Ithaca, NY: Cornell University Press, 1999.

Roth, Benita. *Separate Roads to Feminism: Black, Chicana and White Feminist Movements in America's Second Wave*. Cambridge: Cambridge University Press, 2003.

Royster, Jacqueline Jones, ed. *Southern Horrors and Other Writings*. New York: Bedford Press, 1997.

Rutkoff, Peter, and William Scott. "Pinkster in Chicago: Bud Billiken and the Mayor of Bronzeville, 1930–1945." *Journal of African American History* 89, no. 4 (2004): 316–30.

Sanchez-Eppler, Karen. *Dependent States: The Child's Part in Nineteenth Century America*. Chicago: University of Chicago Press, 2005.

Sawislak, Karen. *Smoldering Cities: Chicago and the Great Fire 1871–1874*. Chicago: University of Chicago Press, 1996.

Schechter, Patricia A. *Ida B. Wells-Barnett and American Reform, 1890–1930*. Chapel Hill: University of North Carolina Press, 2001.

Scott, Daryl Michael. *Contempt and Pity: Social Policy and the Image of the Damaged Black Psyche, 1880–1996*. Chapel Hill: University of North Carolina Press, 1997.

Scott, Emmett J. "Letters of Negro Migrants of 1916–1918." *Journal of Negro History* 4, no. 3 (July 1919): 290–340.

Seraile, William. *Angels of Mercy: White Women and the History of New York's Colored Orphan*. New York: Fordham University Press, 2011.

Sernett, Milton. *Bound for the Promised Land: African American Religion and the Great Migration*. Durham, NC: Duke University Press, 1997.

Sharpless, Rebecca. *Cooking in Other Women's Kitchens: Domestic Workers in the South, 1865–1960*. Chapel Hill: University of North Carolina Press, 2011.

Shaw, Stephanie. "Black Club Women and the Creation of the National Association of Colored Women." *Journal of Women's History* 3, no. 2 (Fall 1991): 10–25.

Shaw, Stephanie. *What a Woman Ought to Be and to Do: Black Professional Women Workers during the Jim Crow Era.* Chicago: University of Chicago Press, 1996.

Smith, Amanda. *An Autobiography of Mrs. Amanda Smith, the Colored Evangelist.* electronic ed. Chapel Hill: University of North Carolina Press, 1999.

Smith, Joan K. "Progressive School Administration: Ella Flagg Young and the Chicago Schools, 1905–1915." *Journal of the Illinois State Historical Society* 73, no. 1 (Spring 1980): 27–44.

Smith, Susan. *Sick and Tired of Being Sick and Tired: Black Women's Health Activism, 1890–1950.* Philadelphia: University of Pennsylvania Press, 1995.

Spear, Allan. *Black Chicago: The Making of a Negro Ghetto, 1890–1920.* Chicago: University of Chicago Press, 1967.

Stenho, Sandra M. "Public Responsibility for Dependent Black Children: The Advocacy of Edith Abbott and Sophonisba Breckinridge." *Social Services Review* 62 (September 1988): 485–503.

Stephens, Richard W. "Birth of the National Vocational Guidance Association." *Career Development Quarterly* 36, no. 4 (June 1988): 293–306.

Stockley, Grif. *Daisy Bates: Civil Rights Crusader from Arkansas.* Oxford: University Press of Mississippi, 2012.

Stovall, Mary E. "The *Chicago Defender* in the Progressive Era." *Illinois Historical Journal* 83 (Autumn 1990): 159–72.

Strickland, Arvarh E. *The History of the Chicago Urban League.* Columbia: University of Missouri Press, 2001.

Stroman, Carolyn A. "The *Chicago Defender* and the Mass Migration of Blacks, 1916–1918." *Journal of Popular Culture* 15, no. 2 (Fall 1981): 62–67.

Summers, Martin. *Manliness and Its Discontents: The Black Middle Class and the Transformation of Masculinity, 1900-1930.* Chapel Hill: University of North Carolina Press, 2004.

Tate, Claudia, ed. *The Works of Katherine Davis Chapman Tillman.* New York: Oxford University Press, 1991.

Taylor, Ula. *The Veiled Garvey: The Life and Times of Amy Jacques Garvey.* Chapel Hill: University of North Carolina Press, 2002.

Tedesco, Laureen. "Progressive Era Girl Scouts and the Immigrant: Scouting for Girls (1920) as a Handbook for American Girlhood." *Children's Literature Association Quarterly* 31, no. 4 (Winter 2006): 346–68.

Torres, Sasha. *Black, White, and in Color: Television and Black Civil Rights.* Princeton, NJ: Princeton University Press, 2003.

Travis, Dempsey J. *An Autobiography of Black Chicago.* Chicago: Urban Research Institute, 1981.

Trolander, Judith. *Professionalism and Social Change: From the Settlement House to the Neighborhood Centers, 1886 to Present.* New York: Columbia University Press, 1987.

Trotter, Joe W. *From a Raw Deal to a New Deal: African-Americans 1929–1945.* New York: Oxford University Press, 1996.

Tsoukalas, Steven. *The Nation of Islam: Understanding the Black Muslims.* New York: P and R, 2001.

Turner, Richard Brent. *Islam in the African-American Experience.* Bloomington: Indiana University Press, 2003.

Valk, Anne, and Leslie Brown, *Living with Jim Crow: African-American Women and Memories of the Segregated South.* New York: Palgrave Macmillan, 2010.

Walker, Lewis, and Benjamin C. Wilson. *Black Eden: The Idlewild Community.* East Lansing: Michigan State University Press, 2007.

Walker, Susannah. *Style and Status: Selling Beauty to African-American Women, 1920–1975.* Lexington: University Press of Kentucky, 2007.

Wallace, Michelle. *Black Macho and the Myth of the Black Superwoman.* New York: Dial, 1979.

Ward, Geoff K. *The Black Child Savers: Racial Democracy and Juvenile Justice.* Chicago: University of Chicago Press, 2012.

Watts, Jill. *God, Harlem, USA: The Father Divine Story.* Berkeley: University of California Press, 1995.

Weisenfeld, Judith. *African-American Women and Christian Activism: New York's Black YWCA, 1905–1945.* Cambridge, MA: Harvard University Press, 1997.

Wells, Ida B. *Southern Horrors and Other Writings: The Anti-Lynching Campaign of Ida B. Wells, 1892–1900.* Edited by Jacqueline Jones Royster. Boston: Bedford Books, 1997.

Whaley, Deborah. *Disciplining Women: Alpha Kappa Alpha, Black Counterpublics and the Cultural Politics of Black Sororities.* Buffalo: SUNY Press, 2010.

White, Deborah Gray. "The Cost of Club Work, the Price of Black Feminism." In *Visible Women: New Essays on American Activism*, ed. Nancy Hewitt and Suzanne Lebsock, 247–269. Urbana: University of Illinois Press, 1993.

White, Deborah Gray. *Too Heavy a Load: Black Women in Defense of Themselves, 1894–1994.* New York: Norton, 1999.

White, Frances E. *Dark Continent of Our Bodies: Black Feminism and the Politics of Respectability.* Philadelphia: Temple University Press, 2001.

White, Graham and Shane White. *Stylin': African American Expressive Culture, from Its Beginnings to the Zoot Suit.* Ithaca, NY: Cornell University Press, 1999.

White, Jr., Vibert L. *Inside the Nation of Islam: A Historical and Personal Testimony by a Black Muslim.* Gainesville: University Press of Florida, 2001.

Wiese, Andrew. *Places of Their Own: African American Suburbanization in the Twentieth Century.* Chicago: University of Chicago Press, 2005.

Wilkerson, Isabel. *The Warmth of Other Suns: The Epic Story of America's Great Migration.* New York: Random House, 2010.

Williams, Juan and Quinton Dixie. *This Far by Faith: Stories from the African-American Religious Experience*. New York: HarperCollins Morrow, 2003.

Williams, Lillian. *A Bridge to the Future: The History of Diversity in Girl Scouting*. New York: Girl Scouts of the USA, 1996.

Wolcott, David B. *Cops and Kids: Policing Juvenile Delinquency in Urban America, 1890–1945*. Columbus: Ohio State University Press, 2005.

Wright, Richard. *Twelve Million Black Voices: A Folk History of the Negro in the United States*. New York: Basic Books, 2012.

Yu, Henry. *Thinking Orientals: Migration, Contact, and Exoticism in Modern America*. New York: Oxford University Press, 2002.

DISSERTATIONS AND THESES

Alexander, Shawn Leigh. "Marcus Garvey and the *Chicago Defender*, 1917–1923." PhD diss., University of Iowa, 1995.

Colson, Myra Hill. "Home Work among Negro Women in Chicago." Master's thesis, University of Chicago, 1928.

Crawley, Charlotte Ashby. "Dependent Negro Children in Chicago in 1926." Master's thesis, University of Chicago, 1927.

Helgren, Jennifer. "Inventing American Girlhood: Gender and Citizenship in the Twentieth-Century Camp Fire Girls." PhD diss., Claremont Graduate University, 2005.

Mack, Ione Margaret. "The Factor of Race in the Religious Education of the Negro High School Girl." Master's thesis, University of Chicago, 1927.

Pardee, Ruth Evans. "A Study of the Functions of Associations in a Small Negro Community in Chicago." Master's thesis, University of Chicago, 1937.

INDEX

Chicago School of Civics and Philanthropy, 49
Chicago Telephone Company, 118
Chicago Tribune, 121
Chicago Union Station, 2, 39
Chicago Urban League Industrial Department, 119
Chicago Urban League, 47–51, 65, 71–74, 119, 144
Chicago Whip, 76, 117
Chicago: academic success of migrant girls in, 99–100; African American frustrations with services, 85; black population growth in, 60; as center of Camp Fire Girls activity, 136; cosmetics companies and hair salons in, 70; cultural and community organizations outreach to black girls, 5; domestic workers' obstacles in, 112; educational opportunities for girls in, 96–97; girls' impressions and views of, 131, 153; as hub of job opportunities for African Americans, 115; lack of placement of black women in jobs, 126; migrant girls balancing educational goals and economic needs, 102; migrants' beliefs and realities of, 168; new privileges and expressions, 66; options for new southern migrants to, 59; popular culture and religious experiences in, 68; storefront churches in, 72; suburban towns near, 3–4; threat of racial violence in, 7–8
Chicago's United Charities, 52
Christianity, 22, 61
Cincinnati, Ohio, 115
City Federation of Colored Women's Clubs, 49–51
civil rights movement, 138, 145, 168
Civil War, 22–23, 97
Clark-Lewis, Elizabeth, 66, 68
Clement, Elizabeth Ann, 160

Clybourne Avenue, 133
Colored Branches of the YMCA, 42
Colored Young Women's Christian Association, 138
Columbia University, 123
community trusts, 165
Conroy, Jack, 79
Cook County Hospital, 53, 151
Cook County, Illinois, 32–33
cotton picker, 3
Court of Domestic Relations, 21, 71, 87, 157, 163
Cox, Oliver Cromwell, 116
Crisis, The, 11

Darkwater: Voices from Within the Veil, 141
De Priest, Oscar, 88
Democratic National Convention, 18
Demopolis, Alabama, 7
Department of Household Administration, 29
Detroit, Michigan, 3, 84, 91, 106
Division of Negro Affairs, 120
"Don't Buy Where You Can't Work" campaigns, 97, 117, 128, 171
Double V campaign, 138
Douglass National Bank, 3
Drake, St. Clair, 111, 119–20, 143
Drew, Timothy, 76
Du Bois, W. E. B., 73–74, 102, 141
Duster, Alfreda, 140

East St. Louis, Illinois, 146
Ebenezer Church, 67
Eckford, Elizabeth, 172
Emancipation, 4, 150
England, 22
Englewood (school), 99
Episcopal School, 25
eugenics, 134
Evans, Mary, 72
Evanston, Illinois, 4, 28